Avoiding Armageddon

Studies in Canadian Military History

The Canadian War Museum, Canada's national museum of military history, has a threefold mandate: to remember, to preserve, and to educate. It does so through an interlocking and mutually supporting combination of exhibitions, public programs, and electronic outreach. Military history, military historical scholarship, and the ways in which Canadians see and understand themselves have always been closely intertwined. Studies in Canadian Military History builds on a record of success in forging those links by regular and innovative contributions based on the best modern scholarship. Published by the University of British Columbia Press in association with the Museum, the series will especially encourage the work of new generations of scholars and the investigation of important gaps in the existing historiography, pursuits not always well served by traditional sources of academic support. The results produced feed immediately into future exhibitions, programs, and outreach efforts by the Canadian War Museum. It is a modest goal that they feed into a deeper understanding of our nation's common past as well.

Andrew Richter

Avoiding Armageddon: Canadian Military Strategy and Nuclear Weapons, 1950-63

UBC Press / Vancouver and Toronto

Michigan State University / East Lansing

09 08 07 06 05 04 03 02   5 4 3 2 1

Printed in Canada on acid-free paper. ∞

National Library Cataloguing in Publication Data

Richter, Andrew, 1965-

Avoiding Armageddon

(Studies in Canadian military history, ISSN 1499-6251)
Includes bibliographical references and index.
ISBN 0-7748-0888-8 (bound); 0-7748-0889-6 (pbk)

1. Canada – Strategic aspects. 2. Canada – Military policy – History. 3. Nuclear
weapons – Government policy – Canada – History. 4. Arms control – Government
policy – Canada. I. Title. II. Series

UA600.R52 2002   355'.033071   C2001-911555-5

Library of Congress Cataloging-in-Publication Data

A catalogue record for this publication is available from the Library of Congress.

Canadä

UBC Press gratefully acknowledges the financial support for our publishing
program of the Government of Canada through the Book Publishing Industry
Development Program (BPIDP), and of the Canada Council for the Arts, and the
British Columbia Arts Council.

This book has been published with the help of a grant from the Humanities and
Social Sciences Federation of Canada, using funds provided by the Social Sciences
and Humanities Research Council of Canada.

Printed and bound in Canada by Friesens
Set in Stone by Artegraphica Design Co. Ltd.
Copy editor: Cheryl Cohen
Proofreader: Morgan Holmes
Indexer: Patricia Buchanan

UBC Press   Michigan State University Press
The University of British Columbia   1405 South Harrison Road, Suite 25
2029 West Mall   East Lansing, MI 48823-5202
Vancouver, BC V6T 1Z2   **www.msupress.msu.edu**
604-822-5959 / Fax: 604-822-6083
www.ubcpress.ca

Contents

Preface

The origins of this book can be traced to many of the principal works in the field of Canadian security, works that have largely assumed Canada was either too weak and/or too disinterested to examine issues of strategy during the Cold War. Unable to identify a national Canadian defence policy, the authors of these studies concluded that Canadians simply accepted the analysis and strategic conceptual frameworks identified and articulated by our alliance partners. In spite of the widespread acceptance of this argument, however, little evidence has been offered to support it.

Based on documents declassified for this study, this book examines how Canadian defence officials (assisted by those in the Department of External Affairs) approached some of the critical defence issues of the 1950s and early 1960s. There are several reasons why this time frame was chosen. Most crucially, the period comprised the years in which the general tone of the Cold War was established for the subsequent two and a half decades. At its start, US-Soviet relations, while tense, had not yet deteriorated to open hostility, and the glow of wartime cooperation, while fading, had not disappeared altogether. Thirteen years later, East-West relations had gone through an extraordinary period of sustained tension, climaxed by the Cuban Missile Crisis of 1962, an event that convinced policy makers on both sides that more accommodative policies needed to be introduced and implemented. Thus, by 1963, the Cold War was ending its first cycle and would soon enter a prolonged period of détente.

The period was also chosen because Canada was a critical Western actor during these years, not as powerful, to be sure, as the United States but quite firmly placed in a "middle" group of countries that included Britain, France, and West Germany. In the subsequent four decades, Canada's status, in the opinion of many observers, has declined – perhaps significantly. Indeed, many pinpoint the start of this decline to the series of defence crises in the late 1950s and early 1960s, years that saw Canada negotiate an air defence agreement with the United States, debate the pros and cons of nuclear weapons acquisition, and become a leading proponent of global disarmament. I wanted to examine these developments in detail and determine whether they offer contemporary observers and policy makers guidance on how to approach controversial issues.

Even though the events and debates in this book took place several decades ago, examining the relevant records was problematic. Indeed, conducting an historically based defence study in Canada is difficult because of the pervasive government secrecy that prevents the widespread release of documents. While a great many records were reviewed and declassified for this project, the number pales in comparison with the total amount that remains closed and kept in storage at government warehouses in and around the Ottawa area. Among access officers at the National Archives of Canada (NAC), I encountered genuine uncertainty over what could and could not be released, much of it linked to a lack of familiarity with recently declassified records collections in other countries. Although the situation has improved over the past couple of years, what is really required is an attitudinal shift to one that places importance on the transparency and openness of historical documentation. Given that the political culture in Canada has traditionally focused on government rights and privileges and has permitted secrecy for more than a century, however, such a paradigm shift seems unlikely.

The majority of documents examined for this study were found at NAC and the Department of National Defence's Directorate of History, which has since been made part of the Directorate of History and Heritage (DHH). Ongoing budgetary problems that have affected staffing levels at both institutions pose a challenge to all but the most dedicated researchers. It took up to eighteen months, for example, to obtain documents that had been requested for this study.

One source of documentation that remains largely untapped is foreign collections, particularly those in the United States. The intimacy of the Canada-US security relationship, and the fact that there were so many defence committees with representation from both countries, ensures that a secondary research option is available to Canadians. While there are not many documents written by Canadian government officials per se in American collections, there are many of broad relevance to Canadian strategic thought, including the records of the Canada-US intelligence boards, those of the Joint Chiefs of Staff, and the personal papers of a wide range of military and civilian officials. Furthermore, each of the American military services maintains its own records collection, and these are also of interest in uncovering the Canadian approach to crucial issues. Key collections in the United States include the National Archives and Records Administration (NARA), in College Park, Maryland, just outside Washington, DC; the US Air Force Historical Office, based at Maxwell Air Force Base, Montgomery,

Alabama; and the US Navy and Marine Corps Archive, based at the Washington, DC, Navy Yard.

The National Archives of Canada in Ottawa houses an impressive collection of historical material. Generally speaking, the collection is well organized. The government archives division is the one that is most familiar with military and defence documents. Researchers should recognize, though, that declassification of documents is a time-consuming process, and that when documents are requested "informally," the results may be disappointing. A "formal" Access to Information request is time-consuming and can be expensive, but ultimately the requester receives a written explanation why certain documents remain classified. The informal option is free and generally fast, but it is also much more likely to result in a decision to keep documents closed, as no explanation is required.

Nonetheless, there are some grounds for optimism for future defence-related projects. The passage of time means that increasing numbers of documents from the 1950s and 1960s can now be released. Also, the continuing declassification of documents in the *Foreign Relations of the United States* series, some of which involve Canada, will result in greater pressure to release additional documents in this country. Last, the enormous number of documents that were reviewed for this study – many of which had never been reviewed before – means that access officers will at least have a record on which to base their future decisions.

The Directorate of History and Heritage maintains its own record collection in Ottawa, and it is a tremendously useful supplement to the material at NAC. Budgetary constraints have left the directorate understaffed and underfunded, however, with the consequences passed down to researchers. During the three years (from 1995 to 1997) in which I visited the directorate's research facilities, the days of operation were steadily reduced, from five days a week to four, and then to just two. Furthermore, parts of the collection still need to be properly reviewed and catalogued. For example, I had been conducting research at the directorate for about a year when I was informed, almost by accident, that there "might" be some papers by R.J. Sutherland (Canada's foremost defence scientist) that had never been properly filed and were therefore not indexed in the main collection. While I am thankful to the directorate for reviewing and opening some of these papers, I was also told that there were dozens of similar collections awaiting proper cataloguing. While the principal collection is gradually being updated and recatalogued, staffing shortages mean that the process is slow. Still, in spite of these difficulties, research at the directorate can be very rewarding, and the staff is helpful and knowledgeable.

The United States' NARA is a truly impressive facility. On the positive side of the ledger, the collection is vast and diverse, the equipment modern and plentiful, and the staff is anxious to offer assistance. There is also a more "open" environment than the one in Ottawa, and it is made clear to researchers that record collections are generally open unless there is a compelling reason to keep them classified. On the other hand, at least at the times when I visited the archives (spring 1995 and fall 1996), parts of the collection had yet to be properly organized, which obviously posed some difficulties. In fairness, it should be noted that the collection was moved in the mid-1990s, and the situation was considerably better on my second visit.

I have worked on this project in one capacity or another since the mid-1990s, and over that time have witnessed a significant growth in interest in scholarly works examining various aspects of Canada's defence history. While this book demonstrates that Canadian defence officials did think strategically and that they reached their own understanding of key issues, the findings are nonetheless preliminary and may need revision as more documentation is released. I hope that with time this study helps to spark a wider debate within the broad field of Canadian security and defence.

Acknowledgments

This book would not have been possible without the help and encouragement of many people. David Dewitt of York University supervised the dissertation upon which it is based, and thus deserves a special note of thanks. Brian Job was my postdoctoral supervisor at the University of British Columbia, and he offered many helpful suggestions and consistently wise counsel. Others who offered comments and feedback include George Lindsey, Harald von Riekhoff, Jack Granatstein, David Leyton-Brown, Frank Harvey, Dan Middlemiss, Reg Whitaker, Joel Sokolsky, and Steven Mataija.

Avoiding Armageddon has been published with assistance from the Humanities and Social Sciences Federation of Canada, using funds provided by the Social Sciences and Humanities Research Council of Canada. During the course of my research, I received financial support from the Department of National Defence Security and Defence Forum and from SSHRC. The book was completed while I was a postdoctoral fellow at the Institute of International Relations at UBC. Others at UBC I wish to thank are Mark Zacher, Ken Carty, Allen Sens, Kal Holsti, John Wood, and Sam Lasalva.

Any book based on historical documentation in Canada faces numerous challenges – from government secrecy to incomplete records collections – and I would be remiss if I did not thank the staffs at the government archives division of NAC and the DHH. I wish to extend my gratitude to Ron Falls, Owen Cooke, and Serge Bernier, each of whom helped ensure that my access requests were dealt with promptly and judiciously. I also appreciated the courteous work of the staff of the NAC Reading Room, who had the unenviable task of making sense of my document requests. I further wish to thank the staff at the Canadian Forces College library in Toronto, in particular Cathy Murphy, who helped me with much of the secondary literature. In the United States, I received helpful assistance from the staff at NARA.

At UBC Press, I wish to thank Emily Andrew, who skilfully guided me through the publication process.

Last, I wish to thank my parents, Maxwell and Iris Richter, for their constant encouragement and support.

Avoiding Armageddon

Introduction

In the early days of a new millennium, and with the Cold War an increasingly distant memory, it is easy to forget that just a few years ago a nuclear rivalry held much of the world's attention and fear. The United States and the Soviet Union faced each other through rival power blocs, each committed to emerging victorious in a seemingly interminable competition. And while the North Atlantic alliance and the Warsaw Pact maintained an impressive array of conventional military firepower, it was nuclear weapons that were most revered for both the physical destruction they could cause and the political power that the threat of their use entailed.

Although it is certainly true that many weapons from the twentieth century have been horrifying – chemical and biological weapons in particular stand out – none have provoked more fear than nuclear weapons. This reaction is forever linked to the searing images of 6 August and 9 August 1945, when the United States detonated atomic weapons over the Japanese cities of Hiroshima and Nagasaki, respectively. With yields of fourteen and twenty kilotons, the bombs completely destroyed the two cities. In short order, far more powerful weapons were developed, and by the early years of the following decade bomb yields reaching into the megatons had been designed and deployed by both the United States and the Soviet Union.

The enormity of the stakes in the nuclear age ensured that strategic thought did not suffer from a lack of either scholarly or popular attention. Indeed, within months of the first atomic explosions, new thinking about military power began to emerge as strategists struggled to make sense of weapons that seemed to turn conventional military wisdom upside down. In fact, the very notion of winning a war quickly came to be questioned by some. As John Baylis and John Garnett have noted, when nuclear war threatened to destroy both the vanquished and victor alike, the long-accepted Clausewitzian idea of war as an instrument of policy suddenly looked quite odd.[1] Author Bernard Brodie, who was to become the most important strategist of the postwar era, wrote in his 1946 book *The Absolute Weapon:* "If the atomic bomb can be used without fear of substantial retaliation in kind, it will clearly encourage aggression. So much the more reason, therefore, to take all possible steps to assure that multilateral possession of the bomb, should that prove inevitable, be attended by arrangements to make as nearly certain as possible that the aggressor who uses the bomb will have it used against him ... *Thus far the chief purpose of our military establishment has been to win wars. From now on its chief purpose must be to avert them. It can have almost no other useful purpose.*"[2] With this statement, Brodie announced that deterrence would become the de facto goal of American defence strategy in the nuclear age. Indeed, observers would be hard pressed to identify a passage in a scholarly work – in *any* field of study – that so accurately predicted a revolution so soon after the transforming event occurred. Still, it was some time before the broader American defence community recognized this change, as there were powerful forces of conservatism at work among the strategic elite.[3]

By the mid-1950s, however, the gestation period of a new generation of strategists came to an end and the modern arms debate, with which we have been familiar since, was born. In the United States, this change was induced by the arrival of the hydrogen bomb, the Eisenhower administration's (somewhat eager) adoption of it, the anticipated introduction of ballistic missiles, and the subsequent articulation of the strategy of "massive retaliation." American analysts and observers, aided by a small group of Europeans, wrote works that revolutionized the study of strategy and began identifying terms and concepts that would largely define the strategic dialogue for the ensuing three decades. The period from 1954 to 1964 became known as the "golden age" of nuclear strategy.[4]

While the strategic studies literature has focused on the scholarly contributions of Americans, almost no attention has been paid to Canadian thinking on nuclear weapons and related issues of strategy. The lack of scholarly attention in the field is directly related to a much larger failing – the general scarcity of literature in the broad area of Canadian security and defence.[5] The reasons for this omission are not clear; over the years, the explanations offered have included Canada's history as a British colony, this country's "unmilitary" nature, and even the contention that there were few interesting Canadian defence decisions and developments in the twentieth century.[6] While, admittedly, several excellent works have been written, the general lack of interest has fed the impression that this country's security arrangements and policies have not been worthy of serious study.

Given the lack of attention to the field of Canadian security, it is not surprising that the specific topic of Canadian strategic thinking has also gone largely unexamined. While a few studies have been published, not one has been based on original documentation – that is, records and files that would reveal the presence or absence of such discussions within

Canada's Department of National Defence (DND). The difficulty in gaining access to government records has been an effective barrier to such research in the past, but this explanation cannot account for the more recent failure of Canadian scholars to investigate this topic. Indeed, considering the recently declassified archival material from 1955 to 1965 leads to questions about the apparent readiness of Canadian security scholars to accept the "findings" of studies based largely on readings of the public record and the secondary literature.[7]

A country's strategic thought can tell us much about the manner in which military and defence issues are approached and about attitudes toward the use of force, as well as enable more general observations about the country's place in the broader political and security environment. Similarly, a lack of strategic thinking can tell us a great deal. Such a failure may be linked to the influence of a conservative and/or authoritarian government, or it can suggest the apparent satisfaction of defence requirements established by a dominant strategic theorist. Perhaps more important, it can signify a denial that there are important defence issues and problems requiring consideration. All countries, though, have such issues to deal with; what they may lack are the observers to recognize and articulate them.

Canada's long colonial dependence on Britain, as well as the close bilateral relationship with the United States, led to a series of studies in the late 1960s and 1970s that argued this country lacked an independent capacity to articulate its interests in a variety of areas, of which defence and security was only one.[8] For the purposes of this study, though, the key claim was that Canada had no tradition of strategic thought, a failure that had left the country with little protection against foreign military doctrines and the defence policies that had resulted from them. This argument was made by Canadian security scholars Adrian Preston and John Gellner, as well as the British strategist Colin Gray.[9] The precise details varied, but each author offered the same basic, somewhat contradictory message: Canada had produced little in the way of postwar strategic thought, and any such thinking that had been articulated was traceable to imported foreign (largely American) concepts. This failure was attributed to Canada's long dependence on foreign militaries for organization, discipline, and philosophy, and the country's practice of identifying national interests in larger alliance terms.

Among the three studies, Gray's is the best known and most widely cited. In his 1971 article, Gray argued that Canadian strategic thought had been more noticeable for its absence than for any contribution made, and to the extent that such thinking had been articulated in this country, "strategic theoretical parasitism" ensured that the contribution had been little more than a copy of the analysis produced elsewhere.[10] Gray explained that the Canadian failure to think strategically was tied to a common Canadian perception – "a widely accepted denial that there were important distinct

Canadian defence problems in need of solution."[11] This denial had led Canadians to examine the defence problems of both the United States and the United Kingdom, countries at the centre of the contemporary strategic debate. However, the costs of this rejection had been substantial, as Canada's defence problems had often been "subsumed" in broader discussions of issues facing the West. According to Gray, Canadian defence issues needed to be considered on their own to reflect Canada's unique international situation. As he noted, "there is a great need both for a Canadian approach to Canadian problems and for a Canadian approach to the problems of international security."[12]

Gray asserted that Canada's strategic "tutelage" by the United States – which had followed an earlier period of reliance on the British – had to end, and that Canada "is in need of more intensive and better informed strategic debate." He argued that the strategic vacuum in Canada had resulted in an environment dominated by "polemicists" and the "strategically illiterate."[13] The situation had resulted not only in a "stale confrontation of extreme and false alternatives," but more important, in questionable defence policies and decisions. Such decisions had often been the result of flawed American strategic analysis that had been "uncritical[ly] transfer[red]" to Ottawa. More sophisticated strategic analysis – at both the public and governmental levels – would result in better defined and more appropriate defence policies. Similarly, Gray suggested that a capacity to produce independent strategic analysis is essential if a country is to devise a defence posture that is politically and militarily sensible.

Gray's article was intended to both encourage greater study of the subject and to challenge scholars to dispute his findings.[14] However, it largely failed to generate further interest or debate.[15] Indeed, despite the passage of time, Gray's study (along with Gellner's and Preston's) has remained dominant in the field.[16] The notion of a strategically disinterested and passive country has become one of the primary tenets in Canadian security, repeated in a wide array of both scholarly and popular works.[17]

This study challenges that interpretation, and demonstrates that Canadians identified and articulated strategic interests independent from those of its allies – in particular the United States. To support this determination, the study evaluates the historical evidence surrounding the development and evolution of Canadian strategic thinking at DND from 1950 to 1963. However, since strategy reflects the interplay of military and political interests, the records of the Department of External Affairs (DEA) constitute an important secondary research focus.[18] Independent Canadian strategic thought is demonstrated in two ways: (1) by comparing and contrasting Canadian conceptual thinking on several core issues with that of key foreign strategists; and (2) by examining the extent to which Canadian interests and concerns determined the recommendations of government officials (and conversely, the role that the external environment played in this process). By disputing some of the accepted premises in Canadian security literature, the study offers scholars a more complete picture of how Cold War defence issues were considered in Canada, and helps identify causal relationships that account for specific developments in Canadian strategic thought.

The book also poses several broader questions that are intended to place it in a more contemporary light. For example, it sets out to challenge the view that the Canadian state has little freedom of action on issues related to defence and security. If evidence of independent strategic thinking were revealed, this would demonstrate that Canada has considerable latitude to explore defence issues and articulate strategic concepts. On the other hand, the failure to uncover evidence of Canadian strategic thought would support the larger contention of the dominance of the external environment in Canadian defence, a framework that sees Canada's choices and options in international politics as severely limited as a result of developments beyond its borders.[19]

In a broader sense, the study represents a test of the peripheral dependence perspective in Canadian foreign and defence policy, which views Canada as a weak and penetrated country with little ability to resist others, in particular the United States.[20] Since emerging in the late 1950s, peripheral dependence has encompassed a broad array of works and philosophies. At its core, though, adherents see the United States as dominant in virtually all aspects of Canadian life, and maintain that Canada has thus been prevented from developing as a normal sovereign state.[21] With regard to defence, peripheral dependence asserts that Canada has had little choice but to negotiate security arrangements with the United States. American military capabilities are seen to be sufficient to deter challenges from alternative powers, and to render unnecessary the active pursuit of consensus and compromise.[22] The result of Canadian activity that arises from the acquiescent commitment to US-dominated military alliances is the active support for American security preferences and defence policies. In the context of this study, peripheral dependence accepts the findings of authors Gray, Preston, and Gellner, and asserts that Canadians were incapable of identifying independent strategic interests and were content to rely upon the interests or findings of others.

The study also examines the manner in which government departments – notably DND and DEA – formulated security interests and reached policy recommendations. Indeed, the period from 1950 to 1963 straddles two radically different phases in the Canadian government's foreign policy decision-making process. According to David Dewitt and John Kirton, the first part of this period, from 1950 to 1957, corresponded to the "era of harmonious segmentation," years in which the bureaucratic leadership of External Affairs was rarely questioned.[23] Beginning, though, with the array of controversial defence issues in the late 1950s, this consensus was replaced by the "era of competitive fragmentation."[24] The latter period witnessed major bureaucratic cleavages based on irreconcilable constructs of where Canada's main defence interests lay, and what the most appropriate steps were to ensure that this country remained an important global actor. In this environment, DND increasingly challenged DEA's dominance, a situation that first became notable with the North American Air Defence Command (NORAD) agreement in 1957, but reached its climax several years later with the bitter dispute over the acquisition of nuclear weapons. The study offers observations on how the two departments dealt with uncertainty, and the steps each took to ensure that it protected its influence within the government.

As for the period itself, 1950-63 was selected for several reasons. First, this interval corresponds with the peak period of the Cold War, and is also the period that largely established Canada's postwar defence and security policy. From a broader perspective, these were the years in which the basic pattern of the US-Soviet relationship was established.

The Korean War marks the start of the period, and forms the point at which the examination of original documentation begins. Before the conflict, the widespread assumption within the Canadian government – as well as the governments of Canada's allies – had been that the threat from the Soviet Union was more political than military, and that hostilities were unlikely in the short term. Almost immediately after North Korea invaded the South on 25 June 1950, however, External Affairs and Defence Department officials became concerned about the immediate danger that the Soviet Union presented. The war sparked a massive Canadian defence buildup.[25] It also led to twin decisions to send troops outside the continent, first to the battlefields in Asia, and then to Europe, where many believed the next Soviet "probe" would come.

Over the next dozen years, the Canadian government faced a series of controversial defence decisions. Indeed, with the rise to power of John Diefenbaker in 1957 – and the subsequent appointment of Howard Green as secretary of state for external affairs in 1959 – Canadian foreign and defence policy entered the most volatile period in the country's history, as the combination of a series of dramatic international events and changes in weapons technology placed new pressures on Canada. Over the course of Diefenbaker's six years in office, several defence-related scandals erupted, each linked to a specific development in the Cold War and, perhaps more important, to the tension in Canadian foreign policy between Canada's traditional allegiance to the West and growing desire to chart a new, more independent course.[26] That tension, in turn, was tied to the impression that the Cold War gave unfair privileges to the two superpowers, and that smaller countries inevitably paid the price of great power irresponsibility.

In the early part of the period, the most significant defence development was the gradual strengthening of the military partnership with the United States. This was manifested in a series of directives that allowed tactical air force cooperation to intensify, the building of a series of radar lines in the Canadian North, and the gradual establishment of a system of binational air defence cooperation (ultimately leading to the NORAD agreement).[27] By the late 1950s, changes in technology were raising a number of difficult questions about Canada's defence preparedness and the roles and tasks of the Canadian military. Caught up in such discussions were concerns regarding the production of the CF-105 Arrow, the jewel of the Canadian aircraft industry and an industrial project of the first magnitude. A further air defence decision involved the Bomarc surface-to-air missile, which the Diefenbaker government claimed could accomplish much the same strategic mission as the Arrow. The decision to acquire the Bomarc and cancel the Arrow in 1959 was controversial, and shattered the domestic consensus that had supported Canadian security policy since the Second World War.[28]

However, the single most controversial Canadian defence issue during this period was the question of the acquisition of nuclear weapons for Canadian forces in both North America and Europe. The Canadian government accepted several nuclear-related NATO directives over the period 1954-8 – and indicated to the United States its willingness to adopt such weapons on a number of occasions – but it apparently did not fully appreciate the obligations that these decisions and directives entailed. Thus, when the time came to actually acquire the weapons in the early 1960s, the government balked. Between 1960 and 1963, the Diefenbaker government followed an incoherent nuclear policy, at times implying that the weapons would be acquired, at other times questioning whether any nuclear commitments had, in fact, been made.[29] The controversy had repercussions during the Cuban Missile Crisis and ultimately led to a serious domestic political crisis in early 1963.[30] In addition, the government's indecision led to an unprecedented US intrusion in Canadian political affairs, which may have had an effect on the Canadian federal election of April 1963.[31] Although Prime Minister-elect Lester Pearson quickly ended the controversy by reaching agreement with the United States to acquire the weapons, many Canadians had been embarrassed by this country's indecision and delay.

In addition to major developments in Canadian defence, the period witnessed enormous changes in the international military/strategic environment. Some of these developments are discussed in Chapter 1, but attention here can focus on two specific ones – the introduction of long-range ballistic missiles and the growth of nuclear arsenals. Ballistic missiles made it possible for a nuclear strike to be delivered within minutes to any target on the planet. This development, coming only a decade and a half after the nuclear age began, had a further revolutionary impact upon strategy and, in particular, the notions of political and operational control that are so crucial to the use of military power. Missiles were also particularly problematic for Canada, as their combination of speed and range diminished the strategic significance of this country's geography.[32] As documented in later chapters, numerous DND officials thought and wrote about the strategic revolution brought about by the development of ballistic missiles.

As for the growth in nuclear arsenals, both the American and Soviet stockpiles increased dramatically during this period,[33] and by 1963 weapons ranged from the relatively small yields of air-to-air nuclear missiles to the multimegaton behemoths that sat atop ballistic missiles. This development presented a major challenge to Canada, which, as already noted, was pulled directly into the nuclear weapons debate of the period. More broadly, the growth in weapons stockpiles resulted in dramatic changes to the ways in which governments and militaries perceived the role of nuclear weapons and the use of force.[34]

These are some of the key defence issues and developments that arose over the period 1950-63. If one point deserves emphasis, however, it is that this was a decisive phase of the Cold War, and much of the thinking was coloured by the common perceptions and expectations of the era.

This book has six chapters. Chapter 1 establishes the historical context of the study by focusing on some of the domestic and international security developments that affected Canadian defence policy from 1945 to 1949. Thus, in addition to examining Canada's early policy regarding nuclear weapons and the evolving defence partnership with the United States, the chapter reviews some of the broad changes in technology, defence, and global politics that occurred during these years, developments that resulted in a radically different security environment than the one that existed at the end of the Second World War.

Chapter 2 examines developments in air defence, and is the first of four successive chapters to focus on recently declassified archival material. Specifically, it looks at how officials in both DND and DEA approached the NORAD agreement, and reviews the various arguments that they raised. It demonstrates that while the two departments approached the concept of a binational air defence command from fundamentally different perspectives, each believed that the recommendations it offered would further Canada's security interests. The second part of the chapter examines how officials in DND approached the development and ultimate cancellation of the Avro Arrow. It reveals the existence of a bitter interservice rivalry between the air force, navy, and army over production of the aircraft, a rivalry that certainly did not help the plane's fortunes. More important, however, it shows that the project's termination was based on an analysis of both short- and long-term Canadian defence requirements, and that the final decision had near-unanimous military support.

Chapter 3 focuses on Canadian thinking on nuclear weapons and strategy, and identifies areas in which the Canadian conceptual approach was different from the one reached in the United States. The chapter highlights Canadian writings on deterrence, strategic stability, the nuclear balance, and nuclear doctrine. To demonstrate the distinct nature of the Canadian observations, the chapter compares Canadian writings with major contributions in American strategic thought from the period.

Chapter 4 looks at the domestic debate on the acquisition of nuclear weapons that took place between 1959 and 1963. The debate represented a watershed in Canadian defence policy, as it not only split the Canadian public but drove a (further) wedge between DND and DEA, a bureaucratic dispute that would linger for years. The controversy also had international repercussions, because the question of nuclear weapons acquisition became a source of bilateral tension in Canada-US relations. As in Chapter 2, the discussion differentiates between DND and DEA approaches, and reveals that the departments came to different recommendations because their fundamental security interests were different.

Chapter 5 examines Canadian thinking on arms control and disarmament, a subject at the heart of the Canadian security debate through the period. Indeed, it was concern over arms control and the spread of nuclear weapons that largely led to the impasse over the domestic acquisition of nuclear weapons. The discussion focuses on the Canadian conceptual understanding of arms control, and how this approach differed from the one that developed in the United States, where the majority of studies were written. As in Chapter 3, there is a comparison with key writings in the field.

A brief note of clarification might be added at this time. Of the four archival-based chapters, two examine Canadian conceptual thinking on particular issues – nuclear strategy and arms control; the other two focus on issues of specific Canadian concern – air defence and the domestic nuclear weapons debate. Thus, a comparison between the writings of DND officials and those of key foreign strategists is conducted in the two conceptually oriented chapters (3 and 5), where it is important to demonstrate the independence, or lack thereof, of Canadian thinking vis-à-vis the accepted approaches in the field. Among foreign strategists, the focus in these chapters is on American civilian observers, who identified most of the major advances in postwar strategic thought.[35] On the other hand, the primary comparison in Chapters 2 and 4 is between officials in DND and DEA, as the intent is to demonstrate that government officials approached Canadian defence issues from a distinctly Canadian viewpoint, and that departmental recommendations were formed on the basis of Canadian interests, not those thrust upon Canada in the external environment. Thus, while different archival chapters render different comparisons, the intent is the same in each – to demonstrate the existence of independent Canadian strategic thought.

Last, Chapter 6 looks at whether and how Canadian strategic thought was reflected in or influenced Canadian defence policy of the period. This is an important question, as the failure to demonstrate a linkage would indicate that departmental studies and reports were essentially bureaucratic exercises, separated from the demands and decisions of policy makers. Although the chapter demonstrates such a connection, it also points out some of the inherent difficulties in doing so, difficulties that are by no means unique to Canada.

In sum, this study explores a series of assumptions that have gone largely unchallenged in Canadian security literature. It focuses on writings and observations of officials within the Department of National Defence that, until recently, were classified. It demonstrates that officials not only approached defence issues from a distinctly Canadian point of view but also identified and wrote about some of the main conceptual strategic theories of the period. As a result, it calls into question Canadian security literature, which has assumed a passive defence bureaucracy, as well as more general works that maintain the Canadian state does not have the ability to formulate its own interests.

At the same time, the study argues that although Canadian defence officials articulated a variety of strategic interests, it would be unreasonable to expect that those interests were always unique. One of the principal claims of the study is that similarities in national strategic thought do not necessarily reveal an inability on the part of one country to identify its interests or a willingness to copy concepts developed elsewhere. Rather, such similarities illustrate the limitations and constraints imposed by the external environment, and the effects that external commitments may have on states. Simply put, no country has the luxury of establishing defence policies and interests – and formulating the strategic thinking that supports them – in a vacuum. The external environment is a consideration in the formulation of defence policies of all states, Canada being no exception. In this regard, the pressures connected with being a member of NATO and a partner with the United States in the defence of North America, while considerable, were no more severe on Canada than were comparable pressures imposed by alternative security arrangements on other states.

Determining the evolution and development of Canadian strategic thought during the early phase of the Cold War helps to clarify how Canada approached that conflict and exactly what Canada's attitudes were toward the use of force during the Cold War, apart from helping to identify the influences that may have been important in shaping those perceptions. As Canada today faces a vastly different global environment, it is more important than ever to have a realistic appreciation of the manner in which issues were considered and approached during this period of the nation's history.

1
The Defence and Security Environment, 1945-9

The period 1945-9 was crucial in establishing the broad parameters of postwar Canadian defence and security policy. While the outbreak of the Korean War in 1950 would force Canada to reformulate defence policy so that it reflected the Cold War more directly, the first few years after the Second World War were nonetheless critical in determining the general approach that the Canadian government would take toward defence issues and problems in the ensuing decades. Several of the defence decisions made between 1945 and 1949 had long-term implications for the shape, structure, and roles of the Canadian military. Outside the country, this was also a time of enormous strategic change. The single most important development was the division of Europe into rival power blocs. In addition, a series of dramatic innovations in weapons technology revolutionized the use of force, and decision makers had to familiarize themselves with an environment in which the use of military power could have devastating consequences. This chapter thus examines several developments, both within and outside Canada, that had enormous implications for the evolution and articulation of Canadian strategic thought in the 1950s and early 1960s.

The Domestic Defence Environment
Defence planning, the nation's early policy on nuclear weapons, and the emerging defence partnership with the United States were the major defence issues of concern to Canada in the immediate postwar period. Not only were these issues important at the time, but the decisions reached in connection with them had repercussions that lasted decades.

Postwar Defence Planning, the Politics of Procurement, and the 1949 White Paper
Canada entered the postwar period with the status of a significant military power. In most measures it ranked fourth behind the United States, the

Soviet Union, and Britain. Within months of VE Day, though, the blueprint for a much smaller defence establishment was in place. Initial postwar funding and force levels were determined at a September 1945 meeting of the Cabinet Committee on Defence (formerly the War Committee), which set the defence budget for the 1946 fiscal year at $172 million. The navy was told to plan for a force of 10,000; the army, a force of between 20,000 and 25,000 (to form the nucleus of a larger body in case of general mobilization); while the air force was reduced to a regular strength of 15,000 to 20,000 personnel and ten squadrons.[1] This was the services' harsh introduction to the fiscal realities of postwar Canada, and it set the tone for defence developments for the next several years. In a political environment in which change was the only constant, and given a strategic environment that was expected to remain stable and relatively benign, the principal objective of the Department of National Defence in the immediate postwar period would be simple survival.[2]

The strategic rationale of the postwar Canadian military was first articulated in 1947, when Defence Minister Brooke Claxton prepared a critical memo titled "Observations on the Defence Needs of Canada." Claxton described the types of roles that Canadian forces should be able to perform and offered a general description of how future conflict could begin and evolve. The minister believed that there were only two possible theatres of conflict in which Canadian forces could be used: Western Europe and North America. It was "very unlikely," however, that Canadian forces would be called upon to fight in Europe within the next five years, mainly because of the deterrent value of the United States and the implicit nuclear threat that US military involvement entailed. With regard to North America, the minister believed that it would be a secondary target in any future conflict, primarily intended to divert valuable resources away from the European battle zone. Future war would unfold in a manner similar to the Second World War, and therefore there was no need to maintain large regular armed forces. The need, rather, was for general training so that this small force "can be the nucleus of a greatly enlarged war effort."[3]

On 9 July 1947, Claxton presented his first estimates speech to the House of Commons, an address that expanded upon the themes discussed in the earlier memo. After reviewing Canada's war effort, Claxton identified three broad purposes for which the country required a military: (1) to defend Canada against aggression; (2) to assist the civil power in maintaining law and order within the country; and (3) to carry out undertakings Canada might assume in cooperation with friendly nations or under any effective plan of collective action under the United Nations.[4] Following this assessment, Claxton listed fourteen long-term objectives of the department, including closer coordination of the armed services, joint intelligence, and planning groups to review defence plans; the maintenance of adequate reserves of equipment and weapons; and closer integration of the armed forces with a view toward standardization.[5] The minister also discussed new weapons introduced during the war – atomic bombs, jet aircraft, and rockets were all mentioned – and concluded that such systems effectively eliminated Canada's traditional sense of isolation and distance. Still, caution was required in assessing how these changes in technology would affect Canada's defence requirements in the long term.

Claxton's speech was noteworthy for several reasons. It represented, as Douglas Bland has noted, the first identification and articulation of distinctly Canadian functions for the military, objectives that were "not driven by external commitments, nor were they foreign to Canadian citizens."[6] The notion, for example, that Canadian forces could be used to carry out international "undertakings," while hardly a radical concept in later years, was still quite novel in the late 1940s. Further, the fourteen objectives formed a fairly comprehensive list, and several found their way into subsequent DND white papers and policy statements.

Despite the attempt at identifying a strategic rationale for the postwar Canadian military, defence spending remained low. This began to change in 1948-9, though, when the defence budget was increased to $269 million. The following year, with Cold War tensions rising still higher, spending grew by almost 50 percent to $385 million.[7] With this increase in funding the minister was able to announce a number of re-equipment programs, which provide a glimpse into the thinking of the department and the relative priority assigned to the services' procurement requests.

The service that was the biggest beneficiary of the increase in spending was the Royal Canadian Air Force (RCAF). In 1948, it took delivery of 85 British-made Vampire jet fighters, 30 Mustangs, and 23 North Star transports resulting in a considerably improved air force in just one year.[8] In addition, pre-production and engineering work began on an all-Canadian jet interceptor, the CF-100, designed by A.V. Roe Canada. These developments represented a significant change, as over the previous few years the RCAF had been compelled to do without any active squadrons, and its skeletal core of 12,000 men had been assigned to administrative tasks and training.[9] However, the growing recognition of the importance of air forces in the postwar world, as well as the costs associated with aircraft production, signalled a sustained period of spending growth.

Despite the general uncertainty of the immediate postwar period, it is possible to detect at least some semblance of strategic thinking regarding the air force's basic mission and equipment. No legitimate security threat existed right after the war, or certainly none that would justify the maintenance of a large air force. That began to change in the late 1940s, when not only did relations with the Soviet Union deteriorate but the Soviets began producing and deploying large numbers of bombers. To defend against this potential threat, aircraft were required to intercept and engage Soviet planes. The rationale behind the acquisition of modern fighter aircraft and the early development of the CF-100 is therefore clear. The air force gave up the strategic-bombing role it had performed during the war and instead put more emphasis on air defence and reconnaissance. While not all of these changes were welcomed by RCAF personnel, there was, at a minimum, an attempt to determine the kind of air force that Canada required and the basic missions it was intended to perform.

The same cannot be said, however, for either the navy or army. The former was in the worst shape of the three services. At the conclusion of the war, the navy had hoped to build a force capable of varied roles, but fiscal restraint resulted in a service unsure of its basic mission or purpose. The Royal Canadian Navy (RCN) was authorized to have 10,000 personnel in 1945; the figure was cut to 7,500 the following year, but recruitment difficulties meant that even this reduced number was not attained. In the early postwar period, there was confusion in both naval ranks and among senior defence officials regarding what the peacetime mission of the RCN should be, confusion that was reflected in a jumble of service roles and tasks.[10]

Although the army did not suffer from the confusion and low morale evident in the navy, it too experienced difficulty in adjusting to its peacetime role. Authorized in 1946 to have an active force of 25,000 and a reserve force of 180,000, the army consisted of only 20,000 men in 1949, at which time Claxton slashed the reserve ceiling to 50,000. The army was organized into five regional commands; its main function during this period was to man the Alaska Highway and various northern installations, and to maintain itself in readiness for the unlikely event of direct attack.[11] To defend Canada in such a scenario, the army formed a brigade called the Mobile Striking Force that could be moved by air and was capable of operating in the polar regions. Also formed during this period were the Canadian Rangers, a part of the Reserve Force that was intended to provide security and surveillance in remote areas along the coasts and in the North.[12] In the absence of any legitimate risk of a land invasion, however, and in the presence of a widespread belief that war in Europe was unlikely, critics questioned the very need for a Canadian army. The scepticism may have contributed to the low priority given to modernizing army equipment during the early postwar period.

In the fall of 1949, Claxton produced his second major statement on defence policy, titled *Canada's Defence Programme*. The document began with a section on the "International Situation" that reviewed the major defence developments of the postwar period. It examined the terms of the recently signed North Atlantic Treaty and discussed the defence implications of Canada's membership.[13] This was followed by a section on the "Defence Objectives of Canada," which described the department's current beliefs on the possibility and direction of future conflict. This latter section began with a review of Canada's defence purposes: (1) to provide the force necessary to defend Canada; (2) to maintain operational staff, equipment, and training personnel that would be capable of rapid expansion; and (3) to develop joint defence plans with other nations.[14]

In a departure from prior statements, the document noted that "the only kind of war which would involve Canada would be a war in which Communism was seeking to dominate the free nations ... Such a war would be a war for survival." This passage indicated the greater urgency with which the government now considered the Soviet threat, and revealed the type of conflict that was considered most likely. With regard to actual conflict scenarios, the paper noted that as a member of an alliance "it is obvious" that Canada would not fight alone against Communist forces. Rather, Canadian defence policy "assumes that our armed forces will be used in association with those of friendly powers."[15] With these passages, the department indicated that the emerging defence partnerships with the United States and the Atlantic alliance now formed the twin cornerstones of Canadian security policy. In short, the paper revealed that Canada viewed its security as indivisible from that of its allies, an appreciation that was frequently – although not always – reflected in the subsequent strategic thinking articulated by department officials.

The 1949 defence program document refined several of the concepts first identified in Claxton's estimates speech of a few years earlier, and it further clarified the strategic rationale for Canada's postwar defence policy. As such, it represents a turning point and forms a natural break in Canada's post-1945 military development. Perhaps most important, the approach that it codified toward the Soviet Union was to remain largely unchanged for the next several decades. Hostility toward the Soviet Union, despite the ebb and flow of the Cold War, was to become the basic assumption of postwar Canadian foreign and defence policy.

Canada's Early Policy on Nuclear Weapons

One defence issue that demanded immediate government attention in the early postwar period was Canada's position regarding nuclear weapons. Decisions on the future direction of Canada's nuclear program, on the cooperation that had existed during the war with the United States and Britain, and even whether or not to pursue an independent nuclear program all had to be made shortly after the war's conclusion. A brief look at how these decisions were reached helps place this country's subsequent nuclear policy in historical context.

The wartime collaboration between Britain, Canada, and the United States resulted in the detonation of two atomic weapons in 1945. Scientists from all three countries had pursued a common objective, and all shared in the knowledge that their efforts had helped shape the final outcome of the war. Despite this "success," however, there remained considerable confusion at war's end over the precise rights and responsibilities of the various parties to the knowledge behind the bomb. Whereas it was clear that the United States had supplied the bulk of the financial, physical, and scientific/intellectual energy of the program, there was no denying that the two junior partners had made significant contributions. In Canada, for example, the British-Canadian Montreal laboratory that operated under the authority of the National Research Council conducted several key experiments, particularly in gaseous diffusion and plutonium separation, while the Eldorado Mine on Great Bear Lake in northern Canada was an important source of uranium for the bomb project.[16]

This trilateral wartime partnership was shattered in 1946 by the US passage of the Atomic Energy Act (the McMahon Act), which prohibited the dissemination of fissionable material to any foreign country. From that point on, nuclear cooperation was confined to the supply of raw materials and the exchange of limited scientific and technical information. While the act produced little response in Canada, it generated considerable resentment in Britain. This was probably a result of the fact that by this time the British had already made the decision to establish their own domestic nuclear weapons program.[17] The Mackenzie King government, in contrast, had decided to focus on the civilian applications of nuclear energy.

The early Canadian position on the control of nuclear weapons was established in a memo written in the fall of 1945 by Lester Pearson, then the Canadian ambassador to the United States, in preparation for a conference between the three nuclear partners.[18] The memo began with a series of assumptions about the nature of nuclear weapons, arguing that the atomic bomb "is something revolutionary and unprecedented; a new departure in destruction and annihilative in effect." It further noted that unless atomic energy was somehow contained, nuclear proliferation would undoubtedly occur, as it was not realistic to believe that other countries would not manufacture their own weapons. The subsequent arms race would lead to "fear, suspicion, rivalry, desperation, and war; only in this case war would probably mean international suicide."

Policy recommendations followed from these observations. The memo suggested that Canada opt for international, indeed for supranational, control. Hence, the knowledge possessed by the United States, Britain, and Canada could be "traded" for a system of control under the authority of the United Nations. Such an offer, proposed in good faith, could be rejected only by those states whose motives were suspect. Pearson's proposed solution to the issue of international control involved a three-step process – prohibition of manufacture, destruction of existing weapons, and the sharing of all basic scientific knowledge. The central provision in this plan was that national manufacture and use of atomic weapons would be banned. The memo also called for the establishment of an international commission "of scientists of world reputation" to conduct periodic investigations of nuclear facilities (a kind of forerunner to the International Atomic Energy Agency). Pearson concluded that without regular inspection, effective international control over nuclear weapons would prove impossible.

The effect of Pearson's memo is difficult to determine, although the document certainly seemed to form the conceptual basis of the Canadian approach to nuclear issues for several years. What is clear is that the trilateral conference ended with a consensus on the need for a new international body, the United Nations Atomic Energy Commission (AEC), whose responsibility would include future efforts at international control. The Pearson memo became one of the few substantive Canadian efforts at analyzing the impact of the nuclear revolution, and for that reason alone deserves careful consideration.[19]

As important as it was, though, the memo did not start from first principles, as it seemed to take for granted that the central question of domestic manufacture had already been determined. Indeed, the Canadian decision not to manufacture nuclear weapons has to this day gone largely unexamined, as if the decision itself was so obvious that no investigation of it is required. This might be linked to the fact that Canadian scholars have failed to uncover any evidence that a debate on the issue took place – either at the governmental or public levels. It appears instead that no formal decision was ever made and that Canadian policy simply evolved after the war along with the realization that a domestic nuclear weapons program would serve no legitimate national interest.[20]

In spite of the lack of investigation, it would be disingenuous to overlook the question of domestic manufacture entirely. In his classic study *Canada's Changing Defence Policy, 1957-1963,* Jon McLin identified two possible reasons for the Canadian decision. First, Canada was not a military power, nor were Canadians a military people, and they thus rejected a weapon whose sole purpose seemed to be the power to hurt. Second, Canada had no strategic need to develop nuclear weapons, as it was inconceivable that Canada would end up in a major military challenge where it could not rely on the assistance of the United States. Taken together, these two considerations were so persuasive that "the Canadian government adopted its non-nuclear course after World War II not so much by deliberate choice as by unconscious assumption."[21] This judgment still appears accurate, as there remains no indication that the Canadian government seriously considered the option of independently producing nuclear weapons.

A more recent book by Brian Buckley argues that because the country's political leaders and decision makers did not see any useful role for a nuclear-armed Canada, there simply was no need for a comprehensive debate on an issue that generated near-unanimity.[22] However, Buckley also suggests that if different individuals had held key positions of power in the mid- to late 1940s, the outcome might have been different. In any event, the latter conclusion seems to fly in the face of the wide range of factors (many of which Buckley discusses) that led to the decision in the first place.

Having decided not to manufacture bombs of its own, Canada focused on the future control of nuclear weapons as well as the international body designed to oversee such efforts, the Atomic Energy Commission. Canada was made a permanent member of the AEC. The first major issue the commission dealt with was a proposal put forward by the American delegate, Bernard Baruch, on the international control of atomic energy.[23] Canada was cautiously supportive of the plan, hopeful that it might lead to more intense discussions. However, the Soviet reaction was entirely negative, and negotiations quickly bogged down in acrimony amid conflicting charges and countercharges. Observers to this day remain divided over which party was ultimately responsible for the failure of the Baruch plan. Few, though, would deny that the plan lacked credibility and may have been little more than a public relations ploy at a time when neither the Americans nor Soviets were seriously interested in the control of nuclear energy or its byproducts.

An additional comment should also be offered regarding the research complex at Chalk River, Ontario. This was a nuclear facility built during the war whose primary purpose was the experimental production of fissile material for nuclear weapons. Based on an advanced heavy water design, the plant produced plutonium at a rate three times greater than that of comparable American reactors of the day.[24] As noted by James Eayrs, most of this plutonium was sold to the United States, although a small amount was kept in Canada for research purposes.[25] Through the revenue acquired as a result of these sales, the Canadian government was able to construct a second, more advanced research reactor (the NRU) at the same location in the early 1950s. Early Canadian nuclear research resulted in considerable expertise, and led in 1952 to the formation of Atomic Energy of Canada, which was designed to market the peaceful application of nuclear energy.[26]

This discussion reflects the ambiguities of Canada's early nuclear policies. As prime minister, Mackenzie King maintained a declared policy that Canada would not manufacture, possess or use atomic weapons, nor would it be party to any agreement that would make Canada the "custodian" of other countries' bombs.[27] In spite of these declarations, Canada's early position on nuclear weapons was inconsistent. On the one hand, Canada was an important supplier of both the scientific knowledge and technical materials needed to produce nuclear weapons, but on the other it maintained an official policy consistent with that of a non-nuclear state. The policy probably reflected what the government *wanted* Canada's position to be. The country's direct participation in the Manhattan Project made any declaration of nuclear "virginity" problematic. So did the construction of US Air Force and Strategic Air Command bases in Newfoundland and Labrador in the years following the war, and the sale of plutonium to the Americans and British throughout the 1950s.[28] Thus, when considering Canada's later protestations on the dangers presented by nuclear weapons, one should not lose sight of the fact that this country was hardly an impartial bystander in the early years of the atomic age.

Unfortunately, the mid- to late 1940s was not the last time that the Canadian government would have to make decisions about the nuclear weapons issue. As discussed in Chapter 4, nuclear weapons, and more specifically the decision(s) to acquire and deploy them, became a divisive issue in Canadian defence policy between 1958 and 1963. For now, though, the important point to note is that Canada's early dealings with nuclear weapons, while hardly controversial, were certainly not as straightforward as the government of the day claimed. It was a pattern that was to be repeated some years later.

The Emerging Defence Partnership with the United States

The extensive wartime collaboration between Canada and the United States led to concern in Ottawa that in the postwar period, the United States would continue to push for measures that the Canadian government might not be eager to adopt. Ottawa realized that North American defence would increasingly be a cooperative affair. However, significant concerns over both sovereignty and the control of forces had not been resolved during the war.[29] Thus, in the postwar period, the Canadian government became increasingly sensitive to the sovereignty implications of new defence arrangements.

Within one year of the conclusion of the war, Canada was in the midst of its first concerted effort to define its postwar security relationship with the United States. Three related issues topped the agenda: a US request to build and staff Arctic weather stations in the Far North; Recommendation 35 from the Permanent Joint Board on Defence (PJBD) that the two countries continue their wartime collaboration on continental defence; and a planning document, the *Basic Security Plan*, drawn up by the Canada-US Military Cooperation Committee (MCC), that called for an elaborate system of continental air defence.[30]

Among the three requests, it was the latter that caught the government most off guard. Canadian political apprehension over the MCC report led to a series of bilateral meetings in late 1946, and a compromise between Canadian and American diplomatic and military personnel was reached.[31]

The US delegation, led by senior State Department official George Kennan, softened (and ultimately withdrew) its demand for a continental air defence system. The basic American message was that there was no rigidity to US thinking, and that any initial steps taken in air defence would be relatively modest and inexpensive.[32] This approach met with widespread Canadian approval, as a policy of firmness and patience avoided commitments that would have been difficult to meet in a fiscal environment where defence issues were not priority items. Nevertheless, the meetings revealed the increased importance attached to continental defence matters, an issue area that would, with time, attract near-constant attention.

With regard to defence cooperation, the wartime military partnership between Canada and the United States had been governed by the *Joint Canadian-US Basic Defence Plan No. 2*, more commonly known as ABC-22, a document drawn up by the joint defence board in the summer of 1941. The plan was intended to ensure that the wartime strength of the United States and the British Commonwealth would be combined in an effective and efficient manner. It was clearly not suitable for the situation at war's end, and the question of what would take its place quickly arose.

In the spring of 1946, the Permanent Joint Board on Defence presented a draft proposal of Recommendation 35, which would govern future military cooperation between the two countries. It ensured continued close cooperation with respect to the interchange of military personnel, standardization of equipment and methods of training, and the free and comprehensive exchange of military information.[33] Despite Canadian political concern about agreeing to a formal bilateral alliance, the federal government gave official approval in the fall to a slightly modified Recommendation 35, which was subsequently renamed Recommendation 36. Concern over the possible Soviet reaction led to a joint decision not to make a formal announcement.

By early 1947, a series of dramatic press accounts made the initial strategy untenable, and Prime Minister King was forced to make a statement to the House of Commons that explained that "in the interests of efficiency and economy" the two countries had decided to continue the wartime collaboration of their defence establishments.[34] This cooperation, which would "necessarily be limited," was based on the principle that each country retained control over military activities undertaken on its territory, and remained free to determine the extent of future military collaboration.[35] While the statement played down the importance of the accord, the obvious conclusion was that Canada had openly allied itself with the United States. Indeed, the 1947 Declaration of Principles on Defence Cooperation (also referred to as the Joint Statement on Defence) was to guide the framework of North American defence until the negotiation of the North American Air Defence Command (NORAD) agreement a decade later.[36]

Also of bilateral concern during this period were American requests for access to facilities on Canadian soil. As James Eayrs has noted, the complexity of the Canada-US defence relationship meant that requests could come via the PJBD, the US embassy, or a variety of military service channels, and "by the summer of 1946 they were arriving thick and fast."[37] American requests included the permanent maintenance of planes and installations at the air force base at Goose Bay, Labrador; the opening of new weather stations in the Arctic islands; construction of new radar stations in the Canadian North; the operation of the Northwest Staging Routes; the maintenance of far northern airfields; and the provision of facilities for various exercises and training programs on Canadian territory.[38] The number of requests was a fairly accurate gauge of American defence interest in Canada, and indicated to the Canadian government the urgency with which the United States was increasingly approaching defence issues that required some degree of Canadian participation and/or agreement.

Particularly difficult to resolve were requests to reinforce and expand the base at Goose Bay and to build and operate a series of radar stations in the Arctic. Regarding the former, the Goose Bay base attracted considerable attention from US Air Force planners in the immediate postwar period, as it was the only one in North America from which bombers might reach Soviet targets with the prospect of safe return. By early 1947, the United States had requested to station both bomber and fighter groups there to augment forces proposed for deployment at Harmon Field, an additional American base in Newfoundland. US officials, in an apparent attempt to convince their Canadian colleagues of the importance with which they viewed the base, noted that Goose Bay "could be said to be the most important all-round strategic air base in the western hemisphere."[39] While Canadians searched for a way to emphasize a non-military aspect of the base, the United States denied the request, and ultimately Canadian permission was granted to station long-range bombers.[40]

The other issue of concern was the construction of radar stations in the Canadian North. As noted, the draft Canada-US Basic Security Plan had called for an elaborate program of air defence, of which one component was to be the rapid construction of a radar network. While the plan itself was dropped, the concept of radar warning was not. By 1949, in the face of mounting pressure to take action, the Canadian government decided to replace the Arctic radar project with a more modest proposal: the Pinetree Line, completed in 1954, consisted of radar stations running the entire length of Canada. While this line was not the most technologically advanced, it was only the first of a series of such radar lines, and would with time herald a new era in bilateral defence cooperation.

In sum, the Canadian government recognized that the war had changed the requirements of continental defence, and Canada was prepared to compromise in order to meet American concerns. Recognizing the enormous power and responsibility that the United States was to play in the postwar period, Ottawa was anxious to take a cooperative role in North American defence. However, this did not mean that Canada meekly accepted whatever defence initiatives the United States proposed. On the contrary, as the discussion regarding the initial MCC proposal demonstrated, Canada insisted that the United States not directly challenge Canadian sovereignty and/or interests.

The expanding military partnership with the United States was driven by several factors: a wide range of political, economic, and historic ties; a growing perception of the Soviet threat as well as a common appreciation of approaches to dealing with that threat; and an increasingly intimate interservice relationship that frequently acted outside the formal parameters of the political executive of either country.[41] Regardless of which factor may have been most significant, the net result was that Canada began to codify its defence relationship with the United States in ways that it had previously avoided.

The International Environment

The immediate postwar years were also critical for a series of external political and strategic changes that were to influence international events for decades. These included the Cold War and the political division that it caused, advances in weapons technology, and the changes in war planning brought about by those advances.

The Beginning of the Cold War and the Establishment of Rival Power Blocs

Interpreting the origins of the Cold War has long been a hotly debated subject in international relations. Liberals argue that the Soviet Union emerged from the war obsessed with security and determined to establish a buffer zone around its borders with the West. According to this view, the West could do little to alter these interests, as Moscow was intent on increasing its global reach.[42] Revisionists, on the contrary, argue that the principal American interest at the end of the war was to make the world safe for American capitalism, and thus the United States never took into consideration the legitimate security concerns of the Soviet Union. The revisionists also point out that the fiercely anti-communist views of the American people, aided and abetted by their political representatives, made any compromise difficult.[43] Still another school blames Stalin, arguing that while his goals were not ideologically motivated, they were vague and ill-defined.[44] His methods of achieving limited objectives created distrust, for even if his actions were defensive they were perceived by the West as threatening to its security.

The common thread in these interpretations is the idea that the Cold War could have been avoided if only policy makers had been sensitive enough to the interests of the opposing side. This interpretation, while appealing, is almost certainly an oversimplification. The fact remains that in the aftermath of the war there was an enormous power vacuum in continental Europe brought about by Germany's defeat, and it would have been difficult to fill this peacefully even among countries with common political and military interests. Given the array of differences between the United States and the Soviets, such an accommodation may well have been impossible. The void in Europe allowed the Soviets to extend their authority into the heart of the continent. In its own interest, the West was compelled to try to mitigate this shift in the global balance of power. Consequently, as the war ended, conflicting strategic interests led to mutual recriminations.[45] This hostile atmosphere naturally affected political relations, which began their downward spiral within a matter of months.

If one had to identify a birthdate for the Cold War, John Lewis Gaddis has argued that February 1946 would be as good as any.[46] In that month, Stalin implied that as long as communism had not replaced capitalism as the most important form of economic organization, war between the two sides was inevitable. One month later, before an audience that included US president Harry Truman, former British prime minister Winston Churchill delivered his famous address in Fulton, Missouri, in which he charged that an "iron curtain" had been rung down across the heart of Europe. The speech accelerated a widespread and growing hostility toward the Soviet Union by comparing it to Nazi Germany. By August – exactly one year after the war's end – US-Soviet relations had declined to the point where President Truman considered using military force to prevent Soviet intervention in the defence of the Turkish Straits.

While Soviet actions were often not as threatening as some US officials made them out to be, a pattern was being established. For Western decision makers predisposed to believe the worst about the Soviet Union and its policies, the ideological tone of Soviet pronouncements confirmed that Stalin would, if he could, exploit systemic developments, vacuums of power, and the popularity of local Communist parties to serve the Kremlin's interests.[47] Signs of Soviet aggressiveness achieved a heightened salience, and conflicting evidence was routinely dismissed. Not that there were, in any event, a shortage of threatening signs. In Poland, Romania, and Hungary, unpopular Communist minorities consolidated their power and began receiving military aid, officer training, and strategic guarantees from the Soviet government. Other flashpoints during 1946-7 included Manchuria, Iran, Greece, and Turkey. Not only did the Soviets rupture the appearance of great power cooperation in the United Nations, but they isolated themselves from international economic cooperation. Their rejection of the

Bretton Woods agreements, the principal Western postwar economic plan, illustrated their penchant for independent and autarkic courses of economic development.

Curiously, however, despite the acceptance by most Western policy makers of Soviet aggressiveness, Western policy lacked a coherent strategy. That changed in the aftermath of a 1946 telegram, written by the American chargé d'affaires in Moscow, which was later revised and published anonymously in the influential American policy journal, *Foreign Affairs*.[48] The thesis of George Kennan's "long telegram" was that the entire thrust of American policy toward the Soviet Union during and after the Second World War had been misguided. That policy, whether in the form of Franklin D. Roosevelt's emphasis on integration or bargaining, had assumed the existence of no structural impediments to normal relations with the Soviet Union. Kennan's argument, on the contrary, was that because of its need for external enemies to justify its own domestic repression, traditional diplomacy could never reassure the Soviet regime. Moscow could be expected to try to expand, taking advantage of every opportunity as it arose. To counteract this, Kennan argued that Soviet leaders were responsive to demonstrations of force, as Russia was fundamentally weak and its rulers would retreat when faced with a determined foe.[49]

As Gaddis has noted, rarely has a single set of ideas had such an immediate impact on a nation's foreign policy.[50] Kennan's paper struck a chord with decision makers in Washington, and within months it had been accepted as official US policy. The strategy of containment brought together the new American interest in maintaining a global balance of power with the perceived Soviet challenge to that equilibrium in a part of the world that could hardly be more pivotal – Western Europe. Kennan's approach formed a tightly focused policy for dealing with the Soviet Union. There were four elements to it: (1) no further efforts would be made to conceal differences with the Soviets; (2) there would be no further concessions in negotiations; (3) US military strength would be expanded and requests for military and economic aid would be looked upon more favourably; and (4) negotiations on a number of different fronts would continue, but only for the purpose of registering Moscow's acceptance of American positions or for publicizing Soviet intransigence for the purpose of winning allies abroad.[51]

While containment involved a more aggressive approach with the Soviets, it was the subsequent enunciation of the Truman Doctrine and the Marshall Plan that revealed a recognition that the Cold War would be a long-term struggle, one that would pit two global systems against one another in a wide range of political and economic contexts. US officials realized that their initiatives would probably antagonize the Soviets, but they felt compelled to take action nonetheless. The United States was caught in a classic dilemma whereby the steps deemed essential to promote its own security clashed with the security imperatives of its adversary. The Soviets, seeing Communists excised from the governing coalitions in Western and southern Europe, and frightened by the spectre of German reconstruction under Western auspices, could be expected to fight back. American officials were willing to accept a further rupture in the US-Soviet relationship be- cause they were convinced that the dangers of inaction exceeded the risks involved in provoking the Soviets.[52]

The gathering storm clouds in US-Soviet relations were reflected in NSC- 20/4, passed in late 1948. Titled "US Objectives with Respect to the USSR," the National Security Council document repeated many of the now- common refrains in US security policy. The main fear pertained to "Soviet domination of the potential power of Eurasia." The aim of US policy was to "reduce the power and influence of the USSR to limits which no longer constitute a threat to the peace, national independence and stability of the world family of nations."[53] NSC-20/4 embodied the core ingredients of US national security policy in the postwar period – globalism and anti- communism. However, the study offered no clear definition of objectives or priorities, no assessment of the attributes and weaknesses of various tac- tics, and no insight into the opportunities generated by prospective rifts within the Communist world.[54]

In early 1950, just a few months after the confirmation of a Soviet atomic test, the basis of US security policy in the Cold War was established. NSC-68 presented the Soviet threat in stark terms, stating that "the Soviet Union has one purpose and that is world domination," and furthermore, "unlike previous aspirants to hegemony, is animated by a new fanatic faith, anti- thetical to our own, and seeks to impose its absolute authority over the rest of the world."[55] US goals were designed to reduce Soviet power on its pe- riphery, establish independent countries in Eastern Europe, and "foster a fundamental change in the nature of the Soviet system, a change toward which the frustration of the design is the first and perhaps most important task."[56] The report, written by Paul Nitze, the director of policy planning in the State Department, urged the rapid expansion of American military ca- pabilities and the strengthening of US allies.

NSC-68 is widely regarded as the first comprehensive statement of US postwar national strategy. For the first time in the post-1945 period, a defi- nition of goals and a general statement of methods oriented primarily to the needs of the Cold War was articulated. It was directed toward the objec- tives of balance and stability in US security policy. That policy was now firmly based on the model of the Cold War, and of the global competition with the Soviet Union that it had spawned. As Melvyn Leffler has observed in his study *A Preponderance of Power,* "in the worldview of NSC-68, there was no room for neutrality; diplomacy was a zero-sum game. The stakes were global preponderance."[57]

Thus, by the start of the Korean War in June 1950, the Cold War global system had largely been established. Two rival power blocs – with hegemonic powers at their helm – were in the process of being formed, and countries around the world were coming under increasing pressure to join one of the respective "camps." The United States and the Soviet Union, as the dominant nations of the new system, had enormous powers and responsibilities. While direct conflict between the two had been avoided, a pattern was being established in which each side would test the patience of the other in an area of vulnerability, pushing it to the point where a direct military confrontation seemed not only possible but likely, as in the case of Berlin. Only at that point did the crisis subside, to be replayed somewhere else under slightly differing circumstances.

As a prominent member of the Western alliance, Canada had to adjust rapidly to the altered global security environment, which it did with energy and enthusiasm. Canadian defence and external affairs officials generally shared the views of their American colleagues on the dangers represented by the Soviets. Canada may have lacked the political compulsion to characterize every Soviet act in the worst possible light, but political leaders nonetheless warned the public of the threat from Soviet policy in order to win acceptance for the increased burdens of taxation and defence.[58]

Canadian policy of the day cannot merely be dismissed as anti-Communist and pro-American, although it certainly was both. As John Holmes has noted, "if the chips were down, Canadian governments and, the evidence suggests, the Canadian public had no doubt which side they were on."[59] This was not so much the American side as it was the side that included both the United States and most of Canada's other allies as well. Canada quickly realized that its interests – particularly those of a political nature – were not always consistent with those of the United States, and it often sided with other members of the West in intra-alliance disputes. At the same time, though, officials in Ottawa realized the "special relationship" that Canada had with the United States, and that there might be occasions where a choice between the two would be required. The ambivalent Canadian policy was to avoid weakening the United States while assisting in the weaving of a larger political web to control the behaviour of all states.[60]

Military Innovation and the Power of Nuclear Weapons

The atomic bombs that destroyed Hiroshima and Nagasaki were the most formidable weapons the world had ever seen, but several years would pass before the full impact of the nuclear revolution was recognized in defence and government circles. Several important military developments took place in the immediate postwar period, including advances in bomber aircraft and the slow growth of the American nuclear stockpile, the Soviet atomic explosion of 1949, and the decision to develop hydrogen weapons.

From 1945 through 1948, the era of American nuclear monopoly, the US system for stockpiling nuclear weapons and making them available for use was extremely limited. Indeed, the precise extent of this was not known until quite recently. For several decades the assumption had been that, as the only nuclear nation, the United States must have had overwhelming nuclear superiority.[61] In fact, it is questionable whether the stockpile in the early postwar years was large enough to be meaningful in a strategic sense. There were, for example, only two nuclear weapons at the end of 1945, nine in July 1946, and thirteen one year later; by 1948, the number had begun to increase more rapidly, with fifty weapons available.[62] Throughout this period a "doctrine of scarcity" existed among US military planners.[63] This was probably a factor in the initial reluctance to develop war plans that took advantage of the American atomic monopoly.

However, the small number of weapons was not the only factor that raised doubts about the possible effectiveness of US nuclear forces. Another consideration was that none of the bombs were stored assembled and it took forty men two days to put each one together. Further, each was a "Fat Man" implosion bomb that weighed about 4,500 kilograms and was relatively inefficient in its use of fissionable material.[64] The bombs were so large and cumbersome that loading one onto a bomber entailed installing a special hoist in a pit, placing the bomb into the pit, rolling the aircraft over it, and then lifting the weapon into the specially modified bomb bay.

The B-29 was, until 1950, the mainstay of the Strategic Air Command and the principal delivery vehicle of the US nuclear forces. Through 1948, there were only thirty specially configured B-29s in SAC modified to carry atomic bombs, all in the 509th Bomb Group based in Roswell, New Mexico.[65] The range of this aircraft was 7,000 kilometres, meaning that its effective combat radius was only 3,500 kilometres; for the bombers to reach targets in the Soviet Union, the United States would have to make use of overseas bases or aerial refuelling. While the latter alternative seemed preferable, it carried additional requirements for the operation and maintenance of several hundred tanker aircraft as well as raised numerous logistical difficulties for the US Air Force. Thus, there was much concern during the immediate postwar period about identifying strategically suitable bases that would permit the refuelling of American aircraft. Attention quickly focused on three main locations for such bases – Europe, the Middle East, and North Africa.

During the period in which base rights in these areas were being negotiated, the most critical US bases were in Canada, Britain, and Japan, which as a result of close security ties were the countries where agreements were reached most quickly. Of these, the UK bases were considered the most vital from 1945 to 1950. Not only could they be a principal launch point for attacks on the Soviet Union but they were also the main recycling centres under US war plans for planes and crews returning from missions originating outside Britain.[66] UK concern over the Soviet threat and the desire to cooperate with the United States on military matters resulted in the rapid negotiation and construction of three SAC bases – at Mildenhall, Sculthorpe, and Lakenheath – and plans were under way to build up to five more.[67] Despite the quick success in negotiating these arrangements, though, it was widely realized in the United States that the best solution would be to deploy longer-range aircraft that did not need forward bases at all.

Concerns about the effectiveness of the Strategic Air Command were greatly reduced in 1948-9, when the force's operational capabilities were improved considerably. First, initial deliveries were made of the B-36, the first truly long-range bomber. Second, an additional long-range aircraft, the B-50 (a modified version of the B-29), was also introduced, although in limited numbers.[68] Last, tanker aircraft for in-flight refuelling became operational (modified B-29s, designated KB-29Ms), although performance limitations meant that this capability remained limited for some years.

As a result of the changes, by 1950 SAC consisted of 120 modified B-29s, B-36s, and B-50s, with six bomb assembly teams trained and organized.[69] Moreover, the introduction of the new aircraft dramatically increased the capability of the United States to project military power; this was clear during the 1948-9 Berlin airlift, when the United States was able to resupply the city through the use of its air forces. Still, concerns over the performance of the new bombers led to limited production runs, and the United States had to remain dependent on overseas bases well into the 1950s, when the more advanced, long-range B-52 began entering service.

As noted, in 1948 the size of the US nuclear stockpile began to grow dramatically. The bomb was increasingly influencing US war plans, and it had come to dominate most conflict scenarios. However, no sooner had the US military finally started to adjust its thinking to include nuclear weapons than the US atomic monopoly was shattered: in August 1949, Western intelligence confirmed a Soviet atomic test. The Soviet Union would not have an operational nuclear force for several years, but such a development was considered a virtual certainty. This had a paradoxical effect in that while it discouraged doctrines based on atomic weapons as a uniquely American advantage, it also locked the United States into a nuclear strategy.[70] In effect, the United States now recognized that in the future all war planning would have to take account of the possible use of nuclear weapons, and strategies would have to be devised that would specifically recognize – and, it was to be hoped, avoid – this possibility. As later chapters demonstrate, US strategists and policy makers quickly came up with doctrines that emphasized the Americans' ability to defeat the Soviets in any nuclear conflict, believing that such strategies would make a Soviet challenge less likely (a view not shared by Canadian officials).

The Soviet Union's ability to compete with the United States in several areas of weapons technology ended up surprising American officials throughout the period. The Soviet development of nuclear weapons came well before US intelligence had predicted.[71] The Soviet challenge in areas of conventional military technology, such as jet engines and radar, was similarly impressive. Soviet technological prowess was further demonstrated by the introduction of a series of bombers in the late 1940s. In 1948, the Soviet Union unveiled its version of the B-29, the Tu-4. Although the aircraft's range was limited, it was capable of return missions to Western Europe and one-way missions to North America, and it demonstrated a considerable ability in aircraft research and design, although it was widely regarded in the West as a virtual copy of the American plane. This bomber was quickly replaced by newer models of indigenous design – the Tu-16 Badger, Mya-4 Bison, and Tu-95 Bear, all aircraft that revealed a Soviet capability roughly comparable to that of the United States. By the early 1950s, then, defence planners in both the United States and Canada realized that the Soviet Union could threaten continental North America with an atomic attack that the air defences of the time would be virtually powerless to prevent.[72]

The response of the United States to the emerging Soviet capability for both the manufacture and delivery of atomic bombs was not to back down but to raise the stakes, moving to the development of hydrogen weapons. This ushered in an age of nuclear plenty and solidified a trend toward ever-increasing levels of destruction.[73] The decision to proceed on such a course was reached only after a divisive debate within the American defence establishment.[74] While the debate was highly charged and pitted fellow scientists against one another, what it overlooked was that the hydrogen bomb did not raise any fundamentally new questions. The "super" certainly increased the amount of destructive power available, but the moral and strategic issues it raised differed from those of a few years earlier only by a matter of degree.[75]

On a purely technical level, however, the hydrogen bomb did differ from its fissionable cousin. Given an atomic bomb to act as a trigger, a "super" required no expensive fissionable material because it was fuelled by hydrogen, the most plentiful element in nature. Each H-bomb was at least a thousand times as powerful as an atomic bomb. With the destructive power now available, SAC planners calculated that they could destroy three-quarters of the population of 188 Soviet cities, with casualties approaching 75 million people, within a matter of hours.[76] Further, unlike the atom bomb, an H-bomb was so powerful that only a few might force another great state to surrender. At the same time, it was difficult to conceive of a situation – *any situation* – in which it would make political or strategic sense to use one.

In sum, by 1950 both the United States and Soviet Union were well on their way to developing large and varied nuclear forces that could be used for both strategic and tactical missions. In addition, the means of nuclear delivery was steadily improving, as aircraft design and performance was in the midst of a revolution (the sound barrier was first broken in 1947), while missile programs in both countries had begun a long process of increased research and funding. These developments were to have enormous implications for the international security environment because they required entirely new modes of thinking – to which Canadians contributed – about the use of force.

As a neighbour and defence partner of the United States, Canada could not help but be affected by these changes. Even though Canada "chose" not to develop a nuclear force of its own, it was a strong supporter of the Western alliance, which by the early 1950s had adopted a strategy based on the early use of nuclear weapons in any future conflict.[77] In addition, Canada was home to several US air and naval bases, many of which played an important role in US strategic planning. The key point to note is that this was a period of rapid military change, and that by the start of the new decade many of the technological realities of the modern nuclear age had entered the defence debate.

The Strategic War Plans of the Superpowers
In the early years of the Cold War, both the United States and Soviet Union believed that the best way to ensure security was by strengthening their military forces. Given increasing political differences, it is easy to understand why both had such views, but the attempts of each side to enhance its own military position only compelled the other to do the same. In short, there was no conception of security as a common problem, no realization that the only change that would be mutually beneficial in the long run was one that made *both* sides feel secure.[78] Further, as a result of differing military capabilities, each took a different path to achieving "security." The United States, as a nuclear power, gradually emphasized its atomic capability, while the Soviets, lacking such a capacity until 1949, believed that massive amounts of conventional weaponry could make up for their lack of nuclear weapons.

Early American thinking on the future role of nuclear forces was contained in the 1945 "Spaatz Report,"[79] which set the conceptual tone for the following few years. While recognizing the powerful military effect of the bomb, the report emphasized the scarcity of the nuclear stockpile and the fact that such weapons would remain prohibitively expensive to produce, which meant that they were unlikely to enter American war plans in significant numbers. These conclusions were largely repeated in a subsequent report prepared by the Joint Staff Strategic Survey, which emphasized that if

the enemy had sufficient "stamina," the atomic bomb might not be decisive.[80] This report further noted that victory in future conflict would still
require physical occupation of the enemy homeland, a conclusion that revealed a basic failure to appreciate the enormity of the change that Hiroshima and Nagasaki represented.

By 1947-8, official US thinking about the atomic bomb began to change.
Several factors accounted for this transformation, but the most important
was the realization that early thinking on the scarcity of the bomb might
have been inaccurate and the recognition that Soviet conventional superiority needed to be balanced by American nuclear power. Thus, at this time,
the US military began designing war plans that took full advantage of the
US nuclear monopoly, placing reliance on a massive atomic blitz in the
opening stages of any future conflict with the Soviet Union.[81] The blitz was
to have two major objectives – to slow down the enemy advance and to
destroy sufficiently valuable social and economic targets as to quickly com-
pel Soviet surrender.[82]

The emerging American emphasis on nuclear weapons meant that its
options in case of a Soviet military challenge were limited. This was revealed during the 1948 Berlin crisis, when President Truman authorized the
use of atomic weapons in the event of war.[83] Although Truman regarded
atomic bombs as horror weapons to be employed only in the last resort, it
was important, if deterrence was to work, that he affirm publicly that he
would not hesitate to use them if necessary.[84] By the turn of the decade, any
remaining US hesitation on nuclear use had been eliminated, and the bomb
began to revolutionize American thinking on the use of force and the possible course of future conflict.

In contrast, early postwar Soviet military doctrine was based on Stalin's
concept of "permanently operating factors." This theory was rigidly adhered
to not only because of Stalin's personal power but also because its merit
seemed to have been demonstrated by the victories of the Second World
War.[85] Stalin contended that to win in battle, a government needed to be
able to depend on a number of constants, such as stability on the home
front and the morale of the army. War was seen as a total clash between
societies, in which all the strengths and weaknesses of the belligerents influenced the final result. In addition, there was a belief that success on the
battlefield was dependent on having varied and capable military forces. Last,
Soviet officials advanced the notion of historical determinism – that is, that
the Soviets had the advantage of representing a superior social and economic form of society, and that their eventual victory was thus inevitable.

As for Soviet views on nuclear weapons, the country spent the period
1945-9 largely playing down their importance. This was not surprising,
given that the Soviets did not yet have such weapons, and that under the

permanently operating factors major changes in strategy were rare and tended to take decades to be fully appreciated and understood. Reflecting this belief, Stalin noted in 1946 that "atomic bombs are meant to frighten those with weak nerves, but they cannot decide the fate of wars since atomic bombs are quite insufficient for this."[86] Indeed, even after the first Soviet atomic test three years later, Stalin continued to issue statements that indicated he was largely sceptical of nuclear weapons.[87] In this regard, it seems likely that given the early US advantage in both weapons design and forces, the Soviets were reluctant to stress a new mode of warfare that would undermine their considerable advantage in conventional forces.

Rhetoric aside, however, the early postwar strategic views of the United States and Soviet Union were surprisingly similar. Both continued to see the next war as a kind of repeat of the Second World War. Each side understood and appreciated the destructiveness of nuclear weapons, but neither thought such weapons would be truly decisive. On the American side, this scepticism was linked to the limited atomic stockpile and the difficulties associated with delivery, as well as some lingering doubts about the significance of the weapons themselves. On the Soviet side, the Stalinist notion of permanently operating factors did not permit any radical changes of strategy. Thus, in many respects, neither country was initially convinced that nuclear weapons represented a true revolution in the use of force.

By 1950, however, this began to change. US government reports recognized the radically different nature of the emerging security environment and the types of conflict most likely to unfold should war with the Soviet Union occur. For their part, the Soviets quickly began concentrating on increasing weapons yields, hoping to nullify American technical sophistication with brute force – a practice that continued for decades. With the growth in weapons stockpiles on both sides in the early 1950s, nuclear weapons not only began to dominate war planning, but increasingly played a critical role in *political* discussions and negotiations. A state of mutual atomic deterrence was coming into being, although it would be some time before defence analysts recognized this new reality. In such an environment, strategic thinking needed to be reformulated to take account of new conditions, a challenge posed to all countries but most of all to those, like Canada, that found themselves on the front line of the emerging global divide and whose defence policies therefore had added symbolic importance.

Looking Forward, Looking Back:
The Canadian Defence Environment in 1950

The years 1945-9 were critical in setting the broad framework of postwar Canadian defence and security policy. Domestically, the period began with the Canadian military reeling under a massive program of demobilization in the aftermath of the war, but ended with funding increases and new equipment purchases, a trend that would grow stronger in the coming years. Further, two issues demanded immediate attention – Canada's policy on nuclear weapons and the emerging defence partnership with the United States. Regarding the former, while Canada decided not to produce nuclear weapons, it had extensive ties to their development, a policy ambiguity that was rarely acknowledged. As for the latter, the Canada-US defence partnership revealed a Canadian appreciation of the power and responsibility of the United States, and a recognition that continental defence cooperation was preferable to unilateral American defence initiatives. The decisions reached on these matters would have enormous implications over the following decade. Last, partly out of a desire to balance this country's ties with the United States, Canada joined an alliance of Western states for whom an attack against one would be regarded as an attack against all.

With regard to developments in the external environment, the combination of the Cold War, military innovation, and changes in strategic thought and war planning resulted in a vastly different security landscape in 1950. The growth of the US nuclear arsenal, combined with advances in aircraft, meant that the United States could now literally destroy the whole of Soviet society in a matter of hours. For their part, the Soviets did not yet have the combined nuclear force of the United States, and would not achieve strategic parity until the late 1960s, but their nuclear capabilities were on the verge of rapid growth and Western policy makers certainly had to assume a considerable Soviet atomic capacity. Indeed, with growing resources of wealth and power, many in the West believed that the Soviets might challenge the United States directly, or more likely, the American commitment to the defence of Europe, an area that was believed to be particularly vulnerable.

This was the strategic environment that Canadian defence officials encountered in 1950. It was one dominated by the global competition for power and influence, and the scientific and technical advances that had made the use of force a deadly gamble. Around the world, analysts struggled to make sense of the new environment, but it was in the United States where the largest concentration of defence observers could be found. This emerging community quickly focused its attention on the nuclear revolution, and the changes that were occurring as a result. In Canada, officials in the Department of National Defence struggled with many of the same issues, although the understandings that were reached frequently reflected different interests, concerns, and values.

2
Canada's Air Defence Debate

Officials in the Department of National Defence dealt with several matters of urgency through the 1950s and early 1960s, but few were as crucial as developments in air defence. Rapid advances in technology were making the air defence mission vital to Canada; at the same time, pressures were rising out of the defence partnership with the United States. This was a time of growing concern over the possibility of a Soviet first strike, particularly in the mid-1950s when Soviet atomic and delivery capabilities improved. Canada was therefore under increased pressure to enhance continental air defences to the point where, at minimum, there would be an effective system of radar warning and a reasonable prospect of significant attrition against attacking aircraft. In addition, because air defence involved several different aspects of defence policy – including hardware decisions, command and control issues, and nuclear strategy – it quickly became an area of serious concern. This chapter examines how officials in both DND and the Department of External Affairs approached the issue, and reveals that while they were generally sensitive to the demands of Canada's powerful neighbour, they also kept this nation's defence and security interests as foremost considerations. It becomes clear, however, that those interests were defined somewhat differently by the two departments, with DND officials stressing the common air defence interests with the United States, while those from DEA emphasized the need to protect Canadian political interests. Thus, while officials disagreed on both the nature of the problem and the preferred solution, they all offered analyses that they believed would further Canada's larger strategic interests. To demonstrate this, the following pages focus on three key air defence developments of the period: cooperation with the United States that ultimately led to the North American Air Defence Command (NORAD) agreement; the Avro Arrow and the interservice debate that it generated; and departmental studies that examined the larger relationship between air defence and nuclear strategy. First, though, come a few background observations on how DND officials viewed the Soviet threat in the 1950s.

Growing Recognition of the Soviet Threat
and Its Implications for Canadian Air Defence Forces

In the late 1940s and early 1950s, officials in DND began adjusting to an air defence environment that had changed greatly since the end of the war. In the immediate postwar period, the quality of Soviet air forces was poor and relations with the Soviet Union were not yet dominated by hostility and conflict. Somewhat surprisingly, however, as relations gradually deteriorated, DND reports and threat assessments continued to emphasize the relatively small likelihood of a Soviet attack. A November 1949 Chiefs of Staff report, for example, concluded that while Soviet leaders' had as their "ultimate objective" a Communist world order under their domination, the continued superiority of Western military forces made it unlikely that the Soviet Union would challenge the political status quo, at least in the near- to medium term.[1]

By the early 1950s, Canadian officials were beginning to reconsider their earlier optimism. By this time, not only had political relations with the Soviet Union deteriorated alarmingly, but Soviet military forces had begun to improve dramatically. Now there was pressure in Canada to ensure that air defences would be effective in an increasingly sophisticated military environment. DND officials began studying these changes in 1950-1, and by the latter year the Chiefs of Staff had accepted that "certain vital and vulnerable targets in Canada are liable to Soviet attack."[2] In early 1952, a general staff report concluded that all of North America was at risk of Soviet atomic attack, and that defensive measures therefore needed to be adopted. As the report noted, "the most probable type of bombing attack that Canadian air defences must be prepared to meet is from groups of Russian bombers carrying amongst them an atom bomb."[3] The report went on to discuss recent advances in Soviet bomber forces; it cautioned against concluding that range limitations, which precluded the possibility of return missions, meant Soviet aircraft were incapable of striking North American targets.

Concern over the Soviet military threat intensified over the following few years as defence officials familiarized themselves with the emerging strategic environment. In 1954, a report on the requirements for the Canadian air defence system highlighted the serious nature of this threat. The document began by noting that, with recent changes in weapons and improvements in Soviet aircraft, "an attrition rate much higher than heretofore required must be inflicted on attacking aircraft."[4] Indeed, the report estimated that a rate of even 90 percent "may not be sufficient" to offer adequate protection to the civilian population.[5] Recognizing that the primary

Canadian interceptor of the day, the CF-100, was incapable of effectively countering modern Soviet aircraft, the study concluded that the only way to redress this imbalance was through the introduction of surface-to-air missiles. This recommendation helped spark an internally divisive debate that would be settled only years later, when the decision to acquire the Bomarc missile was finally reached.

Even when concern grew that ballistic missiles would become the main strategic delivery vehicle of the Soviet Union, defence officials cautioned against neglecting the traditional air defence mission. A prime example occurred in mid-1958, one year after Sputnik had demonstrated the Soviet capability in rockets. Defence officials observed that, due to uncertainties over the range and accuracy of Soviet missiles, "the USSR will be forced to keep bombers in their inventory for years to come" and hence air defence forces – including sophisticated interceptors – would still be required in the future.[6] However, as is discussed further in this chapter, DND officials did not develop a consistent position on this issue, and at other times concluded that aircraft would serve no useful purpose in a strategic environment dominated by missiles. The key point to note is that intelligence estimates of Soviet aircraft production, particularly in the latter part of this period, were to become a highly political exercise with serious implications for both defence procurement decisions and larger issues of defence policy and strategy.

In sum, the size and diversity of the Soviet military force – and, more significantly, the Canadian perception of that force – ensured that Canadian air defences would be at the centre of the domestic defence debate throughout the 1950s. Canadian defence officials believed that due to the nature and severity of the Soviet military threat, measures had to be taken that would contribute to the overall deterrent capability of the West. As becomes clear, enhancing the deterrent and protecting and furthering Canadian security interests were the major Canadian air defence concerns that dictated DND's strategic thinking on the issue.

Continental Air Defence Cooperation with the United States

The increasingly intimate defence partnership with the United States, combined with the gradual development of a radar warning system in the Canadian North, led to growing demands for a formalized system of bilateral air defence cooperation. These demands resulted in the initial announcement of the North American Air Defence Command in 1957. Since the 1987 publication of Joseph Jockel's *No Boundaries Upstairs,* the basic position that Canada adopted during the negotiation of the command has become well known, so this part of the story need not be retold here.[7] What does require attention are the Canadian air defence interests and concerns that were identified before the negotiation of the command, and the manner in which DND and DEA officials articulated them. Especially important is a need to examine *whose* interests were advanced, and *how* those interests were formed. It becomes clear that defence officials emphasized the essential complementary nature of US and Canadian air defence interests in the nuclear age, and that this required novel defence arrangements between the two countries. On the other hand, External Affairs officials were far less enthusiastic over air defence cooperation, although the degree to which they actively opposed such arrangements is a matter of continuing debate. In any event, officials in both departments identified distinctly Canadian air defence concerns that raised difficult questions about defence planning and policy.

Early DND thinking on air defence cooperation with the United States was contained in a 1951 report prepared by the Joint Planning Committee for the Chiefs of Staff.[8] The report recommended "extending and consolidating" the continental air defence warning system through the establishment of increased radar facilities as well as the introduction of more interceptors. The document's principal concern was how radar coverage could be extended to all parts of Canada while ensuring that the Canadian network developed in tandem with the United States. Greater radar coverage was required to alert Canadian air defences of possible enemy air attack as well as to set in motion civil defence plans, the report explained. Even at this early date, however, the ultimate need for "one operational air defence system" was understood. No specific proposals on the division of continental air defence responsibilities were offered, but there was a recognition of the mutual nature of the North American air defence problem, which would require a coordinated response in the future.

DND thinking on air defence was also revealed in memoranda regarding the early 1950s directives that allowed tactical air force cooperation between the United States and Canada to intensify.[9] A memo drafted for the Cabinet Defence Committee in November 1951, for example, explained why the mutual re-enforcement of air defence forces was required.[10] It noted that "after the outbreak of war against a common enemy, circumstances may occur which will require rapid re-enforcement of the air defence forces of one country by the other ... The rapidity with which squadrons can be re-deployed to meet the tactical situation may determine the degree of effectiveness of the air defence system."

In this passage, there was an implicit realization that air defence in North America was the joint responsibility of Canada and the United States, and that mechanisms needed to be established that would ensure efficiency and rationality. By agreeing to terms of mutual re-enforcement, Canadian defence officials recognized that this country's foremost air defence interest was ensuring that the most effective system, *regardless of nationality,* would be in operation during times of crisis. This document is thus significant in indicating a conceptual shift away from a nationally oriented security model and toward a new paradigm that recognized the commonalities in Canada-US air defence interests.

This is not to say, though, that defence officials always viewed Canadian security interests as being synonymous with those of the United States. The documentation reveals numerous instances where officials focused on issues that raised particularly difficult issues for Canada. One such example occurred in 1952, at which time the implications of a proposed North American air defence system were examined in a report prepared by George Lindsey, a member of the Operational Research Group of the Defence Research Board.[11]

Lindsey's report argued that establishing a Distant Early Warning line would be expensive, and that new airfields would be required in the Canadian North that would pose an administrative and technical challenge.[12] However, a more troubling difficulty was raised, one that the author himself labelled sinister. The "defence in depth" concept had essentially been adopted as the de facto guiding principle of North American air defence.[13] Lindsey noted that, as it involved waves of defences gradually claiming greater and greater attrition of attacking aircraft, the best-protected part of the system would be at the southern end – that is, the United States. "If defence in depth is necessary, and is successful," Lindsey noted, "then the place to live is down deep in the system." However, if the enemy believed this to be the case, it would probably concentrate attention on the "outer surface" of the network, which it could attack "without paying an extortionate price." While not specifically identified, the outer surface of the North American network was obviously Canada.

The implications of this finding were left unstated, but were nonetheless quite clear. Lindsey had recognized that Canada's geographic location in the northern half of the North American continent presented difficult defence challenges. He essentially warned that, in the event of a major Soviet air attack, defence in depth would involve considerable devastation over Canadian areas, with lesser damage as one went farther south. To avoid such an outcome, Lindsey suggested, the entire orientation of the North American air defence network would have to be pushed farther north, perhaps to the Arctic Circle and even into Soviet territory. Not only would such a network be prohibitively expensive, but the technical challenges would probably prove insurmountable. The report reveals a distinctive Canadian approach to the air defence problem, and a recognition that Canada's interests were not always synonymous with those of its neighbour.

By 1954-5, the attention of defence planners was increasingly shifting to the question of a new air defence command authority between Canada and the United States. DND's early rationale and position on this issue can be found in a report prepared by the Joint Planning Committee in July 1954.[14] After reviewing the current concept of continental air defence, the report noted that the "coordination of the air defence effort constitutes a major problem due to the division of control which now exists between the various commands." To alleviate the problem, four alternative air defence arrangements were discussed, each involving some type of joint Canada-US command authority.[15]

The findings of this study reveal the uncertainties with which Canadian defence officials approached the issue, and the recognition of the delicate political considerations involved. "Planning and control of air defence should be improved," the study concluded, yet it also recognized that political challenges would have to be overcome before any bilateral arrangement was finalized. While emphasizing caution, the study noted that "the appointment of a separate (Commander-in-Chief) Air Defence with responsibility for planning and an appropriate measure of operational control over all air defence forces allocated to the Canada-US region is desirable." There was also an appreciation that a binational command arrangement would improve the air defence capability of both countries, as the current system was "subject to delays, possible disagreements, and misunderstandings between commands which might impose serious limitations on the ability to deal effectively with air raids." The basic DND rationale for a joint command was thus identified: a new arrangement would offer improved air defences to both Canada and the United States, and therefore reduce the likelihood that a Soviet air attack would succeed.

Two years later, in October 1956, a report on the integration and operational control of continental air defences explored many of the same issues.[16] This report observed that the "effective use of all available weapons can only be accomplished by someone who has sufficient information of the over-all air defence situation to make these split second decisions required to use forces to the best advantage." It thus called for "flexibility of employment of forces" and "decisions necessitated by the tempo of the air battle," conditions that could only be met by a new command authority. "It is therefore necessary," the report concluded, "to have in existence in peacetime the organization which will be required in war." Much of this report dealt with possible chains of command, administrative arrangements, and procedures for the establishment of defence plans, issues that would prove controversial in later years. Once again, though, the main strategic interest identified was establishing and operating the most effective air defence system for the continent, one that would serve Canadian security interests.

An *aide-mémoire*, written for Prime Minister John Diefenbaker in the days immediately before the 1957 news release announcing the air defence agreement, gives a further indication of the interests of defence officials. The document, prepared by General Charles Foulkes, chairman of the Chiefs of Staff Committee, began by noting that "we must continue to provide a reasonable air defence for this country, and it is obvious that these arrangements must be made in collaboration with the US."[17] After reviewing the requirements for air defence, the report stated that "it is quite obvious that international boundaries cannot be respected when fighting an air battle," and that "the whole air defence system must be planned and operated as one single integrated system." The military rationale for the command was thus the enhancement of the continental air defence network and the realization that, on its own, Canada was not capable of fully defending the air approaches to North America. Readers might note that this particular report was part of the package of proposals that the prime minister personally approved on 24 July 1957, thereby leading to the initial air defence agreement.

The emphasis on military efficiency and effectiveness that was the central concern of DND was not shared by the Department of External Affairs, which instead focused on the command's political implications and costs. This approach was first revealed in an October 1953 DEA report.[18] After reviewing developments in US air defence policy, the paper turned its attention to "some problems for Canada." The main problem identified was that "the Canadian Government may or may not be convinced, when US projects are proposed, that they are reasonably necessary when [weighed] against global strategic factors and political obligations overseas." The paper cautioned that Canada would have to carefully consider its national security interest, as it could expect significant pressure – both military and political – from the United States to cooperate in a variety of defence projects. The report suggested that the choice to Canada would increasingly be one of either cooperation or of allowing the United States "to develop and operate [projects] exclusively with US money and men." While no specific recommendation on this question was offered, the report recognized that "the time has come to start thinking seriously [about these issues]." This was an early attempt by DEA to urge caution when evaluating future US defence proposals, while recognizing that the pressure to cooperate might be overwhelming.

A more telling indication of the department's apprehension over closer cooperation between the two countries' air forces was revealed in a 1954 memo prepared by the defence liaison division for the undersecretary. The memo agreed that a single military command structure would lead to the more effective use of Canadian and American air defence forces. It observed, however, that the probable result could be "to have the responsibility for the air defence of Canada, including the command of Canadian air defence forces, vested in a United States officer."[19] Whether Canada was prepared to surrender its sovereignty for purposes of continental defence was, in the division's view, "the most difficult and the most important issue."

Over the next several years, as the continental air defence proposal gained military and political support in both the United States and Canada, External Affairs officials remained largely silent on the issue. The minutes of both the Chiefs of Staff and the Cabinet Defence Committees, where departmental concerns could have been raised most easily, reveal a dearth of DEA comment. This changed in early 1957, a few months after a joint Canada-US military study group recommended the need for an integrated air defence system.[20]

R.M. MacDonnell, the deputy undersecretary of the department, told the Chiefs of Staff Committee in February 1957 that External Affairs was in general agreement with the proposal, but he also stated that the "United States authorities should be reminded that Canadian willingness to agree to joint operational control ... should be met by a corresponding US recognition of the need for adequate consultation with the Canadian authorities."[21] The committee took no action at this time, however, deciding that the matter was too important to be settled in the final days of the Liberal government. MacDonnell's concerns were repeated in a 12 June 1957 DEA memo written by Undersecretary of State Jules Léger for the minister, where it was noted that "Canadian consent to enter into an agreement with the US to set up a single operational commander of air defence forces should certainly provide us with an opportunity ... to reassert the need for close consultation and to impress upon the US Government Canada's special place among the countries allied to the US."[22]

After the announcement of the air defence command on 1 August 1957, External's opposition came into clearer focus. This was first revealed in a September 1957 letter from Léger to General Foulkes.[23] The letter was a clear indication of the poor relations that had developed between the two departments over the issue of the joint command.[24] It asserted that DEA had, from the very beginning of talks, been concerned about the implications of any joint command and had advised that the issue raised an "opportunity which should not be lost to reassert the need for close consultation" and to impress upon the US government Canada's "special" place among US allies. The letter went on to challenge Foulkes on the need for a formal diplomatic agreement for the new command, a point that DND was strenuously denying at the time.[25]

In a February 1958 report, External further attempted to convince DND of the larger political implications of the air defence command. Titled "NORAD – Political Control," the report recognized from the outset that the "most likely" form of attack against North America would be through the air, and therefore air defences "are one of the most important elements of our security forces."[26] However, it was precisely because this defence task was so important that political control needed to be better formalized, so that its operation in times of crisis would be clearly understood. The report went on to recommend the establishment of an "additional committee of Ministers whose terms of reference should give them the scope to consider all matters of common concern to Canada and the US."[27] The central message was that a joint air defence command raised many issues – not all of them military – that needed to be considered by political and diplomatic officials.

Many of these departmental concerns were restated, and several new ones introduced, in External's principal study of continental air defence, which was released in August 1958, four months after the formal exchange of notes on the new command authority.[28] This report, "Continental Air Defence – Foreign Policy Implications," offered comments that went well beyond the establishment of the command; it included general observations on the Soviet threat, Canadian forces in Europe, and even Canada's commitments to the United Nations.[29]

Perhaps the study's most important observation was that in any appreciation of a potential threat, "a balance has to be struck between (a) what the enemy is capable of doing, and (b) what his intentions may be." That encapsulates much of the uncertainty that officials in DEA were feeling at the time. Many in the department did not believe that a Soviet attack was likely in the near term, and that the preparations for imminent conflict in the West were an overreaction to worst-case theorizing and uncertainty over what Soviet intentions were. At the same time, the document acknowledged that air defence preparations had to be taken, a result of the defence partnership with the United States, recent changes in the Soviet force structure, as well as a genuine Canadian desire to improve the defence of the continent.

The study's most revealing comments dealt with the manner in which Canada could most effectively contribute to North American air defence. The report stated that Canada had two options – to cooperate with the United States or to refuse further involvement and accept US mutual assistance. The report did not endorse either option; rather it offered advantages and disadvantages of both. On the plus side, it pointed out that one of the main responsibilities of any government is the "ability to defend sovereignty adequately," and in Canada's case that could be best accomplished through cooperative security arrangements with the United States. Still, the document suggested that the issue was not a simple one, as Canada had to decide how far it could go "in cooperative arrangements designed to ensure its survival in the military sense without jeopardizing, in the political and economic field, the very thing it has set out to protect."

On the option of accepting US mutual assistance, the study offered surprising observations, especially given the fact that since the end of the war the Canadian government had asserted, with a certain amount of national pride, that Canada was the only Western country that had not accepted American aid. The fact that accepting US mutual assistance was even an option, though, revealed how fragile the country's defence position had become, at least according to DEA. The report suggested that by joining an alliance of Western countries (i.e., the North Atlantic Treaty Organization), Canada had already accepted "a diminution of sovereignty," and the negotiation of the NORAD agreement was simply a further step down this path. The study implied that, as the respective military and financial contributions of the two countries were expected to be highly uneven, the command's operation might in fact qualify as assistance, but no clear answer was given.

Last, the study offered observations on the larger nature of the Soviet threat. It recognized that growing Soviet economic strength represented as formidable a long-term challenge as did its increasing stockpile of nuclear weapons. Given this, the report suggested that the Soviet threat should increasingly be seen as an economic/diplomatic one, with subsequent implications for Western foreign policies. The United States could be expected, because of its enormous size and power, to continue to play the central role in the military battle against Communism. However, the report called for Canada to concentrate more in political and economic areas. "Since our resources are not unlimited," it concluded, "it would seem desirable to bear in mind constantly the need for some balance between expenditures in the purely military field and those in the non-military field."

These passages reveal a deep ambiguity over how External believed that Canada could best contribute to the air defence of North America. Unlike DND, External's position on the issue was complex and uncertain, and External did not share the military's overriding interest in ensuring that the most efficient air defence system was in operation. To be sure, DEA was concerned about the security and defence of North America, but just as important, it was troubled by the sovereignty implications of a joint command as well as the larger ramifications of continental defence cooperation. The report reveals a department torn between the country's traditional ties to the West and the growing desire to chart a more independent foreign and defence policy, an option beginning to attract attention. This tension would become increasingly evident over the next few years and ultimately lead to a bitter bureaucratic debate between DEA and DND over the issue of disarmament and the domestic acquisition of nuclear weapons (see Chapter 4).

This discussion indicates that Canadian defence officials articulated a consistent Canadian strategic interest on the issue of continental air defence. That interest was establishing and operating the most efficient air defence system, one that would serve the defence and security interests of Canada. It was believed that such a system would not only protect Canadian and other North American targets in the event of a Soviet attack, but would also help enhance the nuclear deterrent, as the better the defence the smaller the possibility of American nuclear forces being destroyed on the ground in a surprise attack. Thus, to proponents of nuclear deterrence, the command made obvious strategic sense.[30]

The interests of officials in DND can be contrasted with those in External Affairs, as the complex nature of continental defence cooperation raised a number of political challenges that proved troublesome for DEA. External's discomfort with NORAD can be traced to the department's difficulty in reconciling two essentially competing interests – the desire to cooperate with the United States on defence matters while protecting and safeguarding Canadian political concerns.[31] The department trod a fine line on this question, at times supporting the command (and by implication, larger continental defence interests), while at others suggesting that political considerations should take precedence over military ones. Despite External's best efforts, though, the departmental balance was tenuous, and the result was genuine uncertainty over Canadian defence and security goals and an intrabureaucratic feud that would, with time, push Canada to a political crisis.

The crucial point to note is that, even though their findings and recommendations differed, officials in both departments approached the issue with the goal of furthering and enhancing Canada's basic security interests. National Defence officials, concerned over the growth of Soviet nuclear forces and the threat they represented, believed that Canada needed to strengthen its air defences and cooperation with the United States offered the most cost-effective and efficient solution. External Affairs officials, while also concerned about the Soviet threat, saw equal danger in cooperating too closely with the Americans and in any event believed that greater emphasis needed to be placed on non-military matters, where it was believed that Canada could play a more influential role in the future. This was not to be the last time that the two departments disagreed on an issue of central importance.

The CF-105 and the Air Defence Debate

Of the air defence issues that DND officials dealt with during this period, none was as divisive or as controversial as the decision regarding the production of the CF-105 Arrow, a Canadian-designed aircraft that was intended to replace the CF-100. As this program represented such a watershed in Canadian defence policy, a brief review of the project is in order. While the decision to cancel the aircraft was controversial, documents reveal that defence officials believed it was consistent with Canadian interests and priorities, and that it was based on an understanding of particularly Canadian factors – not those imposed on this country by the external environment.

Recognizing that the CF-100 had a minimal capability against advanced bomber aircraft, DND formed a team of specialists in 1952 to identify the requirements of an advanced Canadian air defence interceptor for the late 1950s and 1960s. According to the original estimate, between 500 and 600 aircraft would be needed for the period commencing in 1958. The aircraft was expected to be an all-weather supersonic interceptor/fighter, and was intended to be versatile enough to perform other defence missions should they be required. In 1953, a design by A.V. Roe was selected, preliminary blueprints drawn, and wind-tunnel tests begun.[32] The plane was known as the CF-105.[33]

It is important to emphasize that early in the program the intent was for only the airframe to be designed and built in Canada, as it was expected that the engine, fire-control system, and weapons suite would all be purchased from American manufacturers. Canadian industry and defence officials liaised extensively with their counterparts in both the United States and Britain, and it was determined that neither country was developing a plane comparable to that of the CF-105. By 1955, however, the project had begun to expand dramatically, with decisions to pursue all four components in Canada.[34] Consequently, at the 106th meeting of the Cabinet Defence Committee on 27 September 1955, a decision was made to reappraise the program, and an ad hoc interdepartmental committee was formed.

The committee examined several areas of concern to the project – plans and analysis, comparisons with other programs (aircraft and armaments), cost analysis, separate American and British evaluations, and considerations over Soviet deployments. The conceptual underpinning of the Arrow program was stated early in the report, where it was noted that, "should Russia embark on a war involving thermo-nuclear weapons, a comparatively small number of these weapons ... could wreak havoc on our military installations ... Therefore, North America must devise and create an active Air Defence system which will have a high degree of effectiveness against each succeeding phase of the threat over the years ahead. The existence of such a system, backed up by the retaliatory capability of the West, is the strongest possible deterrent to a nuclear war."[35]

The purpose of Canadian air defence, as noted in this passage, was thus to contribute to and enhance deterrence, since its existence would discourage possible aggressors from attacking. The CF-105 would contribute to the active component of the system and was thus crucial to its overall operation.

However, later in the study a second rationale favouring production of the Arrow was offered. This idea focused on the possible political costs to

Canada if the nation's air defence system was not improved. The study observed that the United States could be expected to take whatever measures were necessary to ensure its own security, even those over Canadian airspace. As the report stated, "it seems safe to assume that the US will seek to provide in Canada an element of the system which they consider essential, which Canada does not provide, either through inability or choice." This passage highlights the fact that in the mid-1950s, Canadian defence officials believed that the improvement of this country's air defence capability was so critical that the United States might incur the political and diplomatic costs associated with taking unilateral measures. This possibility had been considered by External Affairs previously.[36] Its recognition in this context, however, indicates that DND officials were very much aware of the political climate in the United States that was demanding major improvements to the continental air defence system.

The study produced three alternative courses of action. Course "A" involved abandoning the aircraft and focusing instead on making continued improvements to the CF-100; option "B" also involved ending the CF-105 program, and in its place purchasing an American aircraft (the F-102 B was mentioned); course "C" was the only one to recommend continuing the project. The report concluded that option A involved unacceptable risks, while B was undesirable for a variety of reasons, including the fact that none of the proposed replacement aircraft in production were suitable for the mission required, and that by abandoning the project Canada would lose a sophisticated and skilled workforce. Course C was thus deemed preferable: it contributed to the further strengthening of the North American defence system, enhanced deterrence, and ensured that Canada received tangible benefits from the expenditure of large sums of public money (about $150 million by this time).

Three years after that study, though, with project costs spiralling further out of control, a second review of the Arrow was conducted, just weeks after Conservative leader John Diefenbaker had won a massive electoral victory on a platform of reduced government spending and fiscal responsibility. This report was prepared for the Cabinet Defence Committee, and from the start it was clear that the new review would be more concerned about cost overruns and production delays than the earlier report had been.[37]

This study concentrated on four factors that, it argued, had fundamentally altered the air defence mission: (1) The changing nature of the threat. The report, issued just one year after the launch of Sputnik, discussed how the Soviets were on the verge of introducing long-range ballistic missiles, and that in the near future missiles were expected to overtake bombers as the principal means of delivering Soviet atomic weapons. (2) Rapid advances in technology. Advances in aircraft performance had made it increasingly difficult to design interceptors with performance characteristics clearly superior to bombers. In addition, ground-to-air missiles (such as the Bomarc) threatened to reduce or eliminate the requirement for aircraft.[38] (3) The diminishing requirement for the manned interceptor. In the years between 1955 and 1958, the expected production requirement of the Arrow had been reduced from 500 to about 100, which called into question the operational need for the program. (4) The cost overruns. By 1958, more than $300 million had already been spent, and the report concluded that it was difficult to estimate what the final cost of the program would be, as several components (in particular the weapons package) were still not fully developed.

The report also discussed the extensive attempts that had been made to generate foreign purchases of the aircraft, particularly in the United States and Britain. While it noted that both countries believed the Arrow to be impressive in terms of design and performance potential, it described expectations of foreign purchases of the plane or the associated Iroquois engine as unrealistic: both countries had sophisticated domestic aircraft industries of their own that were largely dependent on national purchases. The report recommended three possible courses of action, two of which (again) involved the termination of the project. This report did not offer a specific recommendation. It was clear, though, that it leaned toward the outright cancellation of the project, or at most finishing the forty preproduction aircraft that were in various stages of completion at Avro's main plant in Malton, Ontario. In this report, then, the vital role that the Arrow was to play in the air defence of North America was played down, and in its place a variety of strategic, cost, and technical concerns were identified that raised doubts about the program's continued viability. In the wake of the report, the government decided to give the Arrow a six-month reprieve, after which a final decision was to be announced.

By this point, concern over the Arrow had become the dominant issue in Canadian defence, and had led to a bitter intraservice rivalry over the preferred defence course for Canada. Both the army and navy, services that stood to lose large chunks of their procurement budgets if the Arrow was produced, raised concerns about the project. The army made its points in a particularly comprehensive and systematic manner, and thus its critique of the program deserves careful consideration.

The army (as well as the navy) had been critical of the Arrow almost from the time the project was first proposed. At the 574th meeting of the Chiefs of Staff Committee on 11 February 1955, for instance, Lieutenant-General Guy Simonds, chief of the general staff, delivered a stinging attack on the aircraft. He considered the program "wrong in principle," because it was designed to counter a Soviet bomber threat that was likely to diminish at the very time the aircraft would be entering operational service. The future direction of technological change was difficult to predict, and thus caution was required before such a major defence project could be undertaken. On the basis of both timing and operational need, Simonds questioned "whether such an extensive aircraft program was warranted."[39]

A few months later – at the 584th meeting on 1 November 1955 – the new chief of the general staff, Lieutenant-General H.D. Graham, repeated many of his predecessor's remarks. Graham, though, articulated the fear that had concerned many outside the air force for years – that the Arrow "with all its implications, would consume all of the funds that might be available for defence in future years and would have a drastic effect on the other two services."[40] In this way, the chief of the general staff raised the spectre of an intraservice budgetary tug-of-war, a possibility that would not serve any interest and might leave Canada's defence forces reeling for years, perhaps decades. As the project continued over the next few years, the amy's critique grew sharper.

A 1958 document titled "Review of Air Defence" explained the army's main concern not only with the Arrow but with the Royal Canadian Air Force's larger concept of air defence.[41] The document's main charge was that the Canadian air defence system had been developed without adequate cooperation with the United States, and that the roles Canada had adopted were either altogether unnecessary or duplicated ones the Americans were already performing. The report's most critical accusation, however, was that the deployment of RCAF air defence squadrons had little to do with the defence of Canadian targets, and instead performed a perimeter defence role of American targets while "using Canada as the killing area." This was similar to the charge George Lindsey had made in his 1952 report, although now the allegation was much more explicit. In making this allegation, it should be noted, the army was largely repeating a claim by the Defence Research Board that the RCAF had previously denied with vigour.[42]

The army report recommended major changes in Canada's air defence policy. It suggested that the role and need of the manned interceptor was declining and there was therefore no military requirement for the production of the CF-105, although alternative cheaper aircraft might still be purchased. Furthermore, it concluded that ground-to-air anti-bomber missiles were "unproven," and that the success of this weapon system was unpredictable. In perhaps its most startling passage, the report suggested that the "RCAF has tended to 'tailor' the threat to suit the availability of weapons which it proposes to purchase," a charge that alleged the air force had engaged in deliberate deception to build political and military support for particular weapons systems.

By calling into question the basic air defence concept of the air force, the document revealed a bitter debate within the armed forces regarding which air defence roles and missions Canada should accept, and the equipment that was necessary to perform them. More important, the report raised questions about the national interests served by Canadian defence policy, a charge that was beginning to be made by several observers of Canadian defence.[43] While some disagreement between the services over the air defence mission was to be expected (particularly given the enormous financial expenditures involved), the sharply critical and troubling allegations made in this report reveal a defence establishment increasingly torn apart by the air defence issue in general and production of the Arrow in particular. Shortly afterward, a second army study on Canadian air defence proved equally critical of the government's policy, and bluntly concluded that "investment in a defence against aircraft is not worthwhile."[44]

The air force recognized that the plane's opponents had gained the upper hand, and in the summer and fall of 1958 began a last-ditch effort to save the Arrow. In a memo to Defence Minister George Pearkes dated 21 August, the chief of the air staff, Air Marshal Hugh Campbell, said he believed that it was crucial for Canada to maintain an air defence surveillance capability over Canadian territory, and that an aircraft of the Arrow's sophistication was necessary in light of recent advances in Soviet bombers. Reviewing the surveillance capability requirements, Campbell concluded that the CF-105 had been developed at great cost and to cancel it at this late stage would not only devastate the Canadian aircraft industry, but also leave the RCAF unable to perform one of its basic missions. Campbell wrote that "I cannot associate myself with the decision to cancel the 105 programme but must recommend that it proceed as it is presently planned or, alternatively, to couple the cancellation of the 105 with the procurement of a supersonic interceptor to fill the gap."[45] The latter part of the sentence reveals that the air force appreciated the plane's difficult position, and believed that in the event of cancellation, an alternative aircraft would be required.

This memo led to an *aide-mémoire* prepared for the defence minister by General Foulkes that again considered the political, economic, and military implications of a number of options.[46] While it recognized the impressive performance characteristics of the Arrow and the considerable economic consequences that its cancellation would involve, the main recommendation was that the program should be terminated. Three reasons were offered in the report's conclusion: the Soviet shift to ballistic missiles meant that the requirement for interceptors was declining; changes in technology had resulted in an advanced, ground-to-air missile that was cheaper, more efficient, and more economical to maintain; and the cost of completing the project was "exorbitant," with "no guarantee that these estimated costs will not increase."

Curiously, while Canadian intelligence was concluding that the threat from Soviet bomber aircraft was likely to diminish in the future, this was *not* the recommendation of American officials who were consulted on the issue. The difference in intelligence first became apparent in 1956, and over the following few years gradually intensified. In contrast to the situation in Canada, US intelligence consistently concluded that while Soviet bomber forces were unlikely to grow dramatically from 1960 to 1970, they were not expected to decline, and thus a significant defensive capability against them would still be required.

The intelligence gap grew to substantive proportions with the release of a joint paper, ACAI [Agreed Canadian-American Intelligence] 46, in January 1958. In this report, the United States gave no indication that the rate of growth of Soviet bomber forces was declining, whereas the separate Canadian view was that Soviet bomber production had essentially stopped.[47] In the months that followed, US authorities repeated their view to their Canadian counterparts on several occasions. On 6 August 1958, for example, a telegram from the Canadian Joint Staff in Washington to General Foulkes described a meeting that had been held between senior military officers of the two countries. At the meeting, General Thomas White, chief of staff of the US Air Force, stated that US intelligence believed "a substantial [Soviet] bomber threat would continue for at least ten years," and therefore the two nations needed to maintain active air defences.[48] In spite of the American recommendations, Canadian intelligence remained steadfast in its own conclusion.

Explaining this difference is difficult, because there were so few issues in the period over which the two intelligence communities differed to any considerable degree.[49] One possible explanation is the "bomber gap" thesis that became a major concern in the United States in the 1950s – it held that US intelligence overestimated Soviet bomber production to generate domestic support for US programs. Possible explanations even include a wilful disregard of the available evidence by Canadian intelligence officers to support a decision that had already been made: cancellation of the Arrow. Whatever the reason for the difference, the prediction of a halt in Soviet bomber production, probably followed by their withdrawal from active service, negated the principal rationale for the production of the Arrow.

Following the 1958 Arrow report, as signs increasingly pointed to an intraservice feud and uncertainty grew over the desirability of proceeding with the project, a decision on cancellation appeared almost certain. At the 120th meeting of the Cabinet Defence Committee on 14 August 1958, Defence Minister Pearkes recommended that authority be granted for the cancellation of the Arrow and its affiliated projects. Recent analysis had suggested that surface-to-air missiles would shortly become more effective in defending against manned bombers, he said, and, in any event, it was simply not economical to complete the project.[50] But the minister made a special point to emphasize that the major impetus for the decision was not cost considerations but an intelligence *consensus* that a recent slowdown in Soviet bomber production indicated a decisive shift toward missile production.

One week later, on 21 August 1958, the Arrow cancellation decision was confirmed at a further Cabinet Defence Committee meeting. At the same time, approval in principle was given to the installation of two Bomarc bases, one in North Bay and the other in the Ottawa area.[51] It was at this meeting that the link between the cancellation of the Arrow and the acquisition of the Bomarc was made, a development that would ultimately cause considerable political embarrassment to the government, and something that the Chiefs of Staff had specifically recommended against. The cancellation of the Arrow was officially announced in a statement by Prime Minister Diefenbaker on 20 February 1959, at which time Avro immediately laid off 14,000 people, about 90 percent of its total workforce.[52]

This discussion indicates that the Arrow was the source of much debate within the Department of National Defence, and that there was no consensus over what to do about the costly program. The issue revealed a gulf in thinking between the services. The air force, not surprisingly, insisted that the aircraft would be required if Canada were to carry out the air defence mission it had accepted, while the other services argued that the Arrow was militarily unnecessary and financially unsustainable. Supporters as well as opponents of the plane made strategic arguments, but ultimately it was the combination of the anticipated introduction of ballistic missiles and the cost overruns of the project that led to its termination. There was a general consensus that the Arrow was a fine aircraft, even if praise was often grudging from army and navy personnel.[53] Officials wondered what role the plane would play in an environment where missiles had replaced bombers, and there was also the possibility that in the future a bomber sharing similar performance characteristics could be deployed.[54] Given these concerns, production of such an expensive aircraft could not be justified.

The Arrow decision involved a wide range of considerations, but ultimately came down to factors of relevance to Canada. Each of the studies cited was concerned with the question of how Canada could best contribute to continental air defence at a time when the meaning and requirements of the term had been thrown into question. While the analysis produced was hardly revolutionary in terms of either the issues examined or the conclusions offered, all of the studies reached their findings on the basis of Canadian defence and security interests. It bears noting that while the army may have had its narrow service interest at stake when it criticized the plane, its argument that production of the aircraft would consume much of the procurement budget deserves to be considered in a larger light. The point that production might ultimately have left Canada's defence forces in far weaker shape was a powerful and persuasive objection.

Thus, while views on the Arrow varied, the one finding that an array of committees reached repeatedly was that Canadian defence interests could be better served by not producing the aircraft. Only the air force, which clearly had a vested interest in the plane, remained strongly supportive of it, although even here differences between the RCAF and Avro led to frequent tension.[55] This account thus challenges the external-environment thesis that is dominant in Canadian security literature. Indeed, had this environment been decisive on this issue, Canada would certainly have produced the Arrow, as the United States was consistently supportive of it.[56] On this point, the available evidence refutes the long-standing myth that American pressure was the "real" reason for the project's cancellation.[57] This was, as the documentation clearly reveals, a made-in-Canada defence saga.

Other Air Defence Studies

Continental defence cooperation and the Arrow were not the only subjects of air defence studies completed during this period. Three other studies in particular deserve mention: a report prepared by R.J. Sutherland of the Canadian Army Operational Research Establishment, and two studies by the Defence Research Board, each of which offered observations on air defence and touched upon larger issues of nuclear strategy.

Sutherland's paper was completed in October 1958, shortly after the Diefenbaker speech in which the Arrow was given a six-month reprieve. The report's chief finding was that, with the imminent deployment of ballistic missiles, further investments in air defence no longer made strategic sense.[58] As Sutherland noted, even if a perfect defence against bombers could be developed, this would offer protection against only one of the vehicles of possible future attack. Air defence was of no use against ballistic missiles and thus its utility was declining in the emerging strategic environment.

Sutherland identified three "meaningful" levels of air defence: a level high enough that an attack can be defeated; a level at which doubt is created in the mind of the attacker as to whether an attack will succeed; and a level such that the retaliatory force can be defended. As he noted, "we cannot create more than the last level and investment in an attempt to go beyond this level is wasteful and illusory." This sentence reflected Sutherland's growing belief that defence was becoming less important in the missile age, an observation that he would develop in the future.

Of greatest importance, Sutherland noted that based on current deployment patterns and technological progress, he believed that by 1960 "the era of mutual deterrence" would arrive. As he explained, this was a world in which neither side would be able to use nuclear weapons, as no matter which one struck first the opposing side would retain enough forces to conduct a devastating retaliatory blow. This stood in contrast to the situation thus far in the nuclear age, as US strategic superiority had been quite pronounced, an advantage that the Soviet leadership was undoubtedly aware of.[59]

Just days after Sutherland's study, the Defence Research Board's Working Party for Air Defence Policy released its report.[60] The new study began by noting that a re-examination of air defence policy was appropriate in light of several factors that had arisen recently: (1) the decline of the manned bomber threat to North America, indicating the acceptance of the Canadian intelligence finding; (2) the knowledge that nuclear weapons would be deployed by the United States "and probably Canada" for air defence purposes; (3) the emergence of the ballistic missile threat to North America, with the "implication that cities will replace strategic bases as primary targets for attack within the next few years"; and (4) the realization that the North American defence concept "has not been and probably cannot be" extended to Canada.

The report reached several conclusions. First, "a nuclear air attack against the North American continent is possible by design or by accident." Second, while Canadian cities might or might not be targets of direct Soviet attack, "the Canadian population lies in the area where major air defence battles against manned bombers would be fought." Third, and of most importance, the study argued that active air defence could not significantly reduce the vulnerability of Canadian cities, but it could increase the survival of the US retaliatory force. Given this rather dire analysis, the study concluded that "the dangers of nuclear war are such that the prevention of war should take priority over ameliorating its disastrous effects in case of failure." On a more positive note, it observed that, once both sides had deployed long-range ballistic missiles, neither would deliberately initiate a full-scale nuclear exchange out of fear of retaliation, a finding that echoed Sutherland's report.

Several of the observations reached in these two studies were discussed further in a report titled "Some Considerations Affecting Air Defence Policy," which was prepared by the Defence Research Board in February 1959.[61] This document also examined the implications of recent changes in the Soviet threat, and concluded that it was no longer possible to prevent "large numbers" of nuclear weapons from being delivered against targets in North America. As a result, it was not practical to "provide an effective defence for North America." This study also predicted that the age of mutual deterrence would arrive shortly, as "from 1965 onward, it appears that there will be enough missiles available for either side to achieve virtually complete destruction of the other, irrespective of who takes the initiative."

Given these changes, the report concluded that NORAD's defence posture would be "relevant" only until about 1963, at which time the strategic environment would be radically different. In this new environment, the study suggested that the long-term objectives of North American defence should be: to provide a secure retaliatory force consisting of quick-reaction ballistic missiles in hardened bases; to protect populations by adopting appropriate passive defence measures; to continue research toward attaining an effective anti-missile defence and toward producing more accurate intercontinental ballistic missiles; and to improve the ballistic missile early warning system.[62]

The study identified specific measures Canada could take that would contribute to Western defence. Among short-term tasks, it noted that the priority should be the improvement of the early warning network covering the northern approaches to the continent and a greater capability to guard against surprise air attack. For the longer term, it suggested that Canada concentrate on the improvement of the ballistic missile early warning system and the protection of the population through passive defence measures.

The observations on air defences, weapons deployment, and nuclear strategy offered in these reports reveal a department that was trying to determine how changes in the strategic/political environment might affect future Canadian defence policy. The studies reveal a department very much aware of the defence debates of the day, and one that tried to identify and articulate not only a Canadian role in an international strategic environment that was rapidly changing, but also attempted to predict the future shape and structure of that environment. While these studies hardly constitute a sufficient base from which to reach broad conclusions, they were part of a much larger departmental effort to examine the ways in which changes in weapons technology and threat assessment had fundamentally altered the use of force. Later chapters examine additional studies that complemented and built upon these observations.

The DND-DEA Air Defence Disagreement and Its Significance

National Defence and External Affairs officials approached air defence issues from a distinctly Canadian viewpoint. The debates on both the Arrow and air defence cooperation with the United States reveal that officials reached conclusions based on their reading of Canadian interests, not those forced on Canada by the external environment. It has also been revealed, though, that Canada's approach to air defence frequently coincided with that of its powerful neighbour. In the post-1945 world, both Canada and the United States shared an interest in avoiding a Soviet nuclear attack and in defending the continent as best as possible should one occur. Deterrence was the main means of dissuasion, and strengthening deterrence involved cooperating on a broad array of both passive and active defence measures. The NORAD air defence command was thus in the strategic interest of both countries and had been recommended in several DND studies, while the

Arrow was intended to ensure that any Soviet air attack would be challenged by the most advanced interceptor of the day.[63]

This chapter has also described the difference in views between the Departments of National Defence and External Affairs on the command arrangement reached with the United States. There are three major points to note about this disagreement: (1) both departments believed that their recommendations would enhance Canada's long-term security; (2) the cause of the difference was the diverging interests of the two – DND was principally concerned with operating the most efficient and effective air defence system, while External was concerned about the political implications of any binational command authority; and (3) the disagreement signalled the start of a period of tension between the two that would grow with the decision to acquire nuclear weapons for Canadian forces. Air defence thus foreshadowed a bureaucratic dispute that would dramatically intensify in the coming years.

In sum, Canadian air defence interests reflected larger Canadian security interests, which included the operation of a credible deterrent and the participation in the defence of the West. At a time when the strategic environment was in a period of rapid flux, the air defence mission became one of the major barometers of change. But for all its importance, air defence was just one of several emerging defence issues that transformed the Canadian security debate in the 1950s. Attention now turns to a second, nuclear strategy, where the documentation reveals that Canadian officials challenged American interpretations of some of the key concepts of the nuclear age.

3
Canadian Views on Nuclear Weapons and Related Issues of Strategy

The introduction and subsequent deployment of nuclear weapons represented the most significant military development of the post-Second World War era. In the United States, defence analysts and observers quickly began considering the implications of this revolution, and by the early 1960s a considerable body of literature had developed.[1] In Canada, however, the assumption has been that Canadians were passive consumers of the nuclear doctrines and strategies conceived by their allies. On the contrary, this chapter argues that the Canadian conceptual understanding and approach to deterrence theory and strategic stability, two of the key concepts in postwar nuclear strategy, was distinct from the appreciation reached in the United States. Examining several recently declassified studies prepared by Department of National Defence officials in the 1950s and early 1960s makes this clear. Compared with key contributions in American strategic thought from the same period, the Canadian observations reveal an originality indicative of a community of defence officials determined to reach independent judgments on issues of crucial importance. Indeed, the understandings reached by Canadian defence officials were among the most thoughtful and original of the nuclear age, and deserve to be so recognized by students and researchers in the field.

Two caveats should be made at this point. First, despite the originality of the Canadian observations, this chapter does not address questions related to their possible broader influence in the strategic studies literature. Although the analysis raises such questions (albeit indirectly), direct discussion is left for the book's conclusion. The account of a related concern – the effect that Canadian strategic thinking may have had on defence policy – is the focus of Chapter 6.

An additional caveat relates to the question of who made the major contributions in strategic thought. In Canada, which generally lacked a non-governmental defence community throughout this period, it was up to government officials to identify strategic interests.[2] In contrast, in the United States most of the original contributions of the postwar period came from members of the civilian defence community.[3] The distinction highlights the difference in importance accorded defence issues in the two countries, as well as the attention such issues generated among their respective publics. Therefore, to determine the originality of the Canadian observations, the primary comparison in this chapter is between DND officials and American civilian strategists.

Canadian Views on Nuclear Weapons, 1950-9

Canadian views on nuclear weapons and strategy during the early Cold War can be divided into two periods. In the first, lasting much of the 1950s, defence officials grappled with many of the important issues of the day, and reached conclusions that frequently challenged the findings of American analysts and observers. During the second, from 1959 to 1963, officials grew more confident in their observations, and ultimately offered interpretations that were both innovative and original. The comments that follow are roughly divided according to the two periods.

That DND was intent on reaching its own understanding of the nuclear age was first revealed in a 1951 report prepared by the Defence Research Board.[4] Titled "A Preliminary Assessment of Future Trends in Offensive-Defensive Balance," the document began with a review of how offensive and defensive forces had traditionally approached conflict.[5] It identified and discussed the advantages of the offensive approach, which were primarily linked to military factors such as surprise and strategic flexibility. By the early part of the twentieth century, the study noted, defensive forces had countered most of those advantages through technological advances and training techniques; this had resulted in a rough balance between the two. The introduction of nuclear weapons threatened to permanently transform the situation, though, because there was no effective defence. And yet, with widespread nuclear proliferation expected and with weapons stockpiles among "major powers" numbering in the thousands, the report concluded that a nuclear retaliatory capability would effectively nullify any advantage in striking first.

In a key section, the study noted that "summarizing the atomic situation, it can be predicted that in the next 15 years ... the greatest deterrent to atomic attack will be fear of retaliation." This passage deserves highlighting, *as the recognition that an assured retaliatory capability on both sides would enhance the credibility and stability of nuclear deterrence was a novel concept at the time.* The report's prediction of both vertical and horizontal nuclear proliferation was also noteworthy, because official US policy at the time was that such proliferation could be largely contained.

In the early 1950s, the emerging concept of deterrence was also identified and examined by officials in the Department of External Affairs. A telegram titled "Korea and the Atomic Bomb," for example, discussed Canadian anxiety and uncertainty over the possibility of American nuclear use.[6] Written jointly by Lester Pearson, secretary of state, and Hume Wrong, Canadian ambassador to the United States, the telegram was completed just days after reports indicated that US president Harry Truman was considering using nuclear weapons in Korea in response to the Chinese intervention.[7] It contained the following passage: "The military authorities may argue that the atomic bomb is just another weapon. But in the minds of ordinary people everywhere in the world, it is far more than that and has acquired an immensely greater intrinsic significance ... The psychological and political consequences of the employment of the bomb, or the threat of its employment, in the present critical situation would be incalculably great ... The effectiveness of the bomb as a tactical weapon cannot be fully appreciated. Once it has been used tactically, much of its force as a deterrent may disappear." The telegram went on to note that, although the United States was entitled to consider all available courses of action, consultation in the nuclear age was more important than ever (a point of perennial concern for DEA). It noted that Canada, as a wartime partner in the nuclear weapons project and a respected international actor, was in a unique position to ensure that its concerns were directly transmitted to the United States.

While the telegram was mainly concerned with the tactical use of nuclear weapons in Korea, its general tone suggested the employment of such weapons should be restricted to the gravest of emergencies and even then the utmost caution should be practised. Essentially, the memo indicated Canada's rejection of the military argument that the atom bomb was "just another weapon." Canadians viewed the bomb as the ultimate weapon, and this understanding was the basis of its use as a deterrent.[8]

DND thinking on nuclear weapons was further refined in "Science and Future Warfare," a 1954 report prepared by the scientific advisor to the chief of the general staff.[9] This study revealed that some Canadian defence officials had concluded nuclear weapons were not militarily usable, but that they would have considerable political utility in resolving disputes. The document suggested that, in the future, nuclear-armed countries would effectively cancel each other out as their mutual ability to hurt each other would ensure the avoidance of large-scale hostilities. "As a result," the report noted, "we may have seen our last large scale hot war between the major powers." The study thus extended the principal finding of the 1951 Defence Research Board (DRB) paper: the strategic stability that had been predicted to emerge in the future was now equated with the absence of direct military conflict between nuclear-armed states. Further, the study took an even broader view of nuclear proliferation than the DRB had, suggesting that within five to twenty years, "many countries will be able to manufacture, possess, and use nuclear weapons if they so desire."

It was not until the mid-1950s, however, that Canadian thinking on nuclear weapons and issues of nuclear strategy was placed in its broader political and strategic context. This was the result of separate National Defence and External Affairs departmental reports prepared in 1955, both of which revealed that Canadian officials were developing a distinctive understanding of the utility of nuclear weapons in the Cold War.

In March 1955, senior DEA official George Ignatieff completed a study that represented the department's main effort at evaluating recent nuclear developments.[10] The report's most interesting comments dealt with US-Soviet nuclear deployments and their effect on strategic stability and deterrence. Apparently challenging the belief that had taken hold in DND, Ignatieff warned that the large-scale deployment of nuclear forces could decrease global security. In suggesting this, Ignatieff was cautioning that technical and military advances do not normally occur at precisely the same time in different countries, and thus there was a danger that at times one country's nuclear forces might be superior to others' before parity was restored. During such periods, the risk of nuclear attack increased because of the reduced possibility of effective retaliation.

Ignatieff emphasized the importance of balanced strategic nuclear forces as a way of countering the destabilizing effect that a position of nuclear superiority might offer *because stability could be best assured from the mutual fear of a nuclear exchange.* As Ignatieff observed, "The United States and the Soviet Union now confront one another with the prospect of mutual devastation by thermonuclear and nuclear weapons. It is this prospect, and not the mere existence of such destructive power, which is the deterrent to war ... if the strategy of the nuclear deterrent works, it is because it strikes fear and uncertainty in the calculations of a potential aggressor." In this passage, Ignatieff recognized the fear potential of nuclear weapons. It was a characteristic that the American analyst Thomas Schelling would shortly label "the power to hurt," a power so strong as to forever alter the use of force as a rational object of state policy. The DEA report revealed that the observation on the stabilizing effect of the mutual fear of nuclear retaliation, first offered by DND in 1951, was now acknowledged by officials in both departments as the key to long-term stability.

Canadian views on deterrence were further developed in a major DND report – "Future Canadian Defence Policy" – released a few months later, in July 1955. The study, prepared by the army's Directorate of Military Operations and Plans, focused mainly on the emerging requirements of the air defence mission and how such requirements were being transformed in response to changes in the Soviet military threat.[11] The report noted that nuclear deterrence remained the most effective means of avoiding conflict with the Soviet Union, and that Canada needed to cooperate with the United States in those tasks that improved the operational capability and credibility of the US Strategic Air Command (a recommendation that had also been made in the DEA study).

However, the report's most critical comments dealt with the vulnerability of SAC bases and the chances of a successful challenge of the West's nuclear force. The report built on observations that had first been offered in the department in 1953, when General Charles Foulkes, chairman of the Chiefs of Staff Committee, had warned of the possible danger of a pre-emptive Soviet attack against SAC bases.[12] Now, two years later, the DND report expanded upon Foulkes's earlier warning, and dismissed conventional thinking that presumed the West would be the first to mobilize – and strike – in a crisis. Rather, the report considered the possibility that the Soviets might enjoy the benefit of strategic surprise. Under this scenario, the study concluded that the Soviets might be emboldened to attack first if they believed that they could destroy a large part of SAC's force on the ground. As the report warned, "should the Soviet leaders ever conclude, rightly or wrongly, that by an attack on North America they could destroy a major part of SAC before it could retaliate effectively, there would be little left to deter them from war." As a result, the study recommended that North American air defences needed to be improved.

The possible vulnerability of SAC bases to pre-emptive Soviet attack was being recognized at much the same time in the United States. Indeed, American observers were conceding that the US "mobility plan" was based on a series of dubious assumptions.[13] Nonetheless, the Canadian observation was significant, because the Western defence posture was largely based on the belief that the West had invulnerable nuclear forces that could withstand any conceivable Soviet strike.

Canadian Views on Nuclear Strategy and Doctrine, 1959-63

In the late 1950s and early 1960s, Canadian strategic thinking matured as defence officials explored many of the core concepts of the nuclear age more intensively. From the array of departmental studies that were completed, this section focuses on several of importance that were prepared by one defence scientist in particular and the staff for which he worked.

The scientist in question is R.J. Sutherland, who throughout this period was the most innovative strategic theorist in the country.[14] While Sutherland spent the early part of his career in the DRB and the army, his most significant strategic work began with his affiliation with the Joint Ballistic Missile Defence Staff (JBMDS). This group was formed in 1959 by the Chiefs of Staff to examine the strategic implications of ballistic missiles, but its mandate was quickly expanded and it subsequently explored an array of issues of broad strategic relevance.[15]

Each of these JBMDS reports offered important and original findings: (1) "The Effect of the Ballistic Missile on the Prevention of Surprise Attack," written by the JBMDS in February 1960; (2) "A Military View of Nuclear Weapons," written by Sutherland in February 1961; (3) "Strategic Considerations Affecting Ballistic Missile Defence," written by Sutherland (undated, although probably written in 1962); and (4) "Trends in Strategic Weapons and Concepts," also written by Sutherland in 1963."[16]

The first of these papers examined how the introduction of ballistic missiles would affect nuclear weapons, the thinking regarding their use, and strategic stability in general. It began by recognizing that a "revolutionary change" in military technology was occurring – the shift in nuclear delivery vehicles from bombers to intercontinental ballistic missiles. The study noted that besides their speed, range, and accuracy, missiles robbed an opponent of any significant advance notification of attack, as in the missile age defence planners would have no more than thirty minutes' warning time. This development was contrasted with bombers, whose use required extensive preparations that could be observed and detected through an array of surveillance techniques. Because of the US advantage in both the technical sophistication of its bomber force and its surveillance capabilities, the paper argued that the Americans had enjoyed strategic superiority throughout the postwar period (although whether such superiority had offered the United States any tangible benefit was doubtful).

That advantage, however, would effectively end in the missile age. Once the Americans and Soviets deployed large numbers of land-based ballistic missiles – supplementing their bombers and, soon, submarine-launched missiles – both sides would have the ability to withstand a first strike and still be capable of conducting a punishing retaliatory blow. This development would represent an enormous change in the political/military environment, and herald a revolutionary shift in strategic thinking. Most crucially, the JBMDS concluded that this situation would be stabilizing, as neither side would have the potential to successfully attack first. The concept of stability through assured destruction, first discussed in Canada in the 1951 DRB report, was about to become reality.

In the emerging missile age, the study observed that the primary interest of each side should be to enhance the stability of the nuclear balance. That balance could be ruptured not only by unequal force structures, as Ignatieff had warned five years earlier, but also by the deployment of defensive systems. The main finding that resulted from this analysis was that strategic stability would not be enhanced by agreements to restrict the size of the retaliatory missile force. On the contrary, the report suggested that the larger the retaliatory forces on both sides, "the clearer it will be that neither side can rationally strike first."

The second paper to be examined, "A Military View of Nuclear Weapons," was prepared as background material for a lecture Sutherland gave at Carleton University in Ottawa. In this study, Sutherland described recent developments of interest to both Canada and the West, with conclusions that were novel and far-reaching.

Sutherland began with a review of the nature and possible uses of nuclear weapons. He noted that with recent increases in yields, such weapons would have truly horrific consequences if fired. He also discussed changes in the technological environment, and in particular the increasing accuracy and reliability of ballistic missiles and the effect that such systems might have on future conflict dynamics.

But it was Sutherland's observations on first- and second-strike nuclear forces and on the nuclear balance that deserve careful consideration. He debated the merits of a nuclear posture based on a targeting philosophy of countercity versus counterforce, and recognized that while the former might be open to question, it was preferable from the point of view of strategic stability.[17] As he noted, "If we go for [the enemy's] cities, he will go for ours. This seems rather foolish, from our point of view. We are not interested in a mutual exchange of cities. The answer is that we don't really want to attack the enemy's cities but rather to convince him that he should not attack us at all. We therefore make it clear to him that if he does attack we will assuredly destroy his cities notwithstanding what he can do to ours." To explain this apparent paradox better, Sutherland discussed nuclear doctrine, and in particular the concept of the "rationality of irrationality." In brief, this involves making threats that are recognized as being irrational, but convincing an opponent that one nonetheless means them. Threatening to destroy an opponent's cities was not a rational strategy in the nuclear age, Sutherland observed, because one's opponent could in all likelihood – given a secure second-strike force – do the same. And yet, if one were convinced that a possible aggressor would not attack one's cities because of fear of retaliation, the other side's possible aggressiveness would become comparatively more likely. If, on the other hand, the opponent believed that an adversary would carry out its threat despite the assured destruction he would suffer in return, he would be less likely to consider a challenge in the first place. As Sutherland noted, "we must convince [an opponent] that if the situation arose we would act without counting the cost; in other words, that we would be a little bit crazy."

Sutherland's major conclusion in the paper took issue with the notion of a delicate nuclear balance that had become the accepted wisdom in both the American academic and policy communities. In Sutherland's view, the US-Soviet nuclear balance was *not* fragile and the use of nuclear weapons in any future crisis was exceedingly unlikely. The power available to both sides exercised a strong inhibiting influence against rash military challenges. Further, the anticipated introduction of long-range ballistic missiles was expected to enhance stability, as their deployment would ensure a retaliatory capability on both sides. Sutherland believed that the consequences of a nuclear exchange were so horrific – and he was convinced that decision makers on both sides fully understood this – that no leader would ever authorize the use of such weapons in the first place. As he noted, "there are ... no conceivable circumstances in which anyone would wish to provoke [a nuclear] exchange as a deliberate act of policy." Last, Sutherland explained the distinction between first- and second-strike nuclear forces, noting that the former were inherently destabilizing, as their intent was to achieve strategic surprise, while the latter were designed to be used strictly in retaliation.

A third study, "Strategic Considerations Affecting Ballistic Missile Defence," was essentially a conceptual work that examined deterrence in some detail. Sutherland began the paper with a recognition that deterrence "is a political rather than a military concept." He defined deterrence as the "establishment of such military capabilities as will render unattractive from the point of view of a potential enemy the exercise of military capabilities which the enemy must be assumed to possess." Deterrence could not deprive an enemy of military capabilities – rather it could deny to him "the ability to use such capabilities to his advantage."

Following these remarks, Sutherland examined the political implications of deterrence, focusing on the issue of credibility. Credibility in the nuclear age was argued to be almost totally dependent on what one's opponent believed. The actual policies of a state and the size of its military force were less important considerations than how an opponent believed that force would be used in the event of hostilities. Sutherland argued that a poorly armed opponent might make threats that were more credible than those of a well-armed one, the key factor being how those threats were perceived by potential adversaries and one's past record in carrying them out.

Sutherland also examined the military characteristics of deterrence, noting that deterrence involves a "mixture of unequivocal and ambiguous aspects." He explained that the deterrent force must be capable of inflicting upon the enemy a level of damage that it would find unacceptable under any circumstance. However, Sutherland realized that force structures would probably always be contested, and consequently there is "room for disagreement" regarding specific requirements and weapons systems. There was also, he said, a "fundamental point of disagreement" related to the need for military capabilities over and above a secure retaliatory force.

Sutherland concluded the study with a discussion of the differences between the two principal deterrent strategies – simple deterrence and deterrence in depth. The former was defined as the existence of the minimum force necessary to ensure adequate retaliation, regardless of which side were to strike first (a policy that Sutherland believed Britain "has tended towards"). Conversely, the strategy of deterrence in depth denied that the maintenance of a secure second-strike capability was a sufficient condition of strategic stability. Rather, it asserted that an effective deterrent posture required an ability to emerge victorious in battle (which Sutherland argued was the basis of US military policy). The deterrent strategy adopted by a country was dependent on a number of factors, including political goals and objectives, geographical considerations, and the ability and willingness of the population to devote the necessary resources.

Finally, the fourth study, "Trends in Strategic Weapons and Concepts," was largely a discussion of recent political developments, such as the Cuban Missile Crisis and changes in US foreign policy. However, part of the paper dealt with the stability of the nuclear balance, an area in which Sutherland's conclusions were particularly noteworthy. By 1963, Sutherland believed that the nuclear balance, which he had previously argued was stable, had reached a level of stability where further disruptions were not only unlikely but increasingly implausible. The reason was the "mature" level of many nuclear technologies and the scientific and financial difficulties linked to the introduction of next-generation weapons. Indeed, Sutherland noted that the costs associated with military research and development had reached extraordinary levels, and both the United States and Soviet Union were aware that the arms race – if left unchecked – might yet result in the financial ruin of both countries.

Some of the broader observations that were offered in this study might also be noted, as they are reflective of the wide scope of several DND studies of the period. Thus, Sutherland suggested that if force were to be used between great powers in the future, it would have to be used at lower levels of violence, where modes of thinking were less doctrinally predetermined and remained flexible to changes in the strategic environment. The author noted that the Cold War and the global division that it created were elements of a particular evolution of forces, a system that was increasingly irrelevant in large parts of the world. In many regions, the strain of economic development, weapons proliferation, and the impact of technology were converging to produce a different set of priorities that was not related to the narrow concerns of the US-Soviet dispute. Sutherland cautioned that the agenda of international politics would gradually have to deal with these issues, and the emphasis on security and defence that had been dominant throughout the postwar period would need to be reconsidered.

It should be noted that issues related to nuclear strategy were also examined by the Defence Research Board, although such efforts were frequently overshadowed by the board's main work, which was scientific and technical research. Still, a few DRB scientists can be singled out for their research.

One scientist who achieved considerable recognition was Harold Larnder, an operational research specialist for Britain's Royal Air Force during the war (where he helped develop radar). In a sixteen-year career at DND that began in 1951, Larnder served as senior operational research officer at RCAF Air Defence Command, St. Hubert, Quebec; executive director of the Canadian component of the Canada/US Scientific Advisory Team (CUSSAT); and researcher with the Operational Research Group of the DRB. A focus of Larnder's research was the vulnerability of American bomber aircraft, an issue that, as noted, first attracted department attention in 1953. An additional concern was North American air defence and in particular fighter-aircraft tactics, work that ultimately helped determine the placement of the Mid-Canada Line.[18]

A second DRB scientist worthy of note was George Lindsey. Lindsey was briefly mentioned in Chapter 2 for an air defence report that he produced, but his work revealed an impressive range over his long career at DND (which ended in 1987). While Lindsey's major field of study was operational research, he frequently examined issues of broad strategic relevance. One such example was a 1959 study titled "Active Defence for North America," which explored issues related to the problems of nuclear balance and the risks of escalation.[19] Lindsey observed that, while vulnerability to nuclear attack was regrettable, "our uneasy peace is produced by both opponents' ability to retaliate on the other's cities." He further noted that "a sudden intense program of activity" on the part of one side to develop defences might be considered by an opponent as a "tie-breaker," and "encourage" it to consider making a pre-emptive nuclear attack. Thus, *it was important that mutual vulnerability be maintained to enhance strategic stability.* Lindsey's work, like that of the JBMDS, revealed a sensitivity and awareness to many of the critical strategic issues of the day.

In sum, the studies produced by the JBMDS and its principal strategist, R.J. Sutherland, highlight the issues that were thought to be significant in the nuclear age, and the manner in which Canadian defence officials approached them. The subjects examined in these studies – including deterrence theory, the nuclear balance, and strategic doctrine – reveal that there was certainly no hesitation among Canadian defence officials to tackle difficult and controversial issues. However, to reach judgments on the originality of these observations, it is necessary to compare them with the writings of principal American strategists.

US Strategic Thinking on Nuclear Weapons Issues, 1950-63

The 1950s witnessed a virtual explosion in American writings on the strategic environment. The majority of these writings were composed by members of a rapidly growing civilian defence community, most of whom worked in academia or in the array of policy centres and defence "think-tanks" –

the best-known of which was the RAND Corporation – that were established during the decade. The findings of the civilian strategists were not
always reflected in US defence policy, a point that is made clear in the following account and is discussed further in Chapter 6. Such writings, however, formed the background against which policy was conceived, a
development that decision makers were keenly aware of.[20]

The discussion that follows is divided into specific issues, each of which
received significant contributions during this period. Readers interested in
the evolution of American postwar strategic thought have several sources to
consult, including Fred Kaplan's *The Wizards of Armageddon,* Gregg Herken's
Counsels of War, and Lawrence Freedman's *The Evolution of Nuclear Strategy.*[21]

Deterrence and Avoiding Conflict in the Nuclear Age
Early postwar American strategic thinking did *not* focus on the mutual nature of deterrence and the importance of retaliatory capabilities, but rather
emphasized the need for the United States to intimidate and/or defeat the
Soviet Union through overwhelming military superiority. This stands in
contrast to the thinking that emerged in Canada, and indicates the first of
several areas of conceptual difference between the two countries.

The early American approach toward avoiding conflict in the nuclear age
was contained in National Security Council Memorandum 68 of April 1950.
This document predicted the development and deployment of a Soviet capability to strike in significant strength with atomic weapons against North
America by 1954. To counter this threat, the directive recommended an
ambitious rearmament plan that would ensure US military capabilities were
powerful enough to prevail in any conflict scenario. It therefore called for a
massive arms buildup that would result in the United States having "clearly
superior overall power in its most inclusive sense."[22]

In essence, NSC-68 viewed deterrence as a unilateral concept, in that it
asserted Soviet foreign policy and security challenges would be discouraged
as a result of American war-fighting capabilities. It reflected a traditional
power politics approach, as security could be achieved through the expansion of military power. Indeed, the concept of deterrence implicit in NSC-
68 was reflected in a policy planning staff paper that argued the existence of
two large atomic stockpiles, rather than resulting in a nuclear standoff, might
well "prove to be an incitement to war."[23]

It should also be noted that while NSC-68 did not explicitly state this, US
administrations of the period fully expected to win a Third World War should
it occur and that such a war was expected to include the widespread use of
nuclear weapons. Blunt language to this effect was written into NSC-20/4 of
November 1948 and was reproduced in NSC-162/2 of October 1953 (which
became the basis for President Dwight Eisenhower's "new look" defence
policy).[24] This expectation was further codified in the official US war plans

of the period, which were based on a massive atomic blitz of the Soviet Union in the opening phase of any conflict, a strategy that indicated the United States did not take the possibility of Soviet atomic retaliation very seriously.[25] As a 1954 memo for Admiral Arthur Radford, chairman of the Joint Chiefs of Staff, stated, "we will use nuclear weapons whenever it is to our national advantage to do so."[26]

These directives led to the policy of massive retaliation, which was announced by US Secretary of State John Foster Dulles in January 1954. In the aftermath of the Korean War and the perception that the Soviets had effectively established the "rules" of the Cold War, massive retaliation was designed to reclaim the strategic initiative. According to Dulles, the basic decision was that henceforth the United States would rely on a "capacity to retaliate, instantly, by means and at places of [its] own choosing."[27] While this is not to suggest that the United States would necessarily use nuclear weapons under any circumstance, the intent of the new policy was to introduce an element of uncertainty and ambiguity into the calculations of possible aggressors.[28] President Eisenhower (who strongly advocated limiting defence spending through increased reliance on nuclear weapons) was more blunt than the secretary of state in his description, privately telling a congressional delegation in late 1954 that the strategy was designed "to blow the hell out of [the Soviets] in a hurry if they start anything."[29] The United States was serving notice that, in the future, it would reserve for itself the right to decide where to fight, how to fight, and what the consequences and stakes of that fighting would be.

In essence, massive retaliation threatened the Soviet Union with nuclear devastation in response to foreign policy transgressions. The strategy thus completely failed to appreciate that nuclear deterrence was a two-sided dynamic, and that any use of nuclear weapons was bound to have a disastrous effect on the United States. While the Americans did have a considerable military advantage over the Soviets in 1954, massive retaliation did not grasp the purely temporary nature of that advantage, nor did it appreciate that strategic superiority in the nuclear age offered few tangible benefits in any event.[30] In effect, early US strategic thinking regarded nuclear weapons as the preserve of the United States, to be threatened and used as it saw fit.

It would be misleading to conclude, however, that all American observers shared these official views. One who clearly did not was Bernard Brodie, who was the dean of American nuclear strategists and one of the few prominent civilian defence observers with a background in the social sciences.

In 1946, Brodie contributed to and edited a remarkable book, *The Absolute Weapon,* whose key message was that the destructiveness of nuclear weapons had fundamentally and permanently transformed the nature of war.[31] As the book noted, "the atomic bomb seems so far to overshadow any military invention of the past as to render comparisons ridiculous." Even with the technically limited aircraft of the mid-1940s, Brodie contended that a state possessing atomic bombs could destroy most of the cities of any other power. And yet, the increased effectiveness of bombing would not result in "the apotheosis of aggressive instruments." This was because atomic aggression would be deterred – a word Brodie used from the beginning – as long as potential attackers believed that there was a reasonable chance of retaliation.

In the early 1950s, Brodie joined the RAND Corporation, and with his reputation in strategic studies and defence policy analysis already well established, he immediately became one of the institute's most prominent figures. His initial work focused on target selection in war planning, and the utility of limited war strategies in the nuclear age. Thus, a 1954 article critiqued American war plans and called for greater "sanity" in military planning, noting that "when we talk about an unrestricted general war we are talking about a catastrophe in which there are no predictable limits."[32] In a memo written the same year, Brodie criticized the American political and military establishment, and observed with reference to US war planning that "explicitly we accord the Soviets a nuclear capability, but when it comes right down to drawing the relevant conclusions, it is always we who do the hitting and they who do the suffering ... The Joint Chiefs are obviously still thinking of the SAC-nuclear capability in US monopoly terms."[33] The comment was intended to draw attention to the fact that American war plans were based on the assumption of US strategic superiority, despite the absence of any meaningful level of superiority in reality.

The following year, Brodie wrote "Strategy Hits a Dead End,"[34] perhaps the most critical study of the decade, and one that revealed how Brodie's thinking could change in light of unexpected developments. His argument was relatively simple: hydrogen weapons offered such unimaginable destructive force that their use would hurt the aggressor as much as the defender. As a result, Brodie warned that "strategy" as it had been known for millennia – that is, the use of military power to further a state's political goals – had essentially ceased to exist. The power available to both attacker and defender made the traditional distinction irrelevant, and old principles on the use of force no longer applied. A totally new paradigm was needed to reconceptualize the use and purpose of military force.

There are clear similarities between Brodie's writings and some of the Canadian studies discussed above, in particular those regarding the nature of deterrence, the dynamics of future conflict, and the changes in the strategic environment. And yet throughout his thirty-year professional career, Brodie was the prototypical "outsider," a man whose views were often scoffed at by colleagues in the American defence community.[35] This is not to suggest that he was without influence, but simply to emphasize that many of

his opinions were not widely shared – at least at the time they were originally expressed.[36] His views did not enter the mainstream of American strategic thought until the mid-1960s. Indeed, Brodie's isolation and status as
an outsider were essential to his criticism of his RAND colleagues, which
became a common focus of his work in the 1960s.[37]

When compared with early American directives and statements, though,
the thinking on deterrence that emerged in Canada was both original and
distinct. Unlike the focus on military superiority and first use of nuclear
weapons that permeated American analysis, the emphasis in Canada tended
to be on the need for balanced strategic forces and the dangers associated
with nuclear use. Further, Canadian officials warned of the troubling consequences of nuclear superiority, as it reduced the chances of effective retaliation and therefore made pre-emptive attack more likely. In sum, the early
caution and prudence that was evident in Canada does not seem to have
been a consideration in the United States.

SAC Base Vulnerability and the Nuclear Balance

In the early 1950s, concern began to develop in the United States over the
possible vulnerability of the US nuclear force. The most prominent figure in
this research was Albert Wohlstetter, a mathematician by training who reflected the behaviouralist revolution that was sweeping the social sciences
at the time. Wohlstetter arrived at RAND in 1951, and in the following year
began work with a team of colleagues on a project that examined the security of American Strategic Air Command bases from attack.

Wohlstetter quickly discovered that SAC planning assumed that the biggest challenge facing US bombers was the penetration of Soviet airspace,
while little attention had been paid to the possible vulnerability of the bombers themselves. Wohlstetter's team visited bases to get as much information
as possible on force readiness, warning time, and emergency preparations,
factors that might affect the ability of the strategic forces to survive a surprise attack and conduct a retaliatory strike.[38] The study's operating assumption was that the Soviet Union – not the United States – would attack first
in a future conflict, a premise so dubious at SAC that even considering it
was virtually tantamount to national treason.[39]

Wohlstetter's conclusion was that the Strategic Air Command, which at
the time was relying on using overseas bases from which to fly bombing
missions against the Soviet Union, was vulnerable to a surprise Soviet strike.[40]
His research revealed that while US bomber forces had been expanding steadily for over a decade, the total number of bases where the aircraft were
stationed had remained relatively stable. The result of this investigation
was a top-secret RAND study completed in April 1954, titled *The Selection
and Use of Strategic Air Bases*.[41] Wohlstetter's principal recommendation was
that early warning radar systems around air bases needed to be improved,

and that SAC overseas bases should be used primarily for refuelling, not for complete operations.

The Wohlstetter report attracted considerable interest, but it was some time before its findings were officially accepted. Indeed, for approximately two years, the team that Wohlstetter led was repeatedly rebuffed by US Air Force and Department of Defense officials, who found an array of flaws with the study's methodology and conclusions. The reaction revealed that there were numerous people in official capacities who did not wish to hear that a central tenet of US defence policy might have been based on a faulty premise, one that had been supported for many years. It also demonstrated the continuing tension between the professional military and the expanding civilian defence community, as the former was having difficulty adjusting to an environment where it no longer dominated thinking in the field.

The records of the American Joint Chiefs of Staff indicate that the notion of SAC base vulnerability first attracted official attention in October 1955. A memo for the chairman of the JCS, written by Air Force Colonel William Moore, observed that "SAC is vulnerable if tactical warning only is received" and that a wide array of corrective measures, including dispersal and advanced equipment, were being considered in reaction to the RAND report.[42] At the same time, the document indicates the general reluctance of the joint chiefs to admit to the basic conclusions of the RAND study. In fact, it was not until July 1956, more than two years after Wohlstetter had first raised concerns, that the air force and the joint chiefs agreed on a series of measures that alleviated some of the troubling findings identified in the Wohlstetter report.[43]

The RAND basing study was perhaps the most important example of an emerging type of strategic analysis: one that placed a premium on "hard" data and reflected the behaviouralist revolution then under way. With its elaborate charts and calculations, the study set a standard for what analysis in the nuclear age should be.[44] It implied that one could reach judgments on enormously complex issues based on a strict reading of numbers and figures, and that the most important areas of inquiry were no longer crucial political questions on the use and threat of force and leaders' perceptions of risk. Indeed, the study helped spark fears about Soviet intentions without even examining them. In many ways, it represented an attack on the kind of thinking that Brodie had come to symbolize, and the fact that Wohlstetter quickly became the pre-eminent strategist at RAND revealed where the balance of power lay in the US strategic studies community.[45]

Several years later, Wohlstetter, who unlike Brodie had written only classified studies for RAND, decided to make his concerns public. The result was an article, "The Delicate Balance of Terror," published in the influential American policy journal *Foreign Affairs* in 1959.[46] It is important to note that, at the time, although the notion of American vulnerability had been accepted in the defence community, the same could not be said for the general public, who still believed that strategic stability was essentially guaranteed as long as the United States possessed powerful nuclear forces. Wohlstetter's article challenged that faith, as he wrote that the mere possession of nuclear weapons did not create a nuclear stalemate. Mutual deterrence was not automatic, but would require a continuing effort. Thus, the nuclear balance was "delicate," and because of this deterrence was fragile and could fail. In addition, the article is widely credited with having introduced the terms "first-" and "second-strike" nuclear forces into the strategic studies vocabulary.

All of this should give pause to those who have argued that Canadian strategic thinking was little more than a restatement of American concerns. First, documents reveal that Canadian defence officials recognized SAC vulnerability at roughly the same time as their American counterparts (Foulkes's 1953 memo actually predated the RAND basing study by six months). While Wohlstetter's study was completed in 1954, it was some time before its conclusions were officially accepted in Washington. In fact, it appears that the Department of National Defence may have accepted SAC vulnerability slightly *prior* to the US Department of Defense.[47] A final judgment on this question cannot be reached until all the relevant documents – in both Ottawa and Washington – have been released. Still, the main observation is that Canadian officials identified this concern while it was in the process of being formulated in the United States, which reveals a Canadian sensitivity to one of the most serious strategic problems of the day.

In addition, Wohlstetter's 1959 conclusion that the nuclear balance was "delicate" and in constant danger – which became the accepted wisdom in the United States for several years – was directly challenged in Canada. As discussed, R.J. Sutherland believed that the variety and quantity of nuclear weapons available to both sides had resulted in strategic stability, and thus there was only a slight possibility that either side would run the risk of annihilation to marginally improve its relative position. Sutherland further wrote that strategic stability would be enhanced when ballistic missiles were introduced into force structures in the early 1960s, a direct challenge to the (American) consensus of opinion on the issue, which held that missiles were inherently destabilizing and a threat to global peace.

Last, the lineage of the terms "first-" and "second-strike" nuclear forces also deserves brief comment: the distinction has been called as important to the field of strategic studies as "the law of gravity is to physics."[48] In 1959, the year that Wohlstetter's article was published, the terms were first used in Canada in "Initial Survey of the Ballistic Missile Defence Problem," the inaugural study of the Joint Ballistic Missile Defence Staff.[49] Thereafter, Sutherland began using the terms quite frequently in his writings, including the February 1961 paper discussed earlier. Furthermore, Sutherland's studies used the wording to explain specific differences in nuclear strategy and force structure, whereas Wohlstetter was much less precise as to how the composition of a country's nuclear force could determine its strategic policies and choices. Regardless of who actually first coined the terms, it is important to recognize that, as with SAC vulnerability, DND officials were clearly aware of the emerging strategic discourse. Sutherland and his colleagues at the JBMDS wrote papers that both challenged accepted thinking in the field and pushed the strategic debate into new and unexplored areas.

Strategic Stability

By 1960, the risk of sliding into an inadvertent nuclear war had become a dominant theme in strategic studies literature. The quest was for stability, a situation in which neither side would feel compelled to take the initiative in a crisis, thus setting off a chain reaction that could lead to disaster. Stability in the nuclear age demanded that sufficient military forces of both sides be invulnerable to surprise attack and be available for retaliation, a concept that took some time to emerge. Indeed, as Lawrence Freedman has observed, the idea that it was necessary to convince an opponent that there was no threat to its most critical strategic asset was not one that the military would have conceived on its own, and the US defence establishment was "not overly impressed when the idea was put forward by ... civilian strategists."[50] Similarly, the defence establishment was also concerned that stability demanded a renunciation of the larger goal of American strategic superiority (at least insofar as such superiority entailed a first-strike capability), which had been a central tenet of US defence policy since 1945.

The major American contribution on strategic stability was made by Robert McNamara, defence secretary in the Kennedy administration. Shortly after assuming office in 1961, McNamara began devoting attention to reinforcing stability through a concept that became known as "assured destruction," which reflected the defence secretary's tendency to systemize and quantify. This new measure postulated that after a surprise Soviet strike, the United States should still have enough forces left to destroy the Soviets' industrial capacity as well as a "large percentage" of its population (the figures were estimated at 50 percent for the former and 25 percent for the latter).[51] The idea was that as long as the Soviets knew the United States could effectively retaliate after any nuclear attack, they would be sufficiently deterred. In other words, the emphasis remained on the unilateral ability of the United States to deter the Soviet Union by threatening nuclear devastation in response to any conceivable Soviet strike.

This model was followed, though, by an official recognition that the Soviets had developed a roughly equivalent nuclear capability, and that this was, in fact, a stabilizing development. The new term offered to describe this situation, a slight twist on the original, was "mutual assured destruction," which begat the acronym "MAD."[52] Neither assured destruction nor MAD were really nuclear strategies at all, as both lacked guidelines for the employment of strategic forces should deterrence fail.[53] Rather, MAD assumed that with both sides able to ensure destruction, the risks associated with aggressive action would be so great that deterrence simply would not – indeed could not – fail. Twelve years after NSC-68, and eight years after the enunciation of massive retaliation, McNamara's pronouncement finally revealed that the United States had officially accepted the mutual nature of deterrence and the inherent dangers associated with strategic superiority.[54]

The extent to which official US strategic thinking was altered during this period is clear from McNamara's speeches and writings. In 1963, McNamara argued that a disarming US first-strike capability would not only be extremely expensive and probably infeasible, but that excessive counterforce capabilities might be detrimental to US security. As the defence secretary wrote in a 1963 Draft Presidential Memorandum to President Lyndon Johnson, decreased Soviet vulnerability to an American nuclear attack "may be desirable from the point of view of creating a more stable posture, [and will also reduce the Soviet] incentive ... to make a preemptive strike against [the United States]."[55] Still, as discussed in Chapter 6, some ambiguity in the manner in which MAD was ultimately implemented was accepted.

The works of some of the civilian strategists on this issue might also be noted. Bernard Brodie may have understood most fully the need for both sides to have invulnerable strategic forces. In addition to the findings reached in his 1946 study *The Absolute Weapon,* a second landmark work he completed more than a decade later deserves comment. In this 1959 work, *Strategy in the Missile Age*, Brodie wrote that as long as each side was convinced that it could not emerge victorious in any confrontation, deterrence was unlikely to fail.[56] Of the other analysts who picked up on the concept in quick succession, many argued that by mutual agreement it might be possible to achieve an environment where both sides' strategic forces were secure.[57]

An additional strategist who thought and wrote about these issues extensively was Thomas Schelling, one of the best-known civilian defence strategists of the 1950s and 1960s. In his writings, Schelling was most concerned about how one actor could deter another when the threat of using nuclear weapons seemed so out of proportion to any reasonable political or military goal. The answer that he developed was the "the threat that leaves something to chance." In his seminal 1960 study, *The Strategy of Conflict,* Schelling wrote that it would be absurd for any state leader to order an all-out nuclear attack in response to an enemy transgression; however, one could plausibly threaten actions that might start a semi-controllable chain of events which might ultimately culminate in the use of nuclear weapons.[58] If an actor could thus establish that the manipulation of risk was not a fully controllable process, it followed that a country might be able to use that risk to its strategic advantage. The essential argument was that general war need not result from deliberate decision, and that stability could be enhanced as a result.

One final issue that should be noted relates to changes in US nuclear targeting. In June 1962, US Defense Secretary McNamara gave a speech at the University of Michigan in which he announced important modifications in US nuclear strategy. Rather than relying on a massive strike at the outset of any future conflict (frequently referred to as a "spasm" attack), henceforth the United States would attack only military targets and thereby give its opponent the "strongest possible incentive to refrain from striking [American] cities."[59] As he noted, "principal military objectives, in the event of nuclear war stemming from a major attack on the [Atlantic] Alliance, should be the destruction of the enemy's military forces, not his civilian population."[60] However, while McNamara maintained that cities should not be targeted in any future conflict, the strategy explicitly included the option if the Soviet Union attacked US cities first.[61] In any event, the "no-cities" doctrine was strongly criticized by both American and European observers, and within a year McNamara began backtracking from the announcement.[62]

It is apparent that the thinking that evolved in Canada on strategic stability – and several affiliated concepts – was quite unlike the thinking that emerged in the United States. For example, concern in Canada over strategic stability dated to the very start of the US-Soviet nuclear arms race, and thus there was never a need to highlight the dangers that nuclear superiority posed. The need for stability in the nuclear age was recognized as early as 1951, and the dangers associated with strategic superiority were specifically outlined in the twin departmental reports of 1955. In addition, several DND air defence studies of the late 1950s, highlighted in Chapter 2, concluded that the age of mutual deterrence had arrived, and that with it would come greater stability.[63] The depiction in these studies was very similar to the one that became known as mutual assured destruction in the United States, as it was explained that no matter which side struck first in a future crisis, the other would retain an assured retaliatory capability. Thus, the concept of stability through the threat of mutual destruction appears to have taken hold in Canada well before it was officially accepted in the United States.

As for some of the other subjects raised in this discussion, Sutherland's account of nuclear targeting strategies challenged the 1962 policy recommendation of Defense Secretary McNamara. In any event, the American emphasis on counterforce was quickly withdrawn, a result of both strong allied criticism and a recognition that it might be strategically destabilizing. In addition, while Schelling's work on threat manipulation and nuclear credibility predated some of Sutherland's studies, the latter hardly copied Schelling's findings. On the contrary, Sutherland's observations on the "rationality of irrationality" built on those of Schelling, as they represented a further attempt to ensure that American nuclear threats were credible at a time when Soviet strategic deployments had raised numerous concerns.[64] In sum, the understandings on strategic stability reached in Canada alternatively predated, challenged, and/or extended those reached in the United States.

Accounting for Differences in Canada-US Strategic Thought on Nuclear Weapons

Challenging the central thesis offered by authors John Gellner, Adrian Preston, and Colin Gray that Canadians were passive consumers of strategic thought throughout the Cold War, this chapter has demonstrated that Canadian defence officials did think strategically in the 1950s and early 1960s, and that the understandings that were articulated with regard to nuclear weapons and related issues of strategy frequently challenged those reached in the United States. Canadian thinking on deterrence, strategic stability, and the nuclear balance did not mimic the appreciations reached elsewhere. Rather, Canadian studies and reports reflected a different set of assumptions, beliefs, and expectations.

Documents reveal that Canadian defence officials recognized the enormous implications of large-scale nuclear deployments from the start of the US-Soviet arms race. The 1951 DRB report that first discussed the importance of retaliatory capabilities, and the subsequent departmental studies that examined the notion of balanced forces, are testament to a series of crucial understandings that were reached in Canada early in the nuclear age: that nuclear war was a misnomer; that a deterrent relationship involved two actors and an action-reaction dynamic; and that stability could be best assured through the fear of mutual destruction. While some in the United States reached similar conclusions, NSC-68 and the policy of massive retaliation that followed were based on a fundamentally different conception of military power in which strategic advantage could be quickly translated into military and political benefits. (Indeed, both the concept of limited war in the late 1950s and McNamara's counterforce strategy of 1962 were critiqued along similar lines.[65])

Explaining the differences in national interpretation is not easy. However, conflicting understandings of the international security environment offer one possibility. Convinced that order and stability were the most important objectives of the 1950s and early 1960s, Canadian defence officials identified strategies intended to further such objectives. American strategists agreed on the general importance of the goals, but the means of achieving them were markedly different. For example, American doctrine held that order was worthwhile only if it furthered a US conception of global interests. Thus, the intent was stability, but stability on American terms. Canadians, on the other hand, enjoying the luxury of not being a global

power, were able to take a more restrained and nuanced view. It was anticipated early on that the US nuclear advantage was not expected to last, and
it was thought that the Soviet Union (along with other countries) would
ultimately deploy large numbers of nuclear weapons. As a result, the Canadian conception of deterrence did not prioritize American weapons, nor
did it favour the unilateral ability of the United States to deter the Soviets.
Because the central understanding was different, the conclusions that resulted were also different.

Among American strategists, Bernard Brodie's work stands out as being
most reflective of the understandings reached in Canada. This observation
says something quite revealing about the Canadians who thought and wrote
about strategic issues. As discussed, Brodie was an isolated figure in the
American defence community, and his ideas, while respected (at least by
some), were not widely accepted. Indeed, among the early "makers" of nuclear strategy, Brodie probably had the least direct influence on US defence
policy.[66] The fact that he may have been an important influence on Canadian officials indicates that they were concerned less about echoing whatever was popular in the United States than about reaching their own
understanding of the nuclear age and the changes it had brought about (a
point that will be returned to in the conclusion).

This discussion reveals that at the very peak of the Cold War there were a
number of Canadian defence officials who felt sufficiently knowledgeable
that they began to explore some of the primary strategic concepts of the
day. The understandings reached reflect a far more independent and forward-
looking defence establishment than has previously been recognized. This
account, even in isolation, represents a considerable challenge to Canadian
security literature, which has continued to assert the absence of Canadian
strategic thinking for more than three decades. At the very least, it demonstrates a dialogue and approach that call into question the image of a strategically feeble and passive country.

4

The Canadian Debate on the Acquisition of Nuclear Weapons

The question of whether Canada would acquire nuclear weapons represented a watershed in postwar Canadian defence policy. The issue not only split the Canadian public but drove a wedge between Canada and some of its closest allies, in particular the United States. It also led to a bitter intragovernmental split, as the Department of National Defence became embroiled in a battle with the Department of External Affairs over the issue. This chapter examines how officials in both departments approached the question, and considers the factors that led them to reach such different conclusions. DND stressed the deterrent aspect of nuclear weapons, and how Canada could play an important role in ensuring that the credibility of the West's nuclear force remained strong. Further, DND's position changed as the department gradually shifted away from its initial emphasis on externally based considerations in support of acquisition and moved toward more politically sensitive, domestically driven concerns. External Affairs, on the other hand, stressed the destabilizing nature of nuclear weapons and the fact that any Canadian acquisition would have a negative impact on this country's foreign relations. DEA officials also raised specific concerns over command and control arrangements and the negative international consequences that a Canadian nuclear acquisition might have. In spite of their differences, however, each department strongly believed that its analysis reflected distinctly Canadian interests and concerns. The respective conclusions were thus intended not only to enhance Canada's security but also to further the country's international standing.[1]

The nuclear weapons controversy had its genesis in a series of North Atlantic Treaty Organization directives – passed in the mid-1950s – that committed the Western allies to the nuclear defence of Europe. The first alliance directive to specifically recognize that tactical nuclear weapons would be required in Europe in the event of a Soviet attack was MC 48 ("The Most Effective Pattern of NATO Military Strength for the Next Few Years"), which was passed at a NATO ministerial meeting in December 1954. On its own and regardless of any subsequent development, acceptance of MC 48 – which was signified when no substantive Canadian objections were raised – committed Canada to a nuclear defence role. This was followed by MC 14/ 2 ("The Overall Strategic Concept for the Defence of the NATO Area") and MC 70 ("Minimum Force Requirements for 1958-1963") in 1957 and 1958, directives that further clarified the role of tactical nuclear weapons.[2] By not objecting to either of these directives, Canada unquestionably committed itself, perhaps unwittingly, to the nuclear defence of Europe.

Canada's nuclear commitments went beyond alliance directives to include continental defence arrangements with the United States. Documents indicate that as early as 1950-1, US defence officials raised the possibility of storing nuclear weapons at American-operated bases in Canada.[3] By mid-decade the first requests were received for the "closer integration of atomic capabilities in the defence of North America" – proposals that ultimately included the acquisition of nuclear weapons for Canadian forces. Surprisingly little analysis of these requests was initially conducted by either DND or DEA officials, and Canadian approval was granted. Thus, when examining the nuclear weapons controversy, it is important to realize that there were actually *three* components – weapons for Canada's NATO forces, US requests for storage and overflights, and acquisition for use in Canada.

Perhaps the most useful way to examine the nuclear weapons controversy is by dividing it into two time frames. The first, the 1955-9 pre-negotiation phase, ends with the February 1959 speech in which Prime Minister John Diefenbaker indicated that the government would acquire the weapons. The second period, 1959-63, ends with the pro-nuclear decision of Lester Pearson, the newly elected prime minister. Discussion of the first period reviews the evolution of Canada's nuclear commitments and focuses largely on the minutes of both the Chiefs of Staff and the Cabinet Defence Committees, the two main government bodies that examined and made recommendations on defence policy issues in Canada.[4] For the second period, attention shifts to recently declassified departmental documents and reports, with separate sections for DND and DEA.

The Early Canadian Consensus on Nuclear Weapons, 1955-9

From 1955 to 1959, Canadian defence and external affairs officials generally failed to consider the acquisition of nuclear weapons in a comprehensive and conceptually challenging manner. Seemingly basic questions were apparently not asked, including what purpose nuclear weapons would serve and how Canada's security interests would be affected by the acquisition. Even larger questions on the strategic merits of nuclear weapons were not considered. With the primary decision apparently made by NATO, it was almost as if Canadian government officials concluded that there was simply no reason to examine such difficult issues, although this cannot explain the failure to examine the implications of nuclear weapons acquisition for use in Canada. Indeed, it was not until 1959, at which time the acquisition was growing increasingly uncertain, that strategic rationales both for and against acquisition were developed by both departments. Thus, the early "consensus" was less a result of specific analysis that favoured acquisition than it was the consequence of there being no serious examination of a decision both departments believed had already been made.

In an attempt to alleviate some of the confusion that had been generated with the passage of MC 48 in December 1954, the obligations and implications of the directive were explained in a memo prepared by the defence liaison division of External Affairs in July 1955.[5] There was legitimate uncertainty, the memo noted, over whether the directive ensured that nuclear weapons would be used in the defence of Europe or if it gave member states the right to make that decision on their own. However, the document also stated that "in practice, the distinction between the two approaches is more apparent than real." The question would become academic once NATO forces were organized in such a way that the only defence they could offer was with nuclear weapons – a process that was already occurring because of the failure to meet the conventional force guidelines established at Lisbon in 1952.[6] As the memo summarized, "a decision to put up resistance on a large scale will necessarily mean a decision to fight with nuclear weapons ... [this] seems to flow inexorably from the Council's approval of MC 48." Neither this document nor any other DEA report of the time, though, directly addressed the directive's implications for Canada, in particular its effect on a possible acquisition of nuclear weapons.

The first occasion where the topic of nuclear weapons was raised at the Chiefs of Staff level – even indirectly – occurred at a special meeting of the committee on 18 February 1955.[7] General Charles Foulkes, the chairman, noted that the growth in nuclear stockpiles on both sides meant it was no longer realistic to believe that a future war could be fought without the use of such weapons. This was just one year after the US enunciation of the strategy of massive retaliation and only a few months after the passage of MC 48. In addition, the continuing weakness of the West's conventional forces was a contributing factor to General Foulkes's observation. In an environment in which conventional defences would probably fail within a day or two of a Soviet attack, the general noted that all of the allies needed to reassess the contributions they could make. Foulkes did not specifically discuss the issue of nuclear weapons for Canada, but stated that a further conventional weapons buildup was unlikely given the budgetary environment. The implication – that Canada could make an effective contribution to NATO through the acquisition of nuclear weapons – seemed clear.

It was late 1956 before the issue was raised directly at the Chiefs of Staff level: at a special meeting on 3 October, atomic anti-aircraft weapons for both the US and Canadian air forces were discussed.[8] For the US Air Force, the issue was overflights over Canadian airspace; for the Royal Canadian Air Force, whether the weapons would be acquired and, if so, when. General Foulkes remarked that the questions had been under informal discussion between the countries' militaries for some time, but that all involved recognized the "difficult political problem" the issues raised for Canada. As a result, Foulkes recommended that it was "unwise" for the matter to go to cabinet "until every angle had been explored." At this meeting Jules Léger, the undersecretary of state for external affairs, did *not* raise any specific objections on a possible Canadian nuclear acquisition. Rather, he noted that a change in US law would be required before an exchange of atomic information could take place.[9] He therefore suggested that the matter be raised with the "appropriate Ministers" and that their authority be received before any further discussions on the issue took place. In spite of Léger's suggestion, the committee agreed to conduct further exploratory discussions on the matter.

A few months later, in December 1956, nuclear weapons were discussed for the first time by the Cabinet Defence Committee. The specific issue addressed was the arming of US fighters overflying Canadian airspace, thereby indicating that "every angle" had apparently been explored by the Chiefs of Staff, and that they now supported the US request. The committee recommended that "the US Air Force be authorized, for a six month period, to fly such aircraft armed with these missiles over Canadian territory." It was, in fact, the first of many such authorizations. This meeting thus marked the first time that the Canadian government approved, in advance, the possession of nuclear weapons on or over Canadian territory.[10] Perhaps more important, the meeting also signified the beginning of a period of more intensive discussions with the Americans on several nuclear-related issues, including a possible Canadian acquisition. The minutes of the meeting thus noted that "the US might offer to sell similar weapons to Canada and RCAF aircraft would be equipped with them. Indeed, Canadians would probably be surprised if the request were refused."[11]

By the spring of 1957, military attention was clearly shifting to the acquisition of nuclear weapons for use by Canadian forces. At the 608th meeting of the Chiefs of Staff Committee on 19 March 1957, an array of nuclear weapons systems designed for different defence roles were discussed.[12] First, Air Marshal C.R. Slemon, chief of the air staff, examined the relative merits of the two weapons systems that were being considered for placement on the CF-100 for continental air defence: the MB-1 Genie and the Sparrow missile, both of which were being developed in the United States for use with a nuclear warhead. Afterward, Lieutenant-General H.D. Graham, chief of the general staff, raised an issue of similar importance for the army – the acquisition of nuclear rockets for Canadian forces in Europe. Finally, Vice-Admiral H.G. DeWolf, chief of the naval staff, noted that the navy "had an interest" in both torpedoes with atomic warheads and atomic depth charges. The meeting indicated that, since the raising of the matter the previous October, all three service chiefs had concluded that domestic Canadian nuclear acquisition was now only a matter of time, and thus it was important that each service identify its preferred weapon system at an early date.

These were not the only nuclear roles discussed at this meeting; a new role for the Canadian air division in Europe was also raised.[13] The chief of the air staff observed that "1 Air Division was somewhat concerned about its atomic delivery capability." Air Marshal Slemon stated that with the recent changes to NATO and the expected role that nuclear weapons would play in future conflict, it was only prudent to raise questions regarding the mission at this time. He suggested that the capability to carry "small" atomic bombs "might be necessary" in order to maintain the effectiveness of the air division, thus hinting that a nuclear strike role might be the only legitimate option for Canada's forces.[14] In spite of the radical shift that this mission would entail for Canada, it did not generate much discussion at the meeting.

The meeting concluded with a summation presented by General Foulkes that reviewed the three nuclear "requirements" envisaged for the Canadian forces: (1) a warhead for a missile still to be selected for the air force; (2) atomic depth charges for both the navy and air force; and (3) warheads for either the Little John or Lacrosse short-range missiles for the army. However, the general also stated that "Canada does not have an immediate requirement for atomic warheads for new weapons and therefore there was no reason to press for a change in the US law for a period of at least two years." The meeting concluded with the statement that the "Chairman, Chiefs of Staff, would prepare a policy statement concerning weapons development in Canada for use by the Minister in answering questions which may arise." While Canada's nuclear requirements were thus identified at this meeting, the chiefs concluded that there was no urgency to the issue.

Some of these findings were repeated in an External Affairs brief for the Canadian delegation in preparation for the critical NATO meeting in December 1957.[15] After noting that nuclear weapons had become an integral part of Western defence strategy, the document recognized that the Chiefs of Staff "envisaged" three distinct nuclear roles for Canadian forces and essentially repeated those identified at the chiefs' meeting the previous March. No specific objections to the possible acquisition were raised in the brief. Rather, it stated that one of the most controversial aspects of NATO strategy was the stockpiling of warheads and the related problems "associated with storage, maintenance, and control."[16] Indeed, it was concern over command and control arrangements that would ultimately become one of the department's primary objections to Canadian acquisition of nuclear weapons.

It was at this time that some of the broader implications of Canada's possible nuclear acquisition and involvement with US nuclear forces finally began to be addressed. At a special meeting of the Chiefs of Staff Committee on 18 December,[17] two separate issues were discussed – an American proposal requesting permission to store nuclear weapons at Goose Bay, Labrador, for the Strategic Air Command, and a request to bring about the "closer integration of atomic capabilities in continental air defence." The committee agreed that the first request would "enhance the effect of the policy of the deterrent," thus identifying a strategic rationale that would be repeated many times, not only with regard to this specific request but also as a larger defence of Canadian nuclear acquisition. On the second issue, the committee offered few remarks, except that the proposal was "entirely logical and reasonable." Once again, the External Affairs representative, J.J. McCardle, made no direct comment, but rather advised that "the United States was primarily interested at this time in receiving political clearance" for both proposals.

At a follow-up meeting two days later, McCardle made some additional remarks.[18] He noted that if agreement on the American request for Goose Bay was reached, it would be critical to "remind" the US government of the importance with which Canada approached the issue of nuclear consultation as it related to the employment of SAC forces. At the same time, he suggested that it was "desirable" to inform Canada's NATO allies of the nature of the nuclear discussions between Canada and the United States (which were being conducted in secrecy). Last, he stated that he was reserving final judgment on the matter until some future point. In spite of the non-committal nature of McCardle's remarks, his failure to offer any specific objection to the nuclear proposal(s) was almost certainly interpreted by DND officials as signifying basic DEA approval of them.

In fact, it was not until the spring of 1958 that the Department of External Affairs began to raise particular objections to Canada's nuclear policies. Sidney Smith, the secretary of state for external affairs, who had been largely silent on nuclear issues at previous Cabinet Defence Committee meetings, offered several observations. Most important, he cautioned that the storage of American nuclear weapons in Canada was entirely different from granting permission on overflights, and the implications of any such decision were "very great." Should an agreement on the issue be reached, Smith argued, Canada would at a minimum want some form of "veto authority" on the use of nuclear weapons stored on its soil – much as the British had recently negotiated with the United States.[19] The discussion ended with the committee agreeing to defer any decision on the matter pending further consideration.[20]

Despite doubts, the essentially supportive position of External Affairs with regard to nuclear weapons was revealed in a departmental report prepared for a meeting of the Canada-US Ministerial Committee on Joint Defence in December 1958.[21] This paper did not challenge the basic Canadian decision(s) to acquire nuclear weapons and support US requests for nuclear storage and overflights. Rather, it focused its attention on questions of command and control, and recommended that Canada not seek any special privileges in this regard, as doing so would create an unfortunate precedent (a recommendation that was quickly ignored in any event by the department). The document also suggested that Canada's nuclear acquisition would have to be related to the government's disarmament policy, a potentially troubling problem that could be averted with the recognition that nuclear weapons were required as a "deplorable necessity" given recent Soviet intransigence.

In early 1959, the attention of the Chiefs of Staff Committee returned to the future role of the European Air Division. At a special meeting on 26 January, General Foulkes stated that the present air defence role was a task better left to the Europeans and that the Canadian squadron should accept the nuclear strike mission.[22] This recommendation was further deliberated on 12 March, at which time Air Marshal Hugh Campbell, chief of the air staff, suggested that the strike/attack role "would represent direct support of the principle of a strong deterrent force." Further, by this time several discussions had been held to determine an appropriate aircraft to perform the mission, and the choice had been narrowed to the Lockheed F-104 Starfighter and the Grumman F-11-1F Super Tiger.

On 20 February 1959, in the same House of Commons speech in which the cancellation of the Arrow was announced, Prime Minister Diefenbaker essentially formalized the decision to acquire nuclear weapons. With reference to the Bomarc air defence missiles and the land-based rockets that were to be acquired, Diefenbaker said that "the full potential of these defensive weapons is achieved only when they are armed with nuclear warheads." Diefenbaker further noted: "we are confident that we shall be able to reach a formal agreement with the United States on appropriate means to serve the common objective."[23] While, as was his custom, Diefenbaker did *not* unequivocally announce Canada's intention to acquire nuclear weapons, this was certainly the impression given by the statement (one strengthened by Diefenbaker's closing plea to "recognize the gravity of the decisions that we are called upon to make").

Whatever doubts may have remained regarding the RCAF's future role in Europe were eliminated by a visit to Ottawa by General Lauris Norstad, the NATO commander, in May 1959. In a series of meetings, Norstad briefed both the prime minister and the cabinet on the importance of the strike mission, and stated that no ally was better trained than Canada to perform it. On 2 July 1959 – two days after the Chiefs of Staff Committee recommended that the F-104 be purchased – the government announced that it had accepted the strike role for the European Air Division.[24] Significantly, there was no mention in any of the early public comments that the mission entailed the use of nuclear weapons.[25] In any event, acceptance of this mission clearly constituted a further nuclear commitment that the Canadian government had voluntarily accepted.

In sum, by mid-1959 everything seemed to be in place for the acquisition of nuclear weapons. The Canadian military wanted the weapons, and while External Affairs had not been overly supportive, neither had it been very critical. A series of military hardware purchases – including CF-104 aircraft for the air division in Europe, Bomarc surface-to-air missiles, Honest John short-range rockets, and CF-101 aircraft for use in North America – had either been announced or were in advanced stages of negotiation.[26] Indeed, in late 1958 the cabinet had authorized that senior military officers begin negotiations with their US counterparts regarding the acquisition and storage of nuclear weapons for Canadian forces.[27] A preliminary draft agreement was reached within a few months.[28] When Defence Minister George Pearkes stated during the summer of 1959 that Canada's troops would be armed "as efficiently and effectively" as the troops of its allies, the comment was widely interpreted as indicating that a formal government announcement regarding nuclear weapons acquisition was imminent.

At this very time, though, the acquisition grew uncertain. There were four reasons for this development: (1) the mid-1959 appointment of Howard Green – a man horrified by the prospect of nuclear war and committed to disarmament – as secretary of state for external affairs;[29] (2) Diefenbaker's personal belief that the majority of Canadians opposed nuclear weapons;[30] (3) the initiation of arms control talks between the United States and the Soviets (specifically, talks on general and complete disarmament, reductions of military manpower, and nuclear testing); and (4) the increasing influence of Norman Robertson, the undersecretary, who believed that nuclear weapons would lead to "global suicide."[31] Thus, in 1960, the government began to stress that no decision on nuclear acquisition had yet been made, and no timetable was offered on when one could be expected.

It was at this time that officials in both DND and DEA began to more thoroughly consider the implications raised by the acquisition of nuclear weapons. Once it became apparent that the government was wavering, both departments began identifying and articulating specific rationales to justify their positions. While these rationales were quite different, each believed that the course of action it prescribed was the right one – DND believed that nuclear weapons furthered Canadian political and military interests, while DEA argued that such weapons would do incalculable harm to this country's reputation and integrity, and bring a nuclear conflict that much closer to reality.

The following section of this chapter examines how thinking in DND and DEA evolved over the crucial 1959-63 period. Particular attention is paid to examining the rationales that were offered by both departments, and the extent to which external considerations played a defining role in shaping perceptions. One caveat must be made beforehand: documents relating to the acquisition and possession of nuclear weapons are among the most sensitive in Canada. Despite the declassification of many files for this project, the majority of records remain closed and it is unclear when they might be opened. It is therefore important to stress the preliminary nature of the following observations.

DND and Nuclear Weapons:
Militarily Important, Politically Essential

DND thinking on the acquisition of nuclear weapons underwent an evolution between 1959 and 1963. This change can be seen as a gradual shift away from the largely defensive, passive reasons initially offered to explain the acquisition, toward more active, positive reasons. Further, over time the department gradually began emphasizing the Canadian political interests that nuclear weapons served, a clear attack on the Department of External Affairs and the influence it had acquired on the issue.

An *aide-mémoire* prepared by the RCAF in April 1959 offers a revealing insight into the thinking of DND at a time when the acquisition, while still viewed as probable, was becoming less certain.[32] It focused on the nuclear weapons systems that the United States wished to store in Canada, and identified three: rockets at Goose Bay for US Air Force interceptors, bombs at the same base for the Strategic Air Command, and depth charges and various anti-submarine warfare weapons at the naval base at Argentia, Newfoundland. Each request was examined briefly and supported out of a belief that each would enhance the credibility of the Western deterrent. The perfunctory manner in which the requests were defended is indicative of a department that had probably not given them much thought, as if the "benefits" they offered were so obvious that they scarcely needed identifying.

Perhaps as important as what was contained in the document is what was alluded to. Toward the end was a brief discussion of a possible Canadian acquisition of nuclear weapons; it clearly suggests that the department – or, in this case, the RCAF – was suffering from an acute case of "nuclear envy." The concluding paragraph noted: "It is suggested that any agreement with the US which would permit the storage and use of nuclear weapons for and by US forces based in Canada be contingent upon a definite assurance from the US that similar weapons will be made available to Canadian forces when they have developed the requirement for and the capability to use them." This reveals a belief that the main stumbling block to any future Canadian acquisition of nuclear weapons would be American opposition, which suggests that the RCAF was badly misinformed about domestic developments in Canada. Second, it raises doubts about the "credibility of the deterrent" argument because, if the rationale were indeed true, there was certainly no need to tie acceptance of the US request to future Canadian nuclear acquisition. The document reveals a department or, at a minimum, a service that was unsure of both its own interests and those of the country.

With the government increasingly wavering on the issue, however, DND began articulating more specific reasons favouring nuclear acquisition. A 1960 memorandum prepared for the Cabinet Defence Committee raised a number of arguments.[33] It began by examining the NATO meetings that had resulted in the passage of alliance directives. Thus, the meetings of 1954, 1957, and 1958 were all discussed and reviewed. The intent was to establish that the Canadian government had made unambiguous commitments to acquire nuclear weapons. As the document noted, "these commitments presume a Canadian policy to acquire nuclear weapons, and the absence of a decision to implement such a policy is becoming increasingly difficult to justify."

The memo also raised a series of alternative rationales defending the weapons purchase. It began by emphasizing the "defensive" nature of the weapons, probably in an attempt to overcome public fears over the roles the weapons would perform.[34] In a further attempt to satisfy critics, the report noted that "it would be clearly understood and stated that Canadian action in acquiring ... nuclear weapons and means of their delivery would be subject to any measures of disarmament or arms control agreed between the East and West." DND clearly appreciated how important such concerns had become, and intended to reassure those who believed that Canadian nuclear acquisition was fundamentally incompatible with disarmament negotiations. The paper also commented on the command and control aspect of nuclear weapons, and concluded that the proposed "dual key" arrangements with the United States were acceptable. However, despite the effort at identifying an array of arguments supporting acquisition, DND had not yet indicated how nuclear weapons served *Canadian* interests, a failing that was evident not only to the government but to the public as well.

A more positive attempt at defending the proposed acquisition was revealed in a paper prepared by General Charles Foulkes, the recently retired chairman of the Chiefs of Staff Committee, in March 1961.[35] This paper looked at several issues, including Canada's overall defence orientation, military commitments, and recent changes in the international security environment. Regarding nuclear acquisition, Foulkes argued that "to carry out the tasks that the government has already accepted," nuclear weapons were required for the Canadian forces. He discussed Canadian alliance commitments, and concluded that failure to honour them would not come without political "costs" (although he refused to speculate what these might be). Foulkes maintained that nuclear weapons would almost certainly be used on any future European battlefield, and thus Canadian troops needed the same kind of military hardware as their potential enemies. There were two other points that Foulkes made defending the acquisition – Canadian nuclear weapons, by offering "dispersal of the deterrent," enhanced the credibility of that force; and nuclear weapons offered military advantages over conventional weapons in the air defence role.

Considered together, these three documents reveal a department defending the acquisition of nuclear weapons on several grounds. However, the lack of consistency in early arguments is indicative of a department still developing its position. The emphasis on external considerations was relatively easy to make, but not persuasive. While nuclear commitments had been made, emphasizing them failed to address the benefits that acquisition offered Canada. Indeed, at a time when many observers were arguing that the Western alliance itself was problematic,[36] repeating externally based commitments was unlikely to sway either the prime minister or officials in the Department of External Affairs.

Thus, at this time, DND officials began to develop more focused arguments in favour of acquisition. Officials started stressing the political and military advantages that nuclear weapons offered Canada. Further, detailed criticisms of the continuing policy of nuclear indecision were offered. The new strategy revealed a department concerned by current developments, and intent on ensuring that its voice was heard amid the confusing array of actors in an increasingly politicized domestic debate.

The first indication of the new departmental strategy was a paper prepared in the fall of 1961 by the joint staff. The aim of the report, titled "Nuclear Weapons for Canadian Forces," was plainly stated in the opening sentence: "to present a rationale in support of nuclear weapons for the Canadian Armed Forces."[37] After reviewing the weapons systems that Canada had committed to purchasing, the report turned to examine various objections regarding acquisition that had been raised at both the governmental and public levels. Four such objections were discussed, critiqued, and ultimately dismissed: (1) concerns over the enlargement of the nuclear "club"; (2) the negative implications for disarmament of any Canadian acquisition; (3) the "sacrificing" of Canadian sovereignty that acquisition would entail; and (4) the reduction in Canadian influence that would result from nuclear acquisition.

Some of the paper's principal findings can be briefly discussed. For example, the paper said it was "understandable" that Canada's concern with arms control had led to a delay in nuclear acquisition. However, the report asserted that Canada's disarmament focus was "increasingly difficult to reconcile with Canada's sales of uranium, her purchases of [weapons] delivery systems and her commitment to a NATO nuclear strategy." In the absence of any indication that arms control negotiations were producing results, "neglect of our NATO and NORAD commitments in this context almost amounts to Canadian unilateral disarmament." The report served notice that, from DND's perspective, Canada's disarmament focus was strategically counterproductive and politically questionable. Further, the report's strong language signalled that the department would no longer look the other way in the face of policy contradictions and inconsistencies.

The paper also took aim at Canada's political interests and suggested how the acquisition of nuclear weapons would further them. This led to a discussion of Canada's influence, with the report commenting that while this country's authority among the "non-aligned" nations was uncertain, Canada's voice in the West was not. It was with the nations of the West – that is, the countries with which Canada shared a common political and ideological heritage – that Canada needed to be most concerned. By moving away from these countries through recent policy decisions and initiatives, the report contended, Canada was harming its international reputation and "prejudicing" its future international influence.

In spite of the more aggressive DND approach, the government continued to waver. Indeed, on the increasingly rare occasions when the prime minister spoke directly on the issue of nuclear weapons acquisition, his statements revealed that his government had not yet made a decision, and would not as long as disarmament talks held out some hope of success.[38] Perhaps responding to such developments, in 1962 DND turned the heat up further by challenging – and essentially discrediting – several of the government's nuclear proposals.

Among the proposals critiqued, one initially offered by Prime Minister Diefenbaker himself, but developed in consultation with officials in DEA, attracted the most attention. This so-called stand-by proposal suggested that nuclear weapons could be made available to Canadian forces during an emergency. This would involve agreements with the United States whereby nuclear warheads from nearby American bases could be delivered on short notice to sites in Canada that were equipped with Bomarc missile installations and interceptor aircraft "positioned in readiness" to receive them.[39] Through such an arrangement, the government believed that it could claim to be honouring Canadian commitments, while maintaining that Canada did not have nuclear weapons on its soil. This would apparently satisfy the government's twin desires to be viewed as a trustworthy ally while demonstrating its pledge to arms control.

A September 1962 letter from Air Marshal Hugh Campbell, chief of the air staff, to the chairman, Chiefs of Staff, revealed DND's disdain for the "standby" proposal.[40] It began by noting that eight large cargo aircraft (of the C-130 class) and crews would be required to provide the warhead airlift for the two Canadian Bomarc bases; additional aircraft would be required for the CF-101s. Campbell noted that readying a Bomarc base was a difficult task, and normal operating procedure called for a minimum of fifteen hours. While Campbell acknowledged that this time requirement could be reduced, doing so would require a larger workforce than the one that was planned. The letter suggested that to be a sound option, further agreements would have to be reached with the United States whereby the Americans would "provide additional nuclear storage facilities at bases close to the US/Canada border." This would require an American construction program plus additional loading crews and ground support. The letter concluded that "senior military authorities" of both the United States and Canada did not believe that the proposal was feasible, and it recommended forwarding that conclusion to the prime minister.

In a follow-up letter written a few weeks later, the chief of the air staff further explained some of the same points, but in an even more dismissive tone.[41] In this letter, Campbell noted that there were only two squadrons of transport aircraft in the United States specially trained for the role of nuclear weapons movement, and it was unrealistic to believe that both would be made available to Canada at a time of acute international emergency. Further, the American technicians who handled and fused atomic warheads were in short supply, and the same observation applied to them (i.e., they would probably not be available to Canada in a crisis). Because of these and other considerations, the option was "simply not acceptable" and did not deserve to be investigated further. In spite of this recommendation, though, the proposal was far from dead, as it enjoyed considerable support within External Affairs, which viewed it as one way of providing Canadian forces with a nuclear capability without formally acquiring the weapons.

In the aftermath of Canada's indecision in the Cuban Missile Crisis, pressure to resolve the nuclear weapons impasse intensified.[42] In addition, the first units of the CF-104 squadrons in Europe were expected to become operational on 1 May 1963, and six months were needed after the conclusion of a bilateral agreement for the construction of nuclear storage facilities. This placed the effective decision deadline at 1 November 1962.[43] The Department of National Defence, however, seemed to be at a loss over how to regain the confidence of the prime minister, as by this time Diefenbaker appeared far more sympathetic to the advice of DEA and its vocal minister, Howard Green. Indeed, indicative of DND's loss of bureaucratic influence, the "stand-by" proposal ultimately formed the basis of negotiations for the acquisition of nuclear weapons on the continent in the "framework" nuclear talks that began with the United States on 30 October. Similarly, a fallback DEA proposal, the "missing parts" plan, was also put forward to the Americans over the strong objections of DND.[44] However, the United States was unconvinced of the practicality – let alone the desirability – of either Canadian proposal.[45] By December 1962 the negotiations aimed at reaching a comprehensive nuclear agreement had stalled.

By the beginning of 1963, the nuclear issue was moving rapidly toward a climax. Three separate developments indicated that a resolution was required. First, the outgoing NATO commander, General Lauris Norstad, visited Ottawa in the first week of the new year. At a news conference, Norstad stated that Canada had made an unequivocal commitment to the alliance to perform the nuclear strike role in Europe and that tactical nuclear weapons were required for the mission.[46] Second, Lester Pearson, the Liberal Party leader, announced on 12 January that he favoured the fulfilment of Canada's nuclear commitments, thereby ending a period of confusion for his party that had mirrored that of the government.[47] Third, on 30 January, in response to statements made by the prime minister, the US State Department issued a news release that dramatically challenged Diefenbaker's interpretation of recent diplomatic and military events.[48] In combination with a growing domestic political crisis, the nuclear issue could not continue unresolved for much longer.

It was at this time that the definitive DND paper defending nuclear acquisition was written – by R.J. Sutherland, chief of operational research at the Defence Research Board. In the 1963 document, titled "Some Problems of Canadian Defence Policy," Sutherland addressed the arguments that had been made by advocates on both sides of the debate.[49]

He began his discussion with the nuclear "facts" as he saw them. Sutherland noted that Canada had committed to acquiring weapons systems that were intended to perform a nuclear role, and had made commitments to both NATO and the United States that it would accept and perform a variety of nuclear tasks. He also noted that Canada's nuclear weapons, while not necessarily "defensive" per se, were to be used solely against military targets. Sutherland recognized that failure by Canada to honour its nuclear commitments would carry a "price." Like Foulkes before him, he refused to speculate what that price might be; the implication, however, was such a decision would harm both Canada-US relations and Canada's standing in NATO.

Sutherland believed it was vital that the specifics of the proposed acquisition be understood, and thus he described how the "joint stockpiling" arrangement with the United States would work in practice. He explained that under normal peacetime conditions, the warheads would remain under American control. Indeed, if no emergency were ever to arise, the warheads would never pass into Canadian hands. It was only in an emergency that the US detachment at a Canadian base would release the warheads to Canadian custody, at which time Canada would have authorization to use the weapons. Thus, the contention that Canada would have to use the weapons according to the whims of the US government, as charged by some DEA officials, was false; so was the charge that the arrangement would weaken Canadian sovereignty. As Sutherland argued, the weapons would be stored in Canada under the permission of the Canadian government, and if such permission was ever withdrawn, the weapons would have to be withdrawn as well.

Another frequently raised objection (particularly by the prime minister) was concern that Canadian acquisition would enlarge the "nuclear club." Sutherland countered this point by noting that only countries with an independent capacity to produce nuclear weapons were properly considered "members" of this club. Canada could not become such a member "short of undertaking our own national weapons programme," an option the Canadian government had no intention of pursuing and had in fact renounced fifteen years earlier. In this regard, Sutherland emphasized the distinction between nuclear weapons states and those countries that had such weapons as a result of joint stockpiling arrangements with the United States. The latter "club" was already quite large, and Sutherland argued that its existence had "not yet jeopardized international peace and stability."[50]

Sutherland also examined the military advantages that nuclear weapons would offer Canada. He identified three main ones: (1) nuclear weapons in the air defence role would not only destroy the weapon carrier (i.e., the bomber) but the bomb as well, which would ensure that there would not be a detonation on the ground in the event of a "kill" over Canadian airspace; (2) Canadian nuclear weapons would help eliminate any "gap" in coverage over the air approaches to North America; and (3) nuclear weapons offered the most effective and efficient defence policy, because "the dollar expenditure required in order to produce a given level of defence will be reduced." Considered together, the three advantages constituted a powerful military incentive to acquire nuclear weapons.

Sutherland asserted that the choice essentially came down to two different conceptions of Canada's role in the world. One viewed Canada as a member of the North Atlantic community of nations. If this were accepted as the basis of Canadian defence and security policy, it was necessary for Canadians to recognize a responsibility toward the common defence, and renouncing the military technology required for the task was simply not possible. Nuclear weapons had been accepted as the cornerstone of Western defence, and to repudiate them at this stage was neither viable nor realistic.

The second conception depicted Canada's role in the world as essentially isolationist. In this view, there was no need for Canada to recognize any particular responsibility for the common defence of the North Atlantic community because that burden would be borne by those who had no choice in the matter – in particular the United States. According to Sutherland, there was a segment of the population that viewed Canada's influence in global politics as far more significant than it really was and believed that a Canadian threat to leave the alliance would have a dramatic impact. On the contrary, Sutherland believed that any such move would leave Canada much weaker, and was inconsistent with this country's political, diplomatic, and military history.

Sutherland's conclusion followed. Canada had made nuclear commitments to both NATO and the United States, and in international politics breaking commitments was not something that any state should take lightly. Further, nuclear weapons served Canada's larger political and strategic interests. Sutherland also argued that the critics' case against acquisition had not been well reasoned. He asserted that an isolationist stance would harm this country's short- as well as long-term interests and badly damage relations with Canada's traditional friends. With regard to the Atlantic alliance, Sutherland noted that NATO was, de facto and in practice, a nuclear alliance. Even if Canada was to disavow any nuclear role, Sutherland wondered, what would this achieve? The alliance would certainly remain committed to nuclear weapons, and the only probable effect of such a move would be to complicate defence planning. As he asked, "Can we combine full membership in a nuclear alliance with a policy of extreme nuclear squeamishness?" For Sutherland, to ask the question was to answer it.

Sutherland's report revealed the extent to which DND thinking had evolved in four years. Unlike the early departmental efforts, which largely stressed Canada's commitments, this study attempted to place the decision facing Canada in its broader historical, political, and strategic context. And yet, in spite of this conceptual progression, DND had failed to develop a consistent position on the matter. Whether this failure was ultimately reflected in the government's indecision is difficult to determine, although in contrast with DND, officials in the Department of External Affairs constantly stressed specific reasons that emphasized how nuclear weapons were *not* in Canada's interest.

DEA and Nuclear Weapons –
Militarily Unnecessary, Politically Harmful

External Affairs thinking on nuclear weapons was, in contrast to DND, consistent and clearly articulated. Nuclear weapons, according to department officials, did not serve Canadian political interests, and moreover, acquiring them would send the wrong signal at a time when US-Soviet disarmament talks were just getting under way. Canada needed to explore other options, which it could do because of its leading position in the West and its authority among developing countries. Indeed, the acquisition of nuclear weapons would hurt Canada's reputation in both the West and the Third World, and would result in reduced Canadian influence globally.[51]

An examination of the thinking on nuclear weapons as it evolved in DEA should include recognition of the important role played by a relatively small group of officials. Leading the battle against acquisition were Undersecretary Norman Robertson and External Affairs Minister Howard Green, who together formed a tough and uncompromising duo and largely determined External's basic policy. Allied against them were Arnold Heeney, Canada's ambassador to the United States, and Robert Bryce, who was secretary to the cabinet and, although not an official of External Affairs per se, nonetheless had close ties to the department. The comments that follow focus on departmental documents, reports, and memos, as well as on Canada's position in disarmament negotiations, a position largely determined by External Affairs and one that had a considerable effect on the nuclear weapons debate.[52]

The negative position that External Affairs was taking on nuclear weapons was dramatically revealed in a document prepared by Robertson in July 1959, just one month after the government had formally announced that it would accept the strike role for the air division in Europe. The paper, titled "Nuclear Weapons – Some Questions of Policy," raised a number of concerns, in particular the consequences of nuclear war and the role that Canada could play in ensuring that such a conflict never occurred.[53] The document's opening paragraph asked two fundamental questions: (1) Were the issues that divided East and West sufficiently important to consider settling them by recourse to global nuclear war? and (2) Could policies that considered the possibility of nuclear war continue to be recommended by rational human beings? While Robertson did not directly answer either question, his position on the matter could hardly have been stated more clearly. To Robertson, Canadian acquisition of nuclear weapons would bring the world that much closer to disaster, and therefore DEA needed to do everything in its power to avoid that outcome.

A few months later, External had to develop a response to the US request for nuclear storage rights at Canadian bases – a request that had initially been made several years earlier. A report prepared in October 1959 examined the full implications of the request.[54] External recommended, on the advice of Robertson, that approval "under appropriate conditions" be granted to the United States.[55] At the same time, it suggested that there needed to be a better understanding of the exact role of the bases in US defence planning. In a revealing passage, the report noted: "we believe that failure to grant approval for the storage would have serious repercussions on Canada-US relations, and would lessen our ability to influence US policy on important issues." Thus, concern over the possible American reaction to a decision of non-cooperation at least partly fuelled the Canadian approval. The episode reveals a growing departmental disenchantment with the United States, and concern over its nuclear weapons policy vis-à-vis Canada.

Further DEA concern with the broad contours of US defence and nuclear policy could be seen over department actions on the "Sky Hawk" air defence exercise, which had been scheduled for October 1959. The plan called for Strategic Air Command bombers, in the guise of a Soviet air attack, to attempt to penetrate NORAD defences; in the process, civilian air traffic was to be grounded to permit the employment of electronic countermeasures. Joint planning had been under way since early 1959, but in the wake of Howard Green's mid-year appointment as minister, thinking in the department on such matters had changed and a number of concerns about the exercise were raised. In August, following a recommendation by both Green and Robertson, the cabinet decided that further consideration was required and that formal approval should be withheld.

The Americans were furious, and expressed their "shock" and "gravest concern" at the Canadian action.[56] Robert Bryce, recognizing that Canada had implied on several occasions that it would approve the exercise, made this point personally to the prime minister, but with the memory of the (politically unpopular) NORAD debate undoubtedly still fresh in his mind, Diefenbaker may have believed that his government did not need the attention Sky Hawk would attract. In addition, the prime minister was still smarting from the military advice he had received over NORAD.[57] He may have thought that this was one way of re-asserting his political authority (as it may have been for DEA in general).[58]

One month later, a DEA memo indicated that the department "would be willing" to reschedule Sky Hawk for the following September.[59] As with the nuclear storage request, though, External's approval had less to do with a belief that the exercise was worthwhile on its own merits, and more to do with concern over the long-term damage that could be done to bilateral political relations if approval was withheld. As the memo noted, "we are inclined to believe that failure [to agree to a new exercise] could have serious repercussions on relations between Canada and the US."

The two cases reveal a department that was increasingly troubled by American military actions and policies, and one determined not to let the United States run roughshod over Canadian interests. Still, on both occasions External indicated that it would be willing to reach an agreement with the Americans, which demonstrates that it had not yet adopted the more aggressively negative position that would be in evidence in the period beginning around 1960.

In spite of Canadian apprehension, nuclear talks with the United States continued intermittently during the period. In June 1960, Howard Green reported to cabinet that five separate issues required resolution: (1) storage of air-to-air defensive weapons for US forces at Goose Bay and Harmon Field; (2) storage of nuclear anti-submarine weapons at Argentia; (3) storage of nuclear bombs for the Strategic Air Command at Goose Bay; (4) acquisition of nuclear warheads for Canadian use in Canada; and (5) acquisition of nuclear warheads for Canadian use in Europe. Only the first issue was close to being settled; the others were at various stages of discussion.[60] Indeed, despite the appearance of progress, it was clear that by this time the government was deadlocked on the questions of nuclear storage, and especially on acquisition, with National Defence and External Affairs growing increasingly hostile as the bureaucratic disagreement became more apparent.

In December 1960, Robertson sent Green a memorandum that detailed his thoughts on Canadian nuclear acquisition.[61] This memo followed a meeting of Robertson, Bryce, and Air Marshal F.R. Miller, the new chairman of the Chiefs of Staff Committee, that had been intended to determine if there was any common ground between the two departments.

The memo began by noting that "it would be inconsistent and hypocritical" for Canada to adopt policies that would "compound" the nuclear problem, in light of the expected approval of a Canadian resolution on disarmament by the United Nations General Assembly.[62] Robertson stated that with the growing possibility of some form of détente between the superpowers, Canada needed to avoid taking actions that might "hamper" developments. As for the nuclear talks that were being held with the United States at the time, Robertson noted that "negotiations ... even on a contingent basis, carries [sic] with them an implication of ultimate intention to obtain the weapons," a decision that he believed ran contrary to recent statements by the prime minister. Last, Robertson noted that the conclusion of an agreement for nuclear storage at Goose Bay and/or Harmon Field would have great "symbolic" importance, and would be widely interpreted as the first step in a much broader policy of nuclear acquisition by Canada.

In the fall of 1960, DEA began emphasizing Canada's position in disarmament negotiations to further bolster its position of nuclear delay/refusal. This roughly coincided with the establishment in 1961 of a disarmament division within the department.[63] In particular, a series of resolutions was debated in the UN General Assembly, and the position(s) that DEA took had a direct impact on the domestic nuclear weapons debate. In effect, as long as Canada played a leading role in disarmament negotiations, the longer would be the delay in implementing Canada's nuclear commitments.

A memo prepared by Bryce for the chairman, Chiefs of Staff Committee, in October 1960 revealed the degree to which disarmament had become the defining concern of DEA.[64] It also identified the steps that DND could take at least to remain a player in the determination of Canadian policy, which was an interest of Bryce's, since he was largely sympathetic to DND. The memo noted that it would be prudent to "take into account" the probability that disarmament would continue to be a declared objective of Canada for the foreseeable future. This recognition led to three general defence implications. First, Canadian defence policies "must be capable of acceptance as being cognizant with and not antagonistic to the pursuit of that objective." Second, Canada needed to search for a measure of disarmament that, if agreed upon, would make a positive contribution to both Canadian and Western security. And third, the impact that future disarmament agreements might have on Canadian defence programs needed to be considered.

One month later, in November, General E.L.M. Burns, the disarmament advisor to the government (and later Canada's chief delegate at disarmament negotiations), wrote a paper titled "Argument against the Spreading of Nuclear Weapons."[65] It challenged the notion – widely accepted in DND – that the best way to ensure strategic stability was through the balanced spread of nuclear weapons. On the contrary, Burns lamented that the proliferation of tactical and strategic nuclear weapons was bringing the world steadily closer to conflict, and that deterrence based on the threat of nuclear annihilation was doomed to fail. Burns noted that "if the world was to have a reasonable chance of avoiding nuclear war," the arms race had to be stopped and ultimately reversed. This could be done only if there was broad agreement between the United States and the Soviet Union that the goal was worthwhile and that there were no unresolved issues of such importance that either side would feel the need to resort to the use of nuclear weapons if the issue reappeared. Arms control was the critical first step, and one that many nations could participate in. While Canada did not have nuclear weapons, it could support the goal by not acquiring them in the first place.[66] This was a decision that Burns believed might persuade other countries to similarly renounce their nuclear ambitions.

A few comments can be made on this paper. First, it *directly contradicted* the earlier DEA thinking on strategic stability outlined in Chapter 3, and indicated a move away from the model discussed by George Ignatieff in his 1955 department study. Given this shift, the DND-DEA dispute becomes easier to comprehend. In essence, by 1960 External Affairs had reconsidered its basic position on strategic stability and had concluded that nuclear weapons, rather than encouraging stability as a result of their enormous power to hurt, represented a grave peril because their eventual use was a virtual certainty. Second, the memo revealed a belief that, regardless of Canadian commitments, it was more important for Canada to take a principled position at this time, and thus the country needed to renounce any nuclear ambitions it might have. Variations on these two basic points were to become the core of External's disarmament position, and contain the seeds of the DND-DEA dispute.

The effect of Burns's memo can certainly be seen with regard to Canada's actions on the Irish Resolution, which was debated by the UN General Assembly in December 1960. The resolution contained two parts: the first called upon the nuclear powers to voluntarily declare a moratorium on nuclear weapons, while the second required states without nuclear weapons to declare, on a temporary and voluntary basis, that they would not try to acquire nuclear weapons. The resolution posed particular difficulties for Canada, as it could be accused of hypocrisy if it voted in favour of the resolution while simultaneously acquiring nuclear weapons.[67] On the other hand, External believed that abstaining or voting against the resolution would send a negative signal at a time when disarmament talks were beginning to develop momentum.[68]

DND viewed Canadian support as signifying the country's intent to renege on its nuclear commitments.[69] In spite of DND's advice, Canada voted in favour of the resolution. External Affairs officials argued that in the absence of any agreement on disarmament, interim measures aimed at constraining nuclear proliferation were preferable to inaction. External had again indicated that it viewed the curtailment of the arms race as more important than honouring a Canadian military/political obligation.

Over the following few years, the United Nations debated and voted on a series of resolutions that posed a direct challenge to DND and the possibility of Canada fulfilling its nuclear commitments. Like the Irish Resolution, many either banned nuclear weapons outright (for example, the Ethiopian Resolution) or requested non-nuclear states to enter arrangements not to pursue a nuclear option (the Swedish Resolution). In addition, Canada played an important role in the Ten Nation Disarmament Committee; its successor, the Eighteen Nation Disarmament Committee; and the negotiations on both general and complete disarmament and the non-militarization of space. On many of these issues, Canadian actions were opposed by Washington and many of Canada's traditional allies.

A few months prior to the June 1962 federal election, Diefenbaker asked DND and DEA to prepare papers to deal with the expected opposition questioning of why the government had found it so difficult to make a firm decision on the acquisition of nuclear weapons.[70] DND somewhat grudgingly supplied a paper reviewing recent case histories of allied weapons systems that had been cancelled after lengthy development periods; the intention was to show the fluid nature of the strategic environment.[71] External responded with a statement that essentially supported the prime minister's delay. It noted that many NATO countries had recently conducted defence reviews, and as a result several had decided to change their defence policies and commitments. The report concluded that "apart from the difficulty of predicting the future utility of weapons systems, it might be imprudent to make major decisions at this time on some important defence problems."[72] The sentence seemed to defend Canadian indecision as the most appropriate course of action.

In December 1962, when the nuclear talks with the United States were deadlocked and pressure was building for a resolution, Diefenbaker attended a series of meetings between US president John Kennedy and British prime minister Harold Macmillan in Nassau.[73] Following the meetings, a communiqué was released that contained a proposal for the establishment of a NATO nuclear force composed partly of tactical nuclear forces in Europe. Although Canada's ground and air forces would be included if such a proposal were adopted, there was no indication that any such assignment would alter their role or the weapons systems already planned for them.[74]

Nonetheless, the Department of External Affairs quickly advised Diefenbaker that, as a result of the communiqué, NATO would be reviewing the direction and shape of its military forces, including the question of how political and military control of nuclear forces would be exercised in the future.[75] The communiqué had certainly not been intended to call into question Canada's existing commitments, but to a hopelessly indecisive prime minister the External recommendation provided a further excuse for delay. Indeed, Diefenbaker quickly began claiming that the RCAF role in Europe had been "placed under doubt" after Nassau.

Diefenbaker subsequently made a speech in the House of Commons that seemed to both support and reject nuclear acquisition.[76] In short order, the US government responded with a sharply worded news release, and the Tory government lost a vote of non-confidence and the resulting federal election to Lester Pearson's Liberals. The new prime minister quickly signified his desire to reach a bilateral nuclear weapons agreement, and a comprehensive deal was reached in August 1963. Nuclear weapons were delivered to Canadian forces units in early 1964, and were maintained in this country until the last ones were removed from CFB Comox, British Columbia, in 1984.[77]

As we have seen, from 1959 to 1963 officials in the Department of External Affairs articulated a clear and unambiguous message – nuclear weapons were destabilizing and provocative, and Canada could have a far greater international impact by not accepting them than it could by fulfilling its commitments. The department believed that this was a critical time in world affairs, and that if Canada acquired nuclear weapons it would forgo any hope of playing a leading role in disarmament negotiations. Thus, unlike their counterparts in National Defence, External Affairs officials succeeded in identifying and asserting a consistent strategic recommendation opposing the acquisition of nuclear weapons.

The Differing Strategic Interests of DND and DEA

Canada's tortuous nuclear weapons debate reflected the prime minister's personal ambivalence on the issue. Believing that Canada had international defence responsibilities, Diefenbaker tended to side with defence officials who spoke of Canadian obligations. On the other hand, he was deeply concerned about the tone of the Cold War, and believed that disarmament and arms control represented a promising avenue for reducing US-Soviet tensions. Stranded between the Departments of National Defence and External Affairs, Diefenbaker chose the path of least political resistance – delay.[78] What is remarkable was how long he managed to avoid making a decision on the issue, literally his entire term as prime minister (although that observation is tempered by the fact that his indecision ultimately led to his government's defeat).

Clearly, there was a general failure to seriously consider the implications of nuclear weapons at the time that Canada made its initial commitments. A comprehensive attempt to examine the issues associated with acquisition occurred only after the government began to express reservations over Canada's nuclear roles. During the period 1959-63, officials in both DND and DEA examined the acquisition of nuclear weapons in some detail, although as with the debate on air defence, the two departments came to startlingly different conclusions and recommended very different courses of action.

Defence officials had a difficult time, at least initially, identifying specific Canadian interests that nuclear weapons would serve, preferring instead to stress external commitments. However, the department, probably recognizing that this strategy was ineffective, gradually began to emphasize two distinct sets of arguments for acquisition – one military and the other political. Militarily, DND maintained that nuclear weapons would not only enhance the credibility and viability of the Western deterrent, but would also greatly improve the effectiveness of Canada's air defence forces. Politically, the department argued that acquisition was required if Canada was to remain an important Western actor, as a negative decision would push this country out of the Western orbit and toward the non-aligned group of nations.

One question that could be raised by this discussion is whether DND's analysis on this issue was "legitimate," or whether it was primarily an attempt at simply developing alternative rationales that could be cited to support a decision – nuclear acquisition – that had already been made.[79] As appealing as this argument might sound to some, it misinterprets the evidence presented in this chapter. In essence, this argument is another way of suggesting that all Canadian defence decisions were made in the external environment during this period, and thus Canada had little room to man-oeuvre. As is discussed in the concluding chapter, this underestimates the real influence that Canada had in the postwar period, and the genuine ability the country has in determining its own security policies. It also overlooks the fact that NATO, like other alliances, is a measure in compromise for large and small members alike.

It is true that Canada originally committed to acquiring nuclear weapons as a result of alliance directives MC 48, MC 14/2, and MC 70, and supplemented these commitments with additional nuclear agreements with the United States. On the surface, then, DND's position on the issue was effectively "set." But, faced with a changing domestic political environment, DND developed various rationales for nuclear acquisition, rationales that identified a range of strategic interests that acquisition would serve. These rationales were no less relevant in the wake of Canada's nuclear commitments than they were before such roles were accepted. Thus, while critical evaluation is always a necessary part of scholarship, care is needed to balance the available evidence with the assumptions that all researchers bring to the scholarly table, and to reach a judgment that is both sustainable and supportable. Accepting this criterion, it seems clear that DND recommended actions based on its reading of core Canadian strategic interests.

The Department of External Affairs, on the other hand, argued that nuclear weapons ran counter to Canada's interests, would hurt this country's international reputation, and were strategically destabilizing. While that last point represented a change in departmental thinking from the 1950s, it had become widely accepted not only in Canada but throughout much of the West. Most important, External believed that Canada could not simultaneously acquire nuclear weapons while playing a leading role in disarmament negotiations. It thus persuaded the government to delay any decision on nuclear acquisition while disarmament talks held out some hope of achieving success.

The National Defence-External Affairs split essentially boiled down to differing conceptions of where Canada's primary security interests lay, and how Canada could most effectively contribute to international stability. In contrast to the prevailing thinking in Canadian security literature, however, officials in both departments came to their conclusions on the basis of their reading of Canadian strategic interests. To DND, the continued viability and authority of the Western alliance was critical, and acquiring nuclear weapons was an important development in this regard. The department believed that Canada's security interests were intimately tied with those of the alliance, and thus anything that weakened NATO also weakened Canada. Conversely, DEA officials believed that by the early 1960s, NATO had become little more than a military shell, and that its emphasis on nuclear weapons could lead to disaster. Canada could play a part in avoiding such an outcome only if it had the conviction to take a principled stand against nuclear weapons, even if doing so meant disregarding commitments and distancing this country from its traditional friends and allies. While acknowledging that this was a difficult decision to make, department officials felt that the interests of the international community demanded it.

In sum, Canadian officials did think about the acquisition of nuclear weapons, and their observations and conclusions were largely determined by the department that they worked in. The Departments of National Defence and External Affairs approached Cold War security issues from fundamentally different perspectives, and thus the fact that they did not agree on matters of national security is hardly surprising. As in the chapter on air defence, it is unimportant to determine which department was more "objective" in evaluating Canadian strategic interests. The key point to note is that, after some initial confusion, officials in both departments considered whether and how nuclear weapons served Canadian interests, and the observations that were reached reveal diverging understanding of Canada's role in the world and the manner in which this country could most effectively contribute to international stability and order.

5
Canadian Conceptual Understanding of Arms Control

A paradox of the nuclear age was that as states acquired nuclear weapons for deterrent purposes, some strategists believed that stability was reduced because of the large number of weapons available and the increased possibility of their use. A second paradox was that because nuclear weapons had such enormous destructive power, it was simply not credible to threaten an opponent with their use in response to minor transgressions. The concept of arms control was developed in the late 1950s and early 1960s to counter these paradoxes while ensuring that nuclear weapons remained a credible deterrent. This chapter examines how officials in the Department of National Defence approached and conceptualized arms control.[1] As the intent is to demonstrate the independent nature of the Canadian approach, the comparison is between DND officials and American strategists. In contrast to US observers, Canadians were generally sceptical of both the utility and potential of arms control, and emphasized the possible negative consequences it could bring about. DND officials also made original use of some of the emerging research tools of the day, in particular quantitative methods. The discussion again shows that Canadian defence officials had considerable latitude for independent thinking, and that the image of their passively accepting theories developed in the United States is both inaccurate and misleading.

Arms Control: A Brief Introduction

In the mid- to late 1950s, there was increasing concern in the American civilian defence community that although the United States still had nuclear superiority over the Soviet Union, its advantage was rapidly declining. Strategic stability was widely regarded to have been the result of American nuclear superiority, and the emergence of a nuclear balance was believed to be inherently destabilizing. In contrast to the view in Canada, the Americans had little faith in the *mutual* concept of deterrence. Pressure thus grew to do something before the nuclear balance was irrevocably altered in a direction that could be detrimental to the security interests of the United States.

By 1956-7, a new concept was emerging in the defence communities of several countries, but in particular the United States. Observers concerned about the loss of control and the dangers of nuclear instability began to consider the possibility of regulating the competition in arms. The aim would be to enhance stability while encouraging trust and goodwill to develop in the broader relationship. Indeed, it was suggested that limited technical agreements for alleviating particular causes of anxiety might ultimately result in more wide-ranging agreements that would promote improved political relations.[2] The key consideration was the belief that agreements could reduce the chances of conflict and (somewhat paradoxically) also reduce the level of violence should conflict occur.

When interest in this idea – which was quickly termed arms control – first developed the intent was not to simply update disarmament, a concept that had been discussed for decades with minimal results.[3] The goal of this new process was more limited than the abolition of entire classes of weapons systems; rather, it aimed at a series of mutually agreed-upon adjustments to force structures of indefinite duration.[4] It was thought that such agreements could prevent competition in particularly dangerous military technologies, a reassuring prospect at a time when scientific and military advances were becoming increasingly difficult to control.[5] In contrast to disarmament, then, arms control appeared surprisingly practical; it seemed sensible to trade questionable weapons deployments for improvements in security. Even the staunch American "cold warrior" Paul Nitze initially saw arms control as an "auxiliary to national security policy."[6]

This is not to suggest that there was unanimous support for the concept. Many observers could not comprehend why the regulation of the arms competition was required at a time when the United States still held a clear nuclear advantage over the Soviet Union. In addition, critics noted that cooperation with the Soviets would prove dangerous, because even if agreements were reached their terms would not be respected. Arms control thus had to overcome considerable opposition within the American defence and political establishment before it was taken seriously. However, once it was understood that the basic idea was aimed at managing the arms race instead of eliminating it, arms control began to be considered more favourably.

After several years of apparent scholarly disinterest, an attempt to thoroughly conceptualize arms control was finally undertaken in 1960, when the journal *Daedalus* sponsored a conference that brought together many of the principal American scholars.[7] Organized by Donald Brennan and later edited into a collection of essays, the conference tackled such subjects as the "background" of arms control, the "major policy issues and problems," and the "techniques of arms control."[8] However, overlooked among the papers was a comprehensive look at what arms control was and why it was desirable in the first place. The authors apparently assumed that the definition and requirement of arms control were well understood but that its effects and results were not. Thus, the rationality assumption and realist understandings about the nature of power and interstate relations became a central, if rarely acknowledged, component of early thinking.[9] More important, the *Daedalus* conference and many of the papers published in the subsequent volume reflected a belief that arms control was essentially an apolitical process – that is, political relations and concerns were thought to be outside its direct sphere of relevance.[10] A final assumption was that Soviet specialists would take a similar view of the arms race and the need to contain it, and thus concur with the general American approach.

One scholar who did not take part in the *Daedalus* conference was Hedley Bull, an Australian who in 1961 wrote the definitive early study on the subject, *The Control of the Arms Race*.[11] Bull described the central tenets of arms control as: a concern about the dangers of nuclear war and a dissatisfaction with existing policies; a suspicion of the goal of a negotiated general and comprehensive disarmament agreement; an insistence on the unity of strategy and arms control; a broadening of the scope of the subject and an appreciation of the links between varieties of military activities previously thought separate; a criticism of the assumption that disarmament should be the objective of arms control policy; and a determination to shatter the illusion of disarmament while remaining optimistic about the contribution of strategic theory to the improvement of prospects for international peace and security. Bull's work is considered later in the chapter; it should be emphasized that he was the first observer to examine the conceptual underpinnings of arms control, even though by this time the concept was widely accepted in Western policy circles and negotiations between the superpowers had been under way for several years.[12]

In the interests of clarity, five defining concepts can be identified in early arms control literature. Arms control referred to: (1) formal processes of negotiation between states; (2) the outcome of interstate negotiations; (3) the theory of interstate military cooperation between potential enemies; (4) any activity intended to promote or express interstate military cooperation between potential enemies; and (5) the consequences of behaviour (tacit or formal) for the objectives of arms control.[13] According to Thomas Schelling and Morton Halperin's influential study *Strategy and Arms Control* (also published in 1961), arms control included "all the forms of military cooperation between potential enemies in the interest of reducing the likelihood of war, its scope and violence if it occurs, and the political and economic costs of being prepared for it."[14] Arms control thus represented far more than the negotiation of agreements to reduce or limit arms; rather, it was indicative of a cooperative approach that could establish a broader process of improved political ties. However, it was this very flexibility of the concept that ultimately was to create confusion and uncertainty, as arms control was utilized in situations in which the central actors involved – most notably the United States and Soviet Union – had differing understanding of what "arms control" referred to.

In sum, in the mid- to late 1950s arms control was generally poorly understood and many of its underlying assumptions had not been thoroughly considered. Even when scholarship began to develop in 1960, many assumptions continued to go unexplained. Further, it was widely assumed that the American approach would be shared in Moscow, although few had attempted to explain precisely why the Soviets would necessarily see the issue in similar terms, particularly at a time when the Soviet Union was rapidly expanding its own nuclear forces. This assumption reflected a mistaken belief that strategic stability was an uncontested concept, and that alternative definitions would surely bow to the "superiority" of the Western version. It was not only Soviet observers who would challenge several of these points, however, but defence officials in Canada as well.

Department of National Defence Thinking on Arms Control, 1955-63

Concern about arms control within the Canadian defence department can be divided into two distinct periods. DND officials initially considered the concept between 1955 and 1960, but at the time their attention was largely focused on specific arms control issues and proposals that demanded immediate attention. From 1960 to 1963, officials grappled with what arms control was and whether it represented a worthwhile goal. Because of the greater significance of the latter studies, only brief remarks are offered on the early Canadian approach.

Two arms control issues demanded attention in the mid- to late 1950s: decisions on reductions of military manpower and of nuclear testing.[15] The possibility of "freezing" and/or reducing conventional military forces had a long history, and was first discussed in the postwar period in 1948, when the United Nations Commission for Conventional Armaments (of which Canada was a member) addressed a wide range of proposals, none of which produced significant results.[16] The issue received renewed attention in 1952, when the Disarmament Commission began discussing it. As had been the case four years earlier, progress was slow; the proposal bounced around various UN subcommittees as neither the United States nor the Soviet Union had yet developed a consistent approach.

That uncertainty ended in March 1956, when the Soviet Union proposed strict numerical limits for military forces, including a maximum of 200,000 for Canada – well above the 115,000-man force of the time. The Department of External Affairs reacted with cautious support.[17] DND's position, however, was ambiguous: it indicated its willingness to comply in practice, but showed no enthusiasm for doing so. The department's response was revealed in a memo prepared by General Charles Foulkes, chairman of the Chiefs of Staff Committee, for the minister in July 1956.[18] Foulkes countered with a three-staged "reduction" of Canadian military forces – from 250,000 in the first stage, to 215,000 in the second, and finally to 175,000 in the third, which would still constitute a force 50-percent larger than the one authorized at the time. The general warned that reducing military forces beyond the third level might pose a threat to the future ability of Canada to mobilize in an emergency. In addition, Foulkes noted that Canada's military forces were largely defensive and were barely adequate to meet the country's security needs at present. Last, the general made a vaguely worded threat that because Canada's North American defence commitments were increasing, any agreement to limit or reduce military forces might have a negative effect on Canada's ability to perform its alliance commitments. The point was clearly intended as a warning to DEA, which had previously indicated its preference for multilateral security approaches.

Neither the government nor DEA was much impressed by DND's response. Considering that the goal was to achieve reductions in defence forces, the Canadian military's position foreshadowed later developments in US-Soviet nuclear arms control negotiations, when the limits agreed to by the superpowers actually represented *increases* in total weapons holdings. It was an inauspicious introduction to the subject of numerical limits, and indicative of the kinds of difficulties that many countries had with proposals to limit manpower.

By mid-1956, though, a second issue had begun to attract more widespread attention: the nuclear test-ban talks that had been under way since 1950.[19] Particularly in the West, public concern over nuclear tests had reached unprecedented levels as a direct result of the massive tests that both the United States and Soviet Union had conducted.[20] There was a growing belief that the only way to bring the arms race under control was to stop all testing. Indeed, two years earlier, in 1954, India had proposed an immediate cessation to atmospheric nuclear testing, but at that time the proposal had not attracted Western or Soviet support – although it had generated considerable backing among developing countries and was one of the original causes for the emergence of the non-aligned movement. With the continuing public outcry, however, both superpowers began to reconsider their earlier opposition. In the fall of 1955 the Soviet Union indicated that it favoured an outright ban on nuclear tests, although with uncertain verification provisions it was unclear how effective any such agreement would be. Still, the offer was intended to increase pressure on the West and score Cold War political points, for if no progress was made the Soviets would be able to claim that the West was the stumbling block preventing agreement.

It was at this time that the Departments of External Affairs and National Defence seriously clashed for the first time over an arms control issue. Although DEA believed that limited nuclear weapons testing was necessary, it began emphasizing the need for numerical controls. Thus, with the support of Lester Pearson, Canada became a strong proponent of this concept. DEA maintained that an agreement to limit the size and number of test explosions "could hardly fail to have a great psychological effect despite the absence of any real practical purpose."[21] External further believed that any agreement on testing might appease the demands from developing countries for their total ban, and might also improve the increasingly difficult political situation that the West was facing at the United Nations. As a result, before the UN General Assembly in late 1956, Canada formally proposed that the superpowers set "some annual or other periodic limit on the volume of radiation to be generated by test explosions," an offer that would have resulted in the de facto establishment of a yield limit.[22]

DND responded harshly to the testing initiative, a reaction that underscored the lack of cooperation between the two departments. The DND position was first laid out in an April 1956 document titled "Tests of Nuclear Weapons," which was prepared by the Defence Research Board.[23] The report began by noting that "from a purely technical point of view," nuclear tests were an "essential" element in weapons development. The document further pointed out the ineffectiveness of banning the testing of thermonuclear weapons while allowing testing to continue on fission bombs (an unintended consequence of any agreement to limit yields). The report argued that there was actually little to distinguish between the two, and it was scientifically possible to test elements of a hydrogen weapon in a fission-type device. The report also discussed the problem that effective verification would pose for any such agreement, a concern that DEA had played down in its proposal. Indeed, in light of the Soviet Union's closed nature, it was debatable whether Soviet provisions on verification could ever satisfy Western concerns. Given these considerations, the report concluded that continued testing was required to ensure the effectiveness of the Western nuclear force, and that any yield limit "would not remove the danger" that nuclear weapons posed.

A few months later, the joint staff prepared a second study that re-examined DND thinking on the issue.[24] Although the new study largely repeating the findings of the first report, what set it apart was the discussion of Canada's possible nuclear roles and the implications these might have for any negotiations to limit nuclear tests. The report observed that the "Chiefs of Staff have an interest in the possibility of acquiring atomic warheads" for both guided and/or unguided missiles, and thus "would be unwilling to agree to a serious limitation on the development and testing of atomic weapons for defensive purposes." This report concluded that Canada needed to adopt a cautious attitude with regard to any agreement limiting testing.

Within a few months, the opposition of DND to controls on nuclear tests appeared to have some effect – as did the strong opposition of both the United States and Britain.[25] The Canadian government began pursuing the possibility of registering nuclear tests rather than strictly limiting them.[26] Thus, the Canadian initiative quietly ended. The episode nevertheless offered valuable early lessons in the political realities of Cold War arms control. Ottawa had learned that Canada was of marginal importance in the major security issues of the day, and that when developing arms control proposals it was vital that Canada's major allies be on board. In addition, DEA saw that on an issue of central importance, the United States did not much care about the concerns of the Third World. This was a lesson that the Department of National Defence had already noted, but one that did not carry much weight with officials at the Department of External Affairs. But perhaps the most important lesson was one that went completely unheeded at the time – that Canada needed to have its own bureaucratic house in order before it went on the world stage and made high-profile proposals.

In general, in the early phase of arms control negotiations, DND was largely content to comment on the specifics of particular proposals and did not examine the concept's larger principles. This was hardly surprising, however, as at the time there was a widespread consensus on what arms control was and the benefits it offered. This consensus may have been linked to the fact that arms control revolved around such issues as the test ban and general and complete disarmament (GCD), proposals that seemed to have more in common with traditional disarmament than with arms control per se.[27] This began to change around 1960, when the United States and Soviet Union began discussing a wider range of issues, including concerns over the dangers of surprise attack and the need for adequate communication during times of crisis (operational arms control), in addition to numerical limits on nuclear forces (structural arms control). In effect, it was not until the arms control agenda expanded that DND officials began to explore the concept in a comprehensive and conceptually challenging manner.

National Defence Thinking on Arms Control, 1960-3

Between 1960 and 1963, DND officials examined in detail what arms control was and whether it represented a worthwhile goal. Their observations reveal a department that was carefully evaluating the country's military and political interests, and one that had few misgivings about offering conclusions that challenged the thinking emerging elsewhere. As in prior chapters, the following account highlights specific departmental reports that emphasized some of the common themes of Canadian defence officials.

In May 1960, the Joint Ballistic Missile Defence Staff completed its initial study on arms control and disarmament, titled "Disarmament and the Deterrent."[28] The report began by recognizing that Canada's basic security interest lay in increasing the general level of world security, which could be done by "reducing the risk of thermo-nuclear war." However, repeating the findings of departmental studies on deterrence and strategic stability, the JBMDS found that the establishment of large and diverse nuclear forces by both superpowers had actually enhanced stability, as such forces effectively eliminated the possibility of surprise attack. The paper argued that as long as both sides maintained invulnerable retaliatory forces, the nuclear balance would remain stable.

As a result of that stability, arms control was unattractive. Any attempt at dismantling the deterrent system in place would have detrimental – indeed destabilizing – effects. As the report noted, there simply was no need for unproven measures at a time when the strategic balance seemed assured. Further, the report warned that arms control could actually *decrease* stability, as it could lead to a conventional arms buildup. On this point, the paper's most important passage said that "the abolition of present strategic deterrents would add to general security only if it were possible to establish effective control over conventional armaments, and to strengthen international peace-keeping machinery. If these conditions were not satisfied, the most probable effect of the abolition of nuclear armaments would be to transform the competition for world power into an essentially more dangerous form." Arms control threatened to re-create the military imbalance that the West's nuclear forces had originally been designed to counter, and would thus place the West in a disadvantageous position vis-à-vis the Soviet Union. Negotiations, therefore, had to be approached with caution.

The report offered four specific observations on arms control: (1) the nuclear balance would be rendered more crucial and less stable as a result of an agreement; (2) an adequate balance of conventional forces did not exist, and yet pressure on such forces would increase in the wake of any nuclear agreement; (3) elimination of nuclear weapons is virtually impossible to confirm; and (4) nuclear weapons can always be re-introduced because the knowledge about producing them can never be eliminated.

Given these considerations, the JBMDS concluded that reduction or elimination of nuclear weapons would not make the world a safer place. The nuclear stalemate had had the merit of "making any form of war less likely," as neither side could emerge victorious. However, with fewer weapons, the security dynamics between the United States and Soviet Union would change dramatically. If both sides had smaller nuclear stockpiles, the side that struck first might have a legitimate chance of avoiding effective retaliation. In this environment, the security dilemma would become more acute as both sides would "feel compelled to take precautions which, in the eyes of the opponent, are threatening and provocative."

Last, in a passage that would be proven remarkably accurate, the report predicted that if the primary goal of arms control was to establish a maximum limit of permitted weapons, the exercise would inevitably result in the identification of a numerical figure that satisfied the "worst case" scenarios of both sides. With that figure determined, there would be an incentive to "build up to it," because both sides would naturally conclude that the other would take full advantage of every permitted weapon. In an indirect way, the report warned that arms control might actually enhance arms races rather than reduce them, a prediction that was proven accurate with the first US-Soviet Strategic Arms Limitation Treaty of 1972.[29]

A few months after this report was prepared, the Defence Research Board released a conceptual study on arms control. Written by G.D. Kaye of the Defence Systems Analysis Group (a DRB subcommittee), this study was equally cautious of arms control, although its methodology was a combination of quantitative research and game theory, approaches that had begun attracting attention among American social scientists. Titled "A Model for the Study of Stability, Arms Control, and Disarmament," the paper asked whether a stable nuclear balance could exist.[30] Assuming that it could, the paper also questioned whether it would be feasible to take remedial action to maintain that equilibrium when the balance changed. Last, the paper considered whether such remedial action could be compatible with arms control (and possibly disarmament). To help with answers, a series of mathematical models was designed and examined.

The paper explained that there were two types of nuclear balance, the "subcritical" and "stable deterrent" states. The subcritical was defined as one in which neither side could destroy the other regardless of which side struck first, while the stable deterrent condition was one in which both sides could inflict unacceptable damage on the other. The study observed that the subcritical state was "intrinsically" more desirable, since the nuclear balance was less likely to be disturbed by accident, miscalculation, or irrationality, and had fewer consequences if disturbed. However, the document recognized that it was the second state, that of stable deterrence, that more closely reflected the strategic reality between the United States and Soviet Union.

The aim of the models (which largely focused on the requirements for stable deterrence) was to explain the shifting nuclear balance and determine the conditions under which strategic stability could be best assured. The paper considered whether limiting the number of nuclear weapons was both technically feasible and desirable, or whether such limits simply raised doubts about the stability of deterrence. The models demonstrated that above a certain level of weaponry, stability does not increase (termed the "unconditional brink level"). This raised the question of whether it was possible to reduce that level "as low as possible," so that "we can maintain an effective deterrent with [fewer] missiles."

Kaye's analysis of possible targets in the United States and Soviet Union revealed a crucial fact – that because of the much higher proportion of American industry and population concentration, a fundamental target imbalance existed that was "impossible to remedy," and resulted in a situation where the critical missile stock level for the United States was about three times that of the Soviet Union. Further, if it was assumed that the Soviets could tolerate a "high damage level," while the tolerance level for the United States was "completely unknown," the imbalance might be "as much as [a factor of] 10 or more."[31] Kaye argued that this difference posed enormous, probably insurmountable, difficulties for any arms control negotiations, because it meant that the United States would be reluctant to conclude an agreement in which there were balanced (i.e., equivalent) nuclear reductions. Thus, because of the considerable uncertainties involved, the "instability measure," and arms race dynamics, the subcritical deterrent state was unlikely in the near- to medium term.[32] Nuclear deployments on both sides could be expected to continue, even though past a certain point there would be no (relative) increase in security.

In conclusion, Kaye argued that arms control could be beneficial under controlled circumstances, but that it should be approached with caution. He observed that it was possible to reduce weapons stockpiles, but only to a level where both sides retained an assured retaliation capability – those weapons necessary to inflict the minimum damage could never be negotiated. Because that level was hard to calculate, Kaye warned that concluding substantive agreements would prove difficult. The two sides would have to concur on an array of questions, and failure to reach agreement in any one area would probably result in general failure. Last, arms control was only applicable in limited situations and its larger political promise remained unproven.

Many of Kaye's ideas on arms control were developed further in a paper he published in the 1961 edition of the *RCAF Staff College Journal*.[33] In this article, he again employed the tools used by systems analysts and game theorists to determine how a city could best be defended in the nuclear age.

Kaye examined two alternative models to city stability: the "all or nothing approach," which asserted that safety from attack was achievable through arms control/disarmament or through a pre-emptive strike, and the "moderate approach," which was comparable to the theory of deterrence.

Kaye concluded that the "all or nothing approach" (concentrating on the disarmament option) was valid only "in a very restricted range of situations," the main difficulty being that while the process of disarmament was taking place, there would be "increasing instability and freedom from attack begins to depend more on the opponent's good will than on his self interest." On the other hand, the "moderate approach" actually enhanced strategic stability, and thus "a state of mutual deterrence can be maintained fairly easily so long as weapons stocks exceed some minimum level." Although that level was not identified, the author stressed the need for "large weapons stocks," which promoted "optimum stability."

At the same time, Kaye recognized that arms control could help the deterrent relationship "if we re-define arms control as agreement(s) on restrictions which will tend to preserve the stability of mutual deterrence." He described specific examples of arms control that, if used wisely, could enhance stability – control by numbers, control by quality, and control by inspection.[34] For example, regarding the first measure, Kaye maintained that both sides could accept an upper limit on missile stocks, but he again argued that limit would have to be high enough so that it would not negatively affect strategic stability. Thus, while Kaye did not dismiss the promise of structural arms control, his analysis revealed that caution would have to be employed and that any agreements should not jeopardize basic strategic equilibrium.

A paper prepared by the joint staff in January 1961 attempted to further develop a distinctly Canadian arms control approach based on national interests.[35] It began with a review of recent arms control/disarmament developments. The paper said "it is assumed that the prime objective is to further Canadian security by advancing the cause of international security and stability through the medium of disarmament under effective international control." It recognized that disarmament negotiations had become increasingly important and that, as a result, Canada needed to follow such developments closely. Further, because of Canada's limited size and power, the report suggested that the country could most effectively contribute to arms control by assisting in the "negotiations and implementation of disarmament agreements among the major military powers," a passage that probably reflected DND's discomfort with External's increasingly independent arms control agenda.

The report's main argument was that Canada should not place its pursuit of disarmament before its larger obligations to the North Atlantic Treaty

Organization. The document warned that arms control could drive a wedge between alliance members, because some countries had indicated a desire to pursue it with greater fervour than others. On this point, DND's position was quite clear – Canada was first and foremost a NATO member and should abide by alliance policy. As the report concluded, "it is considered in the interest of Canadian security to encourage the pursuit of disarmament collectively within NATO, rather than unilaterally." Unilateral initiatives represented a danger to the alliance and eliminated the possibility of presenting a unified response to the Soviets.

On the specific question of reductions of nuclear weapons and vehicles, the joint staff largely repeated the findings that the JBMDS had offered the year before. It noted that as the security and numbers of deterrent forces on both sides increased, so did strategic stability, and "Canadian security interests will not be served by any action which reduces this stability." However, like Kaye's papers, the study identified several arms control measures that it believed could positively influence strategic stability. Such steps included: concluding agreements on nuclear weapons testing (which indicated a departmental shift from the position of the mid-1950s); lowering the risk of war by accident or miscalculation; and reducing and gradually eliminating vulnerable delivery systems such as bomber aircraft. In spite of these recommendations, the report highlighted the need to "achieve the widest public recognition of the increasing stability involved in the strategic nuclear deterrent concept to ensure that this is not prejudiced by ill-considered attitudes towards nuclear disarmament."

An additional paper completed by Kaye in February 1962 summarized his thinking – and more broadly that of the department – on arms control. This paper, "Subjective Aspects of the Strategic Nuclear Balance," also utilized quantitative research methods and game theory to reach conclusions on strategic stability.[36] Beginning with the relatively simple case in which two actors each have 100 missiles, the paper examined increasingly sophisticated mathematical models, including those that took into account the deployment of anti-ballistic missile systems; a variety of delivery vehicles; the possible actions of allies; as well as a number of other factors, including such subjective considerations as political leadership and popular support. Much of the study was concerned with the conditions under which strategic stability declines and the likely response of a nuclear-armed state to a situation in which it believed that the military balance was turning against it.

Kaye argued that under such conditions a country would be more likely to panic. This actor would be liable to use force out of concern that if it did not, it might be damaged or destroyed in a pre-emptive attack by its adversary. A second likely response, if given sufficient time, would be to embark on an arms buildup. While a military increase is often intended to redress a force imbalance, the opposing side rarely interprets developments in the same way and often concludes that this could be the prelude to an attack. At best, opposing states view any military increase with suspicion and concern; at worst they view such actions as aggressive and react accordingly. Kaye's model again demonstrated that *stability was best assured when both sides had roughly equivalent (and large) nuclear forces and when such forces expanded and declined at roughly similar rates.* Instability was created when the balance was altered, especially suddenly or unexpectedly. Arms control could be effective in limiting these changes, but only to a relatively small degree.

The department's pre-eminent strategist, R.J. Sutherland, also wrote on arms control. This was not a particular focus of his research, but one of his papers – "Disarmament and Arms Control" – was one of the few departmental efforts to examine both operational and structural arms control.[37]

Two themes were evident throughout the study. First, arms control could not change the basic dynamics of global politics, and thus force would remain the final arbiter of disputes. On this point, Sutherland reviewed arms control attempts in both the nineteenth and twentieth centuries, and focused on efforts such as the Hague conferences and the 1932 World Disarmament Conference. Although he recognized that these meetings had resulted in some agreements, Sutherland questioned their importance, noting that they had not prevented subsequent conflicts. Second, Sutherland noted that prior arms control negotiations had frequently set unreasonable goals, and thus several efforts had essentially been bound to fail. By way of example, Sutherland examined the "fantasy" goals of recent negotiations, particularly regarding general and complete disarmament. He reviewed contemporary Western and Soviet proposals, and argued that both sides had made sure that their advantage in particular weapons systems would be protected – despite the apparent finality of the professed goal. Sutherland maintained that the two sides had been equally responsible for the GCD "fiasco," which had done considerable damage to the future prospects of arms control.

As for the general importance of arms control, Sutherland admitted that he had underestimated its significance in the past. Although he stressed that such accords had rarely had a "major" effect on military capabilities, they were "a symbol of the movement towards mutual accommodation between the United States and Soviet Union, and they represent a significant commitment of prestige on the part of both governments." For that reason, Sutherland believed that arms control deserved to be the object of continuing negotiations, provided its limitations were appreciated.

The most significant obstacle preventing a broad-based accord was the contrast between US and Soviet strategic forces. Sutherland noted that the United States, the leader of a large and geographically diverse alliance, had developed a balanced triad (air-, land-, and sea-based) of nuclear forces, while the Soviet Union, a Eurasian land power, had overwhelmingly stressed its land-based weapons. Limiting particular weapons would therefore prove difficult, as each side could be expected to protect the system(s) in which it held an advantage. Further, the two countries did not share similar attitudes toward nuclear weapons; the Soviets had no equivalent fascination with the Western concept of deterrence, and tended to view such weapons as an additional, albeit important, source of military power. Thus, in a final analysis, Sutherland was rather pessimistic on the future of arms control, although he did believe that agreements could have a positive influence on larger political relations.

Officials in DND clearly had conceptual difficulties with the theory of arms control. Rather than viewing it as a step to enhance strategic stability, Canadian officials were more likely to voice concerns over the dangers that arms control presented and the false expectations that it raised. This is not to suggest that every DND study spoke negatively of arms control, but each of the works examined in this chapter expressed caution in evaluating its potential. As Chapter 3 highlighted the work of Robert Sutherland on nuclear strategy, this chapter has focused on G.D. Kaye of the Defence Research Board, the DND scientist who conducted the most intensive study of arms control. What remains to be determined is whether the observations offered in Canada differed from those developed elsewhere.

Conceptual Thinking on Arms Control, 1959-63

Major works in the field of arms control were written by civilian strategists (most of whom were American). Indeed, four books published between 1960 and 1963 are widely regarded as classics in the field: *The Control of the Arms Race*, by Hedley Bull; *Strategy and Arms Control*, by Thomas Schelling and Morton Halperin; *Arms Control, Disarmament, and National Security*, edited by Donald Brennan; and *Arms Reduction: Programs and Issues*, edited by David Frisch.[38] While the precise argument varied, each book offered the same basic message – arms control is capable of contributing to the stability of the military environment by means of conscious cooperation, or even collaboration, between potential adversaries. Further, it was argued that arms control agreements could reduce the likelihood of war, the damage that might be suffered should war occur, and the economic burden of defence preparations.[39]

Strategic Stability and Arms Control

Four key studies – works by Bernard Brodie, Hedley Bull, Malcolm Hoag, and Thomas Schelling and Morton Halperin – represent different streams of thought on arms control from the period under consideration. While three of the four are American, this focus is consistent with the dominant role that US strategists played in the development of arms control theory.

Bernard Brodie was one of the first civilian strategists to attempt an examination of both the operational and structural variants of arms control. In his 1959 study *Strategy in the Missile Age,* Brodie noted that the US-Soviet arms race was threatening to spin out of control, and that measures to contain it deserved careful study.[40] He criticized the "military mind" for dismissing arms control in the past, suggesting that "military thinking has to move beyond its traditional fixation on immediate advantage."[41] As he further noted, "we ought not to look askance at measures for slowing or otherwise alleviating [the arms race] simply because those measures involve certain finite risks." Specifically, Brodie believed that measures designed to reduce the possibility of surprise attack could not only lessen the chances of conflict, but were consistent with the US commitment to the strategy of deterrence.[42] A variety of other measures might offer further positive strategic benefits, although Brodie believed that many of these depended on the establishment of trust, which would prove difficult to negotiate.

Brodie suggested that the best way to reduce the danger of surprise attack was to lessen the incentives for one, which could be done by encouraging deterrent – rather than aggressive – policies. The most effective strategy for this was through procedures whereby both sides could assure themselves that deliberate attack was not being prepared. Brodie noted that, as a key motivation behind an enemy attack is the belief that an opponent is preparing one of its own, measures that reduce the probability of accidental outbreak of war also lessen the possibility of preventative war.[43]

To Brodie, the key variable – and question mark – in this equation was technological change. He believed that technology could disrupt the nuclear balance and therefore limits on its development could enhance stability. As Brodie observed, "nothing which has any promise of obviating or alleviating the tensions of [the present] situation should be overlooked."[44] In sum, Brodie adopted a cautiously positive attitude toward arms control, believing that it could enhance stability and reduce the possibility of surprise attack.

The concept of stability and the role that arms control could play in enhancing it was further considered by Hedley Bull a few years later. Indeed, this question lay at the heart of *The Control of the Arms Race,* a book that largely focused on whether large-scale arms reductions were feasible and whether nuclear proliferation could be contained.

Bull's basic position was that arms control held enormous promise. The possibility of reaching agreements to limit weapons deployments had an obvious appeal, but also raised a number of difficult issues. First, Bull recognized that there was no guarantee that even if such measures could be negotiated, the arms race would not be resumed at a later date. Should this occur, the competition that would develop would be even more severe than the initial one, as both sides would be starting from a lower level of weaponry and would feel pressure to quickly achieve a position of strength.

Bull examined other difficulties with arms control. He noted that agreements could result in dramatic changes to the balance of power, something that he believed should only be done with caution. He argued that the balance of power, which helped preserve the independence of states, was an essential element in global politics. As he noted, the balance prevented "the society of sovereign states from being transformed by conquest into a universal empire."[45] While power balances were hardly a guarantee against conflict, Bull argued that in comparison with possible alternatives – that is, hegemony – balances should be viewed more favourably.

At the same time, though, Bull noted that adjustments in armaments and alliances were the primary means by which balances of power were normally upset; a state could increase its military strength by enlarging or improving its own military forces, or by gaining allies or depriving its opponents of them. He further observed that, by fortunate circumstance, the two superpowers had acquired roughly equivalent military forces, which had "provided a modicum of security." This balance should not be disrupted, and yet it would be, he believed, without the negotiation of arms control agreements, as it was only through the regulation of the arms competition that the US-Soviet strategic balance could be preserved. The present environment was therefore most unusual, in that stability could be jeopardized by both the absence as well as the negotiation of arms control agreements.

Bull noted that there were "powerful arguments" that suggested the maintenance of a stable nuclear balance required cooperative arms control measures. This hardly meant that the competition in weaponry had to be ended in all fields, however. On the contrary, Bull believed that competition had created the US-Soviet balance in the first place, and that balance "may even be served by the further prosecution of the arms race in certain fields."[46] Nonetheless some degree of limitation was required, which would involve difficult decisions regarding the reduction of some weapon systems while others would be preserved at their present strength. Thus certain types of weapons, such as re-enforced missile sites, were stabilizing, while others – including anti-ballistic missiles and civil defence preparations – tended to undermine the strategic balance. The key lay in making the appropriate distinction and persuading one's opponent that both sides could benefit from cooperative measures.

A third contribution of note in the arms control literature was a 1961 article by Malcolm Hoag, an analyst who began his career at the University of Illinois, moved to the RAND Corporation in 1952, and then joined Robert

McNamara's team of "whiz kids" at the Pentagon in 1960. The Hoag article, "On Stability in Deterrent Races," was an examination of the difficulties in maintaining stability in an environment where security was not dependent on political relations but on the fear of nuclear retaliation.[47] Hoag explained that in the absence of positive political ties, only three courses of action were open to states – to attack, to cultivate peaceful relations, or to run the risk of being attacked.[48] In the nuclear age, the third possibility raised the spectre of complete destruction, and thus there was constant pressure on states to introduce strategies that ensured a pre-emptive attack was carried out when it seemed certain that an opponent was preparing to strike. Such a strategy entailed an obvious risk, but the dynamic of nuclear weapons and the impossibility of defending against them formed a powerful rationale in favour of it (Hoag was obviously not persuaded that the variety and growth of nuclear forces had created a situation of strategic invulnerability). It was because of this possibility that Hoag believed arms control offered a useful approach to reducing tensions.

According to Hoag, arms control represented the best hope for maintaining security in an uncertain strategic environment. Such agreements could enhance stability and alleviate some of the pressures that military and political officials dealt with. Unlike most observers of the day, Hoag argued that such agreements could be both formal and informal, the latter offering an avenue that not only might prove easier to implement, but could lead to further agreements. At a time when making concessions of any kind was politically difficult, unilateral measures aimed at strengthening deterrence while reducing the sources of instability offered considerable promise. Indeed, Hoag believed that the most effective measures were those that would reduce the possibility of an accidental nuclear war without alarming potential enemies about nuclear credibility and thus potentially weakening deterrence.

A fourth major arms control study was the 1961 book *Strategy and Arms Control,* co-authored by Thomas Schelling and Morton Halperin. Its fundamental premise was that the strategic environment had become dangerously unstable, the result of both the introduction of large numbers of nuclear weapons and the accompanying fear of being caught unprepared and losing one's forces in a disarming first strike. Thus, the book focused on the importance of communication and reassurance in international politics. As the authors noted, "we believe that something in the way of rules, traditions, and clearer expectations about each other's reactions and modes of behaviour may reduce the likelihood of military action based on mistake or misunderstanding."[49]

Written at the peak of the Cold War, the book emphasized the mutual nature of the security problem, and the mutual solutions that were required to solve it. In short, both the United States and Soviet Union had a common interest in inducing and reciprocating restraint, in offsetting some of the characteristics of modern weapons, and in ensuring that armaments and force postures did not worsen their underlying conflict.[50] Arms control could help alleviate these problems, although caution was required to ensure that the adopted measures had the desired effect. Indeed, unlike many of the other studies of the period, Schelling and Halperin's book acknowledged the need to treat arms control critically and to carefully monitor its impact. As they noted, arms control "can reduce tension or hostilities; it can reduce vigilance. It can strengthen alliances, collapse them, or make them unnecessary. It can create confidence and trust or create suspicion and irritation. It can lead to greater world organization and the rule of law or discredit them."[51]

Perhaps most critical for the purpose of this discussion, however, was the realization that reductions in weapons could be destabilizing. To demonstrate this, the authors briefly considered some models of weapons deployment, and concluded that "beyond a certain point ... reduction [in weapons holdings] may increase both the fears and the temptations that aggravate the likelihood of war."[52] And yet, while this possibility was recognized, it is important to note that the discussion on "stability and size of forces" was very brief (two pages), and was certainly not given much emphasis in a book that largely stressed arms control's promise and potential to enhance strategic stability. Overall, then, Schelling and Halperin believed that – while it was by no means a perfect solution – arms control offered the prospect of a more stable and predictable international security environment.

This review of four major studies in the arms control literature reveals a strikingly different emphasis than the Canadian works. While there was universal agreement that arms control was not a solution to the Cold War, there was clearly more enthusiasm for such measures in the United States. Even traditional realists such as Bernard Brodie and Thomas Schelling seemed more optimistic on the potential stabilizing role of arms control than Canada's Robert Sutherland and G.D. Kaye. As discussed, the key consideration in the Canadian studies was ensuring that agreements did not disrupt or diminish the forces necessary to maintain stable nuclear deterrence. In this regard, a frequent emphasis was that arms control might threaten stability by reducing the mathematical certainty of retaliation.

Although there was some recognition of this in several of the studies reviewed (in particular those by Brodie and Schelling and Halperin), the emphasis of early arms control literature was quite different in that there was a far greater faith in the ability to regulate the arms race in a manner that ensured and protected strategic stability. Indeed, while Schelling and Halperin acknowledged the potentially destabilizing aspect of arms control, they were nonetheless far more positive on its larger promise than were Canadian defence officials. Thus, rather than emphasize the stabilizing aspect of balanced nuclear forces, much of the arms control literature assumed that such deployments would ultimately lead to disaster, without ever precisely explaining why this would necessarily be the case. In this regard, one can see similarities with DEA's analysis of nuclear weapons. Part of the explanation may have been the American understanding of deterrence, which, as noted in Chapter 3, was slow in appreciating the advantages of mutually invulnerable forces and retaliatory capabilities. Thus, this may have been the response of a community concerned and intimidated by the rapid growth of Soviet nuclear forces. In any event, the cautiousness and uncertainty evident in DND arms control studies was not apparent in the United States, and is a further example of Canadian defence officials articulating an understanding of an important strategic issue that differed from the consensus view in the United States.

Lastly, a brief comment can be offered on how the US government approached arms control in the late 1950s and early 1960s. During this period, the United States was primarily concerned with negotiations over a nuclear test ban, the dangers of surprise attack, and the talks on general and complete disarmament. The results of each of these sets of negotiations was mixed at best.[53] Perhaps surprising, though, is the degree to which the arms control theories and concepts developed by the civilian strategists and thinkers underlay US policy (particularly given the differences between these communities noted in Chapter 3). As Robin Ranger has noted in his study *Arms and Politics, 1958-1978: Arms Control in a Changing Political Context*, "the American scientists' input to [arms control] policy making was ... influential."[54]

The key development explaining this association was the establishment of the Arms Control and Disarmament Agency (ACDA) in 1961.[55] This was an agency where "the technical arms control thinking of 1958-1962 was *de rigueur*."[56] ACDA and the civilian observers shared underlying assumptions about the benefits of arms control and the dangers of unregulated arms competitions. Perhaps most critically, they also shared the belief that arms control was primarily a technical, rather than a political, process. Thus, US arms control policy quickly focused on specific weapons deployments and the nature and types of military forces.

The US government's affinity for technical solutions was first revealed in discussions at the Surprise Attack Conference of 1958. The US contingent emphasized those weapons systems that they believed led to strategic instability, while the Soviets were more concerned with political areas of conflict that they concluded could trigger a larger showdown. Similar difficulties quickly developed in the GCD talks and in the Campaign for Atom Free

Zones in Europe. In essence, the dispute revolved around the divergent arms control goals of the United States and Soviet Union, and the basic failure of the two countries to agree on a common frame of reference – a problem that would plague US-Soviet arms control throughout the Cold War.[57] However, in spite of the lack of results in superpower arms control negotiations during the 1960s, ACDA maintained a strong grip on US policies until the later part of the decade, at which time changes to the National Security Council ensured that alternative views received more consideration. Thus, during the late 1950s and the 1960s, there was much in common between official and unofficial thinking on arms control, which helps explain why arms control was consistently pursued by the US government.[58]

The Use of Game Theory and Quantitative Research Methods
The use of game theory in international politics was originally developed by the mathematician John von Neumann in the 1920s.[59] It became popular in security studies only when it began to be used as the methodology in a wide range of works by civilian defence scientists in the United States, particularly those by Herman Kahn, Oskar Morgenstern, and Thomas Schelling. The importance of game theory was that it provided a means of reducing strategic problems to a manageable form in which the dilemma and the paradoxes of the nuclear age could be exposed and solutions explored. As Lawrence Freedman has noted, game theory "exemplified a certain type of thinking, presenting it in its purest form."[60]

Among postwar strategists, the one who became best known for his use of game theory was Schelling. Game theory allowed Schelling to consider how the actions of one actor influenced those of others. Among his major findings was the recognition that in most conflict situations even adversaries share common interests and a degree of mutual dependence. Thus, most conflicts are variable-sum games in which adversaries are engaged in both coercion and cooperation (what Schelling called "non-zero-sum games").[61] While all the actors have a common interest in reaching an outcome that is not mutually destructive, they differ over the precise form of the solution. As Schelling noted, the mix of conflict and cooperation differ along a range of possibilities from precarious partnership to incomplete antagonism. A related focus of his work was the utility of tacit bargaining and the tendency of adversaries to cooperate informally on issues of importance.[62] While much of his work on game theory was theoretical and abstract, the larger implication of Schelling's research was clear – game theory could alert decision makers to responses and policies that could jeopardize the fragile stability of the US-Soviet relationship.

In particular, Schelling was concerned about the dangers of accidental nuclear war, and he argued that if such a war were to begin between the superpowers, it would most likely be sparked by the "reciprocal fear of surprise attack."[63] Schelling used game theory and mathematical models to demonstrate that the United States and Soviet Union needed to reach agreements restricting the deployment of weapons systems that were both vulnerable to attack and made opposing forces vulnerable as well. Schelling argued that counterforce weapons upset the stability of the nuclear balance and heightened the incentives to launch a pre-emptive first strike.[64]

Schelling further understood that the use of game theory involved many uncertainties and that these could be exploited by rational players in conflict situations. Indeed, in *The Strategy of Conflict,* Schelling identified what he termed "strategy with a random ingredient." When considering the randomization of threats and promises, Schelling highlighted the fact that a promise is costly when it succeeds, a threat when it fails. When making a threat, there is always a risk that it might have to be carried out, and a further risk of inadvertent fulfilment even if the adversary complies with one's demands.[65] Thus Schelling developed the notion of a "fractional threat" – a threat that carries the risk but not the certainty of being carried out. This, in turn, provided the basis for his subsequent elaboration of "the threat that leaves something to chance," a concept that was one of Schelling's most distinctive and important ideas.[66]

Among the mathematical models that were developed for game theory, the two most popular were the prisoner's dilemma and chicken. The rules of the former essentially force potential collaborators into conflict; those of the latter encourage a mutually tolerable result while carrying the possibility of an unacceptable outcome. The important point to note is that both models demonstrate the significance of the expectation of future interaction. They reveal that how a player performs in one game affects calculations of his likely performance in the future. Thus, if a player defects in one contest he increases his possible problems for the next time, when other players can be expected to be more cautious in how they proceed against him.[67] If, on the other hand, over time an impression of weakness is created, the adjustments to behaviour can create dangerous instability, either because a player seeks to compensate for his image or his opponent seeks to exploit it. Both models reveal the dangers of stalemate in iterated play, although they also highlight the possibilities of risk taking in an uncertain environment where there is the potential of being rewarded.[68]

Even though game theory was used extensively in studies on strategic stability, its specific use in arms control literature was quite limited. For example, while Schelling made considerable use of it in his 1960 book *The Strategy of Conflict,* game theory played only a small role in his major arms control study, *Strategy and Arms Control.* Neither was it explained or used in Bull's or Brennan's work, the two most influential studies from the period. Indeed, among the other major studies, only Seymour Melman's *Disarmament: Its Politics and Economics* and J. David Singer's *Deterrence, Arms Control, and Disarmament* made substantive and sophisticated use of game theory and other forms of quantitative analysis.[69] While several works revealed a general familiarity with game theory, many simply contained a discussion of the utility of the prisoner's dilemma model, as if it were the only insight that game theory could offer the broader subject of arms control. In this regard, one can conclude that while game theory was important in establishing the conceptual framework of arms control, the insights that it offered were not fully realized or appreciated in many of the early works.

Given the limited use of game theory in early arms control studies, the work of Canada's G.D. Kaye can be viewed as both original and distinctive. Like Schelling, Kaye appreciated that game theory offered critical insight into strategic stability, as the nuclear balance revolved around issues of numerical advantage and the perceptions and expectations of others. Unlike the work of most American observers, however, Kaye's modelling revealed that arms control's overall promise was slight, while its potential to destabilize the strategic environment was considerable.

One indication of the importance of Kaye's work was a December 1960 Defence Research Board memo in which it was noted that "various groups in the US were interested in the model and analysis developed by Mr. Kaye."[70] This memo did not identify the "groups" in question (outside of noting that "most of the interested parties are in the Washington area"), but documentation from the period indicates that Kaye and several other DRB scientists met regularly with arms control specialists in the United States, particularly with those at the Arms Control and Disarmament Agency. Additional memos and reports further reveal that, while the arms control community in Canada was small and lacked the research budget of Canada's larger neighbour, American arms control specialists were impressed with the Canadians' work and were eager to share views with them.[71]

In any event, Kaye's use of quantitative analysis in his studies indicates a willingness to apply novel approaches and methodologies to emerging problems. His research revealed that although arms control could help reduce the total number of nuclear weapons holdings, it could not progress far without challenging the essential stability that arms control was intended to strengthen in the first place. Kaye's mathematical models were instructive in demonstrating this, although over time a considerable body of arms control literature would emerge that made much the same point. Indeed, it might be noted that the American critique of arms control that developed in the 1980s had much in common with Canadian studies of the 1960s.

The Gradual Disillusionment with Arms Control and the Canadian Critique

Arms control would ultimately achieve widespread scholarly and public acceptance, and arms control structures have become near-permanent instruments of diplomacy. Nevertheless, success in the arms control field was, until recently, distinguished largely by its absence. This is not to suggest that arms control theory, as conceptualized in the early 1960s, was necessarily wrong. It was surely correct to maintain that, through dialogue, each side could alleviate those fears on the part of the other that tend to spur needless strategic overreaction.[72] If dialogue and technical discussions could proceed, effectively decoupled from changes in political relations, was it not reasonable to anticipate that cooperation would prove sustainable, and limited technical agreements would lead to less limited ones with greater political content?

And yet, any objective analysis reveals that the record of arms control never matched the initial promise – at least while the Cold War raged.[73] Part of the difficulty was no doubt related to flaws in the conceptual component of the theory. Arms control processes exist precisely because states have interests in conflict, while the fact of conflict precludes arms control agreements of more than marginal strategic significance. Weapons have always served political ends, and particular states of weapons balance or imbalance cannot be frozen or closely controlled in their evolution so long as nations view their armaments as principal instruments in prosecuting competing political ends.[74] If one believes that arms control processes can promote substantial changes in the military environment, one must also endorse the belief that armaments can be decoupled from political conflict.

It is evident that Canadian defence officials approached arms control far more critically then their American counterparts through the 1950s and early 1960s. In essence, Canadian officials believed that measures designed to reduce or eliminate weapons systems threatened to transform the nuclear balance. Most important, the military redundancy that had been developed over time and at great expense would be called into doubt should particular weapons systems be reduced and/or withdrawn. At lower force levels, Canadian officials believed that either the United States or Soviet Union might be tempted to use force to resolve disputes, as the traditional dynamics of the security dilemma would again come into play. Those dynamics ensure that the steps that one country takes to improve its security diminish the security of its rival. In an environment in which total weaponry had been reduced, officials would need to monitor the situation more carefully, as the side that struck first might be able to escape retaliation. Thus, far from the stable environment that arms control supporters believed would result from agreements, Canadian officials reached a very different understanding.

The Canadian critique can be compared with more recent works on arms control that appear to share several of the same concerns. Among critics, the best known is Colin Gray, who wrote one of the three articles on Canadian strategic thought that this project has challenged.[75] Gray has written that arms control's position of authority among both the academic and defence communities in the United States resulted in an unwillingness for many years to examine its basic premises. As he has observed, in the 1970s arms control came to be regarded as "the high road to peace – a belief or item of faith, which vote-seeking Western politicians of all political stripes did not dare challenge."[76] Because of its close association with "peace," anyone opposed to the concept was quickly labelled as being in favour of war. However, with the election of Ronald Reagan as US president in 1980, the American mood shifted as concerns over Soviet compliance in arms control agreements resulted in increasing calls to examine the potential risks of measures that reduced military deployments.

In the last decade and a half, a considerable body of literature has emerged that has reconsidered some of the primary assertions of arms control theory. Among scholars who re-evaluated their earlier work, Thomas Schelling is the best known. In a 1986 article titled "What Went Wrong with Arms Control?" Schelling argued that the "emphasis on numbers" that came to dominate arms control negotiations in the 1970s devalued both the worth of the agreements that were reached – much as the Joint Ballistic Missile Defence Staff had warned in 1960 – and the utility of arms control more generally.[77] But some of the other critiques have gone well beyond challenges over tactics. In his 1992 book *House of Cards: Why Arms Control Must Fail,* Colin Gray identifies four propositions central to the theory of arms control that he believes are flawed: (1) weapons and arms buildups are a critical cause in the outbreak of war; (2) arms races are always unstable; (3) the behaviour of "revisionist" states can be modified through agreements and treaties; and (4) arms control agreements automatically lead to enhanced stability.[78] Gray's major conclusion is that the more arms control is needed, the less likely are the prospects of anything substantial being negotiated. A key component of his argument is that strategic stability remains a poorly understood concept, and the relationship between weapons deployments, vulnerability, and risk taking evades simple explanation. Gray further argues that weapons per se are not destabilizing, and that large quantities of them make little difference in terms of conflict dynamics and/or the possibility of conflict occurring in the first place.[79] Thus there are notable conceptual similarities with Canadian studies completed more than three decades earlier. Indeed, during most of President Reagan's term in office, many of the arms control weaknesses identified by Canadian officials were accepted at an official level, as the administration emphasized the destabilizing nature of weapons reductions and the futility of reaching agreements with the Soviets.[80]

Overall, the thinking on arms control that developed in Canada in the late 1950s and early 1960s was distinct from the dominant approach that emerged in the United States at the same time. Documents reveal a department that was very cautious on the possible benefits that arms control could offer. Whereas the principal studies (and observers) in the United States emphasized the advantages that would result from lower force levels, Canadian reports emphasized the potential dangers. Having identified Canadian strategic thinking in four different areas, attention now shifts to an examination of whether and how Canadian thinking was reflected in the defence policy decisions of the day.

6

Links between Canadian Strategic Thinking and Defence Policy, 1950-63

An issue that remains to be addressed is whether Canadian strategic thinking had an influence on defence policy, or whether it existed in a bureaucratic vacuum, separated from the daily demands of policy and decision makers. A thorough examination of defence statements, speeches, and minutes of committees reveals that important Canadian policies and initiatives were first identified in departmental documents. There are reasons, though, to be cautious about reaching broad conclusions on the importance of strategic thinking strictly on the basis of its policy relevance. An array of obstacles ensures that the work of government officials – as well as other interested observers – is just one influence among many that decision makers consider. Further, while it is admittedly an important concern to some, influencing policy is frequently not the main objective of defence observers, who can be more interested in creating and defining the strategic dialogue within which policy debates take place. Thus, the importance of Canadian strategic thought exists independently of any direct policy linkage. Before the connection between Canadian strategic thought and defence policy is studied, however, a brief review of major policy decisions of the period is called for.

Decisions in Canadian Defence Policy, 1950-63

Defence policy underwent considerable change in the years following the immediate postwar period. The first major defence development of the post-1950 period was the outbreak of the Korean War. As a result of the conflict, Canadian defence objectives were expressed more precisely. According to *Canada's Defence Programme, 1951-52*, the roles of the Canadian military were: (1) the immediate defence of Canada and North America from direct attack; (2) the implementation of any undertakings made by Canada under the Charter of the United Nations, the North Atlantic Treaty, or other agreements for collective security; and (3) the maintenance of an organization to build military strength in the event of total war.[1] With a clear defence statement, military planning became more predictable. The threat to North America and Europe was no longer an issue, and the need to re-equip Canadian units and integrate them into the North Atlantic Treaty Organization and North American defence was not in doubt. The domestic defence debate thus turned from questions regarding the need for a Canadian military – which had dominated the discussion in the late 1940s – to rationalizing and prioritizing equipment requirements.[2]

Among the critical decisions that had to be made were concerns regarding Canada's alliance commitments. Shortly after formation in 1949, NATO developed three separate commands: Supreme Allied Commander, Europe (SACEUR); Supreme Allied Commander, Atlantic (SACLANT); and Commander-in-Chief, Channel (CINCHAN). The alliance sought to maintain standing forces under each, and Canada was asked to contribute. In response, Canada largely structured its armed forces to meet NATO needs. The army commitment was for an infantry division, with one brigade group (approximately 6,000 men) stationed in West Germany and the balance in Canada ready to reinforce upon mobilization. The air force had an air division (6,500 men, comprising 12 squadrons with a total of 272 aircraft) stationed at bases in France and West Germany. Naval and naval air forces in the Atlantic were almost entirely earmarked for SACLANT as Canada assumed responsibility for a large part of the defence of the North Atlantic.

As the Canadian government was making major commitments to NATO, its bilateral security relationship with the United States became increasingly cooperative – and formalized. Under the Military Cooperation Committee and the Permanent Joint Board on Defence, the two countries jointly developed a series of plans for the land, sea, and air defence of the continent. Most important, in 1958 the North American Air Defence Command (NORAD) was established. While its formation was the subject of considerable debate (at least in Canada), in many ways a binational command made strategic sense in an increasingly integrative and cooperative air defence environment. While NORAD supported NATO to the extent that it helped defend the North American region, there was no direct link between the two save for reporting on general North American defence efforts through the Canada-US Regional Planning Group, a fact that caused some political embarrassment in Canada.

The 1950s saw Canadian defence policy – in its political, strategic, and even economic dimensions – become increasingly linked with Western collective defence efforts dominated by the United States.[3] But the decade also saw Canada assume defence roles that would distinguish it from its allies. Under UN auspices, Canadians served in a number of peacekeeping and peace observation missions. Indeed, as a result of the 1956 Suez Crisis, Canada's secretary of state for external affairs, Lester Pearson, helped define modern peacekeeping by proposing the deployment of an international force between Israel and Egypt. The initiative, which earned Pearson the Nobel Peace Prize, inaugurated a Canadian role as a provider of peacekeeping forces. In addition, Canada became a strong supporter of arms control, and advanced several proposals. The decision to expend resources on both peacekeeping and arms control was consistent with Canada's overall approach to foreign and defence policy in the postwar period. Above all, Canada sought to promote international order and stability, and saw in the furtherance of these goals the means of enhancing its own security.[4]

Alliance commitments led to confusion over defence and security policy in the period beginning around 1960, particularly with regard to nuclear weapons. While the government of John Diefenbaker had a difficult time deciding whether to acquire the weapons, it had no similar difficulty accepting alliance policies that relied on nuclear weapons to deter the Soviet Union. Canada contributed in several ways to the successful functioning of nuclear deterrence, including: (1) as a direct supplier of uranium and enriched plutonium to the United States; (2) by complying with NATO directives that called for the deployment (and use) of tactical nuclear weapons in Europe; (3) by granting the US Air Force permission to operate two major air bases in Canada, one at Goose Bay, Labrador, the second at Harmon Field, Newfoundland; (4) by cooperating with the United States in the air defence of North America; and (5) by cooperating with the US Navy in the naval defence of the North Atlantic. As a result of these roles, Canada's support of nuclear deterrence was unambiguous. Indeed, according to authors William Arkin and Richard Fieldhouse, Canada was "unique in the thoroughness of its support of the US nuclear infrastructure ... second only to West Germany in hosting nuclear-related facilities."[5]

The nuclear weapons controversy ended in the summer of 1963, a few months after the Liberals, under the leadership of Lester Pearson, won the federal election. A priority of the new government was to improve bilateral relations with the United States, which had been badly strained over the previous few years.[6] By quickly indicating Canada's willingness to address American concerns, Pearson hoped to solidify Canadian influence in NATO and enhance Western alliance cohesion in general.[7] As had previous Liberal governments, Pearson viewed participation in Western collective defence as the cornerstone of Canadian defence and security policy.

In 1964, the new government released the first defence white paper since Brooke Claxton's 1949 document. The paper reaffirmed the existing roles of the armed forces in NATO and NORAD, but sought ways in which Canada could make a more identifiable, cost-efficient contribution. Peacekeeping received particular emphasis, as did the protection of national sovereignty. But the most far-reaching change (at least on a military level) was the government's stated intention to integrate and unify the services by abolishing the army, navy, and air force as distinct entities and to create a single service – the Canadian Forces. This step was taken, with controversial results, between 1964 and 1968 under the leadership of Defence Minister Paul Hellyer.

Strategic Thinking and Defence Policy, 1950-63

It is not a simple task to document that strategic thinking had a direct effect on Canadian Cold War defence policy. Policy making in Canada – in defence and security as well as other areas – is the result of a wide array of pressures and constraints, of which the analysis produced by government officials is only one.[8] Other considerations may include economic, legal, and social concerns, domestic political factors, the media, external pressures, and Canada's federal structure – few of which are ever specifically identified. In addition, it should be noted that government policy must satisfy several bureaucratic actors before being adopted, and the preferences and concerns of those actors may change over time. Thus, while there are opportunities to influence the policy process at several different levels, an unambiguous indication of influence is unlikely.

Three sources of defence policy are considered in the following account: (1) the Department of National Defence's annual defence statement, supplemented by the 1964 *White Paper on Defence*; (2) speeches by political authorities and senior military officials; and (3) the minutes of the Cabinet Defence Committee meetings. Only the first is a formal source of policy, but speeches and the minutes of the CDC normally foreshadowed official decisions, and thus the author considers them legitimate sources as well. For each, two indications are interpreted as signifying possible influence – references to passages that can be directly traced to studies written by DND officials, and evidence that the conceptual thinking implicit in a policy decision (or the broader dialogue underlying it) can be linked to a department report.

The first source of policy to be considered are the annual statements of defence objectives, which were released by the department between 1950 and 1960 (most often under the title *Canada's Defence Programme*). While the statements generally shied away from controversial or difficult issues, some did comment on matters of major importance, including strategic stability and nuclear weapons. Indeed, many of these statements accepted the mutual nature of deterrence and the importance of mutual vulnerability, concepts that were introduced in DND studies in the 1950s.

The 1955-6 edition of *Canada's Defence Programme* is one document that considered the dangers of the nuclear age.[9] In the section "Nuclear Bombs and the Future," DND revealed that it had little faith in the possibility of the West emerging victorious from a nuclear conflict. The document read:

"For North America, the possibility appears for the first time of an attack that could cripple the military and industrial potential of Canada and the US. Should we ever be attacked with thermonuclear weapons, it is plain that our immediate problem would be national survival. Everyone not directly involved in an urgent military role would immediately be caught up in the problem of rescue, rehabilitation, and the maintenance of immediate services."[10] The department – and by extension the Canadian government – recognized that in any nuclear exchange, North America would be damaged just as badly as the Soviet Union. The reference to "national survival" as the "immediate" problem after a nuclear attack suggests there was no assurance that Canada and the United States, even if they initiated the conflict, could survive a nuclear exchange. The implication was that the West needed to respect Soviet military power, as any misjudgment could result in catastrophe.

Emphasizing the horrific damage that would result from a nuclear conflict, the report further noted that "in wars of the past, families, towns, and even sizeable communities have been destroyed, but thermonuclear weapons confront us with the possibility that major nations and perhaps the whole of mankind might be wiped out in consequences of future war."[11] The report thus stressed that damage might not be limited to any particular geographic region, but that the effects of a nuclear exchange would be global in scope.

Several DND studies examined in earlier chapters reflect similar concerns. Chapter 3, for example, reviewed the Canadian appreciation of deterrence and the enormous damage that the Soviet Union could inflict on North America. Canadian studies and reports accepted the fact of Soviet nuclear equivalence, even if Soviet strategic forces were numerically smaller than those of the United States. These understandings, however, were not shared in the United States. While individual American strategists recognized the damage that could be done to their country in a nuclear war, the official policy of massive retaliation maintained that the United States could not be appreciably hurt by the Soviets, and that the United States would retain the right to unilaterally decide the tempo, severity, and consequences of future conflict.

Subsequent National Defence statements show an appreciation of the importance of nuclear weapons and the deterrent that they offered. Thus, when the federal government proved unwilling to acquire nuclear weapons for Canadian forces in the late 1950s and early 1960s, this did *not* reveal a reluctance to support the policy of the deterrent. The Canadian acceptance of nuclear deterrence was first revealed in the early 1950s.[12] It was not until the release of the 1957 *Report on National Defence*, though, that this acknowledgment was unambiguously stated. The report noted that "the best way to reduce the possibility of war of annihilation is to make plain to a potential aggressor that collectively the NATO allies have built up their forces primarily as a deterrent to war. The foremost element of these forces is retaliatory striking power, provided by the US Strategic Air Command with nuclear weapons produced in that country; it is being supplemented by the United Kingdom in that regard."[13] The emphasis on nuclear deterrence was the frequent – perhaps the dominant – concern of DND studies of the period, and the acceptance of it indicates a bureaucratic victory for the department over the Department of External Affairs. While not strictly opposed to nuclear weapons, DEA wished to see their overall influence decrease.

In the 1960 departmental statement, there was an explicit recognition that stability was the result of the nuclear stalemate, not nuclear superiority as frequently argued in the United States. Thus, this report observed that "the combination of the development of the nuclear bomb with new and faster means of delivery has created what has been described as a nuclear stalemate. In other words, the Communist world recognizes that a nuclear war with the west would only end in mutual destruction."[14] Later in the same report, it was observed that "rather than try to win a war, [NATO] must prevent a war because we know that it really means mutual destruction in many parts of the alliance and the world – as long as an act of aggression fails to materialize, then our efforts and those of our allies can be considered successful. We will have succeeded in deterring war."

The conceptual linkage with several of the departmental studies examined in earlier chapters is clear. The notion that stability was the result of the threat of mutual destruction was a frequent focus of Canadian strategic thought. R.J. Sutherland wrote on several occasions about the necessity of preventing superpower war, as the weapons available to both sides could turn any conflict into a holocaust. Additionally, there was a recognition that nuclear conflict was unwinnable, and it was therefore absurd to think about "victory" in the nuclear age. Overall, Canadian policy on deterrence and strategic vulnerability evolved in a manner consistent with departmental studies, which challenged the prevailing thinking in the United States.

A recent article by Joseph Jockel and Joel Sokolsky is of note in this regard. The authors argue that although the Canadian government paid lip service to mutual assured destruction (MAD) and other doctrines that emphasized the mutual nature of deterrence throughout the Cold War, in reality Canadian forces played an active role in US nuclear strategy, which was based on a war-fighting doctrine.[15] Jockel and Sokolsky cite Canada's support of the US policy of deterrence, as well as the array of nuclear roles that Canadian forces accepted, as proof of their charge. Thus, they claim that Canadian governments intentionally and consistently misled the public about the realities of Canadian nuclear strategy, as there was a contradiction between Canadian declaratory and actual nuclear policies.

Jockel and Sokolsky raise several interesting points, but some of their specific charges are open to challenge. For example, they fail to place the Canadian experience in its larger context, thereby giving the impression that the contradiction between declared and actual nuclear policy was somehow unique to Canada. In fact, it was not. This discrepancy was also evident in the United States: at the very time that Defense Secretary Robert McNamara was officially adopting assured destruction/MAD in the early 1960s, the Pentagon was preparing much more detailed and flexible war plans for use against the Soviet Union. Part of the explanation for this discrepancy was McNamara himself. He did not believe that the existing war plan (called the Single Integrated Operational Plan, or SIOP) contained sufficient nuclear "options," and that there needed to be a clear distinction between counterforce and countervalue targets.[16] American war plans evolved over the following two decades, and ultimately led to the adoption of Presidential Directive 59 in 1980, a strategy that considered the possibility of fighting a protracted nuclear war – one largely based on Herman Kahn's concept of·"escalation dominance."[17]

Indeed, from 1960 to 1980 (but particularly 1960-74), at the very time that US war plans were growing increasingly complex and flexible, the US government maintained a declaratory emphasis on assured destruction/ MAD.[18] The privileged position of MAD was essentially codified in the arms control negotiations of the late 1960s and early 1970s, particularly in the Strategic Arms Limitation Talks, which were largely based on the notion of preserving a rough nuclear balance in which both the Americans and Soviets could ensure an effective retaliatory capability. These ideas were not substantially challenged until President Richard Nixon appointed a new secretary of defense, Melvin Laird, who was on record as being critical of McNamara's assured destruction concept, although it was some time before Laird's critique could be translated into actual policy options.[19] Thus, rather than being a uniquely Canadian contradiction, the gap between declaratory and actual nuclear policy was observable in several Western countries, particularly the United States.[20]

More important, though, is the question of significance. There is certainly ample evidence, as Jockel and Sokolsky cite, that Canadian forces prepared to play a role in offensive nuclear strikes against the Soviet Union – the air division in Europe being the best example. However, does this preparation necessarily imply that the Canadian government had parted ways with the notion of mutual destruction? In other words, does the fact that Canadian forces trained in offensive nuclear roles mean that they were effectively contradicting MAD?

On this question, there is room for several interpretations, for much depends on whether NATO (and by implication, Canadian) forces would actually strike first in a nuclear exchange. In fact, NATO policy on this issue was ambiguous. There was certainly the possibility of Western forces using nuclear weapons first – for example, the alliance consistently refused to issue a "no first use" pledge – but this was by no means assured. In fact, the declared position of NATO was that it would *not* be first to use military power to change the political status quo.[21] Thus, simply because Canadian forces were trained to use nuclear weapons in an offensive capacity – and some of the roles themselves were offensive – does not mean that the Canadian government anticipated that Canada or, in a broader sense, the West might emerge unscathed in a nuclear conflict, or that this was even the intent. Nor was there necessarily a contradiction between offensive nuclear missions and MAD, for the reality was that the possibility of the West destroying the Soviets' retaliatory capability in any nuclear strike was exceedingly small, a prospect appreciated by military planners on all sides.[22]

Overall, then, while Jockel and Sokolsky's recent article raises a number of interesting questions, it does not refute the fundamental premise of this chapter – that Canadian policy on nuclear weapons and deterrence evolved in a manner that was broadly consistent with Canadian strategic thinking as articulated by defence officials in the 1950s and early 1960s.

Returning to the examination of defence policy, perhaps the clearest indication of the influence of Canadian strategic thought on the policy process is the February 1964 *White Paper on Defence*. On the surface, it falls just outside the time frame of this study, but it was largely written in 1963. This paper represented a return to the policy fold for DND, and reflected a turn away from the increasingly neutralist foreign and defence policy that had emerged over the previous few years at the Department of External Affairs.

The section titled "Considerations Affecting Future Policy" reads almost as if it were lifted from one of R.J. Sutherland's departmental studies. On the issue of weapons deployment and strategic stability, the white paper noted that "military technology must be expected to go on changing rapidly. As long as the US and the Soviet Union both possess the ability to inflict unacceptable damage on the other, regardless of quantitative disparities in striking power, calculated all-out thermonuclear war would be irrational and is, therefore, improbable. However, in the absence of a settlement of major East-West political problems, the maintenance by the West of the capacity to deter thermonuclear war will remain an essential military and political necessity, with the main responsibility resting on the strategic resources of the US."[23] The conceptual linkage with several of the Sutherland and JBMDS papers is so unambiguous here as to indicate a clear example of the influence of Canadian strategic thought. Sutherland wrote on several occasions that nuclear war was both unlikely and irrational, and in spite of the nuclear buildup – or rather because of it – strategic stability was assured.

The white paper contained further passages that appear to contain – or at the very least are reflective of – additional recommendations of DND studies.

For example, on the question of nuclear weapons for Canadian forces, the paper explained that the decision involved three main considerations: (1) the costs and consequences of joining the "nuclear club"; (2) Canada's political responsibilities as a member of a nuclear alliance; and (3) the availability of nuclear weapons to Canada's armed forces. The paper discussed each of these factors, noting that the first was largely "fictitious," the second revolved around Canada's desire to remain a full member of the alliance, and the third was "subordinate" to larger political concerns. In both tone and content, the arguments were reflective of Sutherland's 1963 paper on nuclear weapons, "Some Problems of Canadian Defence Policy."[24]

The influence of strategic thought on Canadian defence policy can be illustrated not only by looking at specific passages in departmental reports and statements but also by examining speeches made by cabinet ministers and senior government officials. For example, a speech delivered by Defence Minister Ralph Campney in 1956 made reference to the consequences of the use of nuclear weapons by either side: "Once full-scale war becomes a suicide pact as it would be today – the victors would win little more than an atomic ash heap. War can therefore no longer be regarded by any nation, even the most cold-blooded aggressor, as an instrument of national policy. The unleashing of war today would bring down on the instigator such appalling forces of retaliatory destruction as can stagger the imagination."[25] The passage reveals that at the very time that massive retaliation was the official strategic policy of the United States, the attitude of Canada's minister of national defence toward nuclear conflict was substantively different, and focused on the mutual dangers and consequences of a nuclear exchange (i.e., a "suicide pact"). Any use of force, according to the minister, would have devastating consequences.

Many of these observations were expanded on in a speech delivered to the House of Commons in June 1956, when Campney spoke on "Nuclear War and the Deterrent."[26] On the issue of war avoidance, he noted that "the threat of war continues. As long as this is true, our best hope is, undoubtedly, in the maintenance of a strong and compelling deterrent." Rather than emphasize the unilateral ability of the United States to obliterate the Soviet Union, though, Campney's focus was on the preservation of deterrence through strong nuclear forces that Canada contributed toward. As the minister explained, US strategic forces needed to be defended by radar, air defence, and an effective military command and control structure, and Canada participated in all these missions. Provided that nuclear forces were properly deployed, defended, and maintained, credibility was assured because any attack would result in a devastating retaliatory blow. In this context, one should recall the air defence studies examined in Chapter 2, which discussed the purpose of enhanced continental air defence cooperation.

A speech made by Defence Minister Douglas Harkness in February 1961 is notable for the observations that it offered on the use of force and Canada's larger defence commitments.[27] Harkness noted that "despite the rhetoric, there is no doubt that force, and the threat of force ... has not yet been renounced as an instrument of policy." The statement highlighted the growing gulf between DND and DEA, because it came at a time when Howard Green, the secretary of state for external affairs, was arguing that military force was declining in utility. In a similar fashion, Harkness also commented on the calls for Canada to become a neutral country. He said "it may be tempting to make a virtue out of the wish to save on defence expenditures, but I for one am convinced it would at best give us only momentary notoriety after which we would find, as one writer recently put it, that we 'should be relegated to the rear ranks of the neutral chorus.'"

A few remarks on these observations are in order. First, the recognition that force remained a central aspect of global politics was made in several JBMDS and Sutherland studies in the early 1960s. While seemingly a trivial point, at the time many observers were suggesting that force would play a reduced role in resolving future disputes.[28] Further, the dismissive comments on the possibility of Canada becoming non-aligned stand in clear contrast to statements made by several DEA officials. The precise identity of the "writer" Harkness referred to cannot be firmly established, but the passage is clearly reflective of Sutherland. Last, in the final paragraph of the speech, the minister noted that "if Canada is to maintain her position of self-respect and influence in the councils of the world, she must continue to play her part in contributing to the combined strength of the West in protecting nuclear power which has prevented ... a general war from breaking out." With its emphasis on Canadian political interests and how those interests could not be divorced from security policy, the passage is reminiscent of several JBMDS studies.

One of the most unambiguous examples of the influence of R.J. Sutherland's writings came in a speech delivered by Air Marshal C.R. Dunlap, chief of the air staff, to the National Defence College in Kingston, Ontario, in July 1963.[29] This speech, coming shortly after the federal election in which the Liberals were returned to power, represented an attempt to set the record straight on the question of Canada's defence commitments to the West and the precise nature of the nuclear dispute.

In the early part of the speech, Dunlap addressed the recent controversy. He noted that nuclear weapons were "the most frustrating problem ever faced" by the Royal Canadian Air Force, and that the lack of a decision had been "highly embarrassing" both at home and abroad. He noted that the indecision had been detrimental to the morale of the service. While the air marshal appreciated that all opinions needed to be considered in an election campaign, he noted that "it is stretching credulity" to suggest that this was a reasonable explanation for the "many completely inaccurate statements made on defence matters [during the campaign]," an indication that the military did not believe that the basic facts of the dispute had been widely understood.

However, a focus of Dunlap's speech was the future role of the European Air Division, which at the time was in the process of acquiring the nuclear weapons with which to perform the strike-reconnaissance mission. Dunlap expressed serious reservations about the role. He noted that the Soviets appeared to be stressing a non-nuclear position, and if this trend were to continue, it "might well influence the attitude of our government." He further stated that "the government is sensitive about nuclear weapons generally and particularly sensitive about our strike role ... If even a tenuous case can be made for a conventional role for the Air Division, then it is quite possible that our assignment might be changed when the time arrives to replace the CF-104s."

Since this speech came at the very time that the nuclear weapons controversy was finally being resolved, it is puzzling why the air force's top-ranking official would speak out on the possibility of changing the role of the air division. And yet Dunlap's address came only two weeks after R.J. Sutherland had written an internal departmental report on the CF-104 that raised several concerns.[30]

Sutherland's paper examined the specific issue of future procurement of additional CF-104 aircraft, and whether Canada intended to retain eight operational squadrons of aircraft in Europe into the 1970s. If indeed this was the government's intention, Sutherland believed that a decision on future procurement would be required before 1964 – a consequence of operational attrition and the lengthy production schedule of the aircraft.

A careful reading of the report indicates that Sutherland had significant reservations about the nuclear strike mission. He noted that the CF-104s were in a vulnerable situation, and in a crisis they would present a tempting military target for Soviet attack. Indeed, their very vulnerability might lead the Soviet Union to launch a pre-emptive strike. Sutherland also discussed the negative effect that the French refusal to cooperate in NATO nuclear planning was having on Canadian forces.[31] Together, the various problems raised fundamental questions about the desirability of the strike role. Sutherland also challenged the strategic rationale of the mission, noting that its first-strike nature meant that the force was "not a junior Strategic Air Command but a tactical theatre force having a limited operational mission."[32]

Other departmental studies came to similar conclusions. As far back as March 1960, the department had recognized that the air division was vulnerable to Soviet attack, and could not be considered part of the "secure"

NATO retaliatory strike force. This was the main finding of a JBMDS report titled "The Vulnerability of ACE Air Strike Forces to Ballistic Missile Attack."[33] This report, which examined a number of conflict scenarios, concluded that the air division presented a tempting target to Soviet military forces. "USSR planners are likely to consider air strike forces as high priority targets," it noted. While the report identified defensive measures that could reduce the vulnerability of the force, most of these steps – such as aircraft alerts and hardening of bases – were unlikely to have much effect.

It is clear that the vulnerability of the RCAF's European Air Division was recognized as early as 1960, and that a debate on a more acceptable role for the division originated within DND long before politicians raised public doubts about the role in the late 1960s.[34] While these concerns were not immediately translated into specific mission alternatives for the RCAF, it is important to emphasize that the military recognized problems with the assignment, a point that has gone unrecognized in the literature.[35]

The third and final source of defence policy being considered in this chapter are the minutes of the Cabinet Defence Committee. Such records can offer a direct indication of the influence of strategic thought, as the committee frequently listened to presentations by defence officials immediately before making a recommendation of policy – which then went to full cabinet.

A committee meeting held in November 1953 provides an early example of how the strategic thinking articulated in a departmental report affected a subsequent policy decision.[36] As noted in Chapter 3, an October 1953 memo prepared by General Charles Foulkes, chairman of the Chiefs of Staff Committee, was the first occasion in which a Canadian defence official recognized the possible vulnerability of the US Strategic Air Command to attack.[37] The prospect raised several questions and concerns, because the possibility of US forces being destroyed on the ground in a surprise strike was anathema to US defence planners.

At the November meeting, Foulkes reiterated the possibility of a Soviet strike directed against the strategic forces of the United States. He noted that recent Soviet advances in weapons technology gave the Soviets an ability to strike North America with devastating force, and SAC was an "attractive" target. This account led to a committee decision to recommend approval of a request for work to begin on a new radar "fence" proposed for the fifty-fifth parallel, which would ultimately be called the Mid-Canada Line. The decision to recommend approval at this meeting was unexpected, as the radar proposal had been discussed between the two countries' militaries for several months and little progress had been made. At this time, though, political and military objections were overlooked, and the need for a new radar system, one that would help protect US nuclear forces, took precedence. The realization that US strategic forces were vulnerable to Soviet attack appeared to outweigh any objections, and the radar line received speedy authorization.

The importance of SAC and the workings of deterrence were the focus of the 103rd meeting of the CDC, held on 24 January 1955.[38] During the meeting, the US Air Force base at Goose Bay came up for discussion. It should be noted that, at the time, the United States was negotiating a final arrangement for the base, which many observers believed was the most important outside the continental United States.

The question of increased personnel and tanker aircraft stationed at Goose Bay was raised at the CDC meeting. The minutes note that "SAC was a vital element in the defence of the free world, and to refuse a request such as this, which had been made in accordance with the original agreement for leasing Goose Bay, would be embarrassing and difficult. As part of the Canada-US region, we had an obligation to our NATO partners to support SAC operations." The meeting went on to note that Canada, as a strong supporter of NATO, was not in a position to reject the request. Canada had indicated its support for nuclear deterrence on several occasions, and the Goose Bay request was intended to strengthen that policy.

On this issue, several DND studies had recognized that the core of the Western deterrent was the US Strategic Air Command, and that Canada would be placed in a difficult position whenever the United States made requests regarding SAC facilities. DND had not concluded that every such American proposal would have to be approved; however, there was a recognition that, as the leader of the Western alliance, the United States needed some latitude in how it wished to structure its strategic nuclear force. In reality, this meant that American proposals aimed at strengthening deterrence could only be rejected in light of the most serious reservations. At this meeting, in the absence of such concerns, the motion was accepted and the United States was granted permission to increase the personnel stationed at the base, as well as to establish an aerial refuelling squadron.

Further comments on SAC were made at a meeting of the Cabinet Defence Committee on 13 June 1956.[39] At this time, the committee was considering additional US requests to station tanker aircraft and construct tanker bases in the Canadian North. The bases would permit SAC to refuel bombers as they overflew Canada. Agreeing to the bases would thus increase the effective range of SAC bombers, which would better enable them to complete their passage to targets and return.[40]

During the meeting, a series of arguments was raised on the importance of the request and its connection with deterrence. While SAC had not been "assigned" to NATO, its "deterrent effect was the most important single element in the defence of the organization." Also, it had been "clearly implied in the past" that one of Canada's roles in NATO was to "support the strategic bombing effort of the US ... The need for such bases was difficult to dispute."

Following these remarks, there is a passage that recalls department reports examining deterrence and the manner in which it works. The minutes of the meeting read: "In large measure, war had been avoided because the Russians now thought that if they attacked there would be prompt retaliation by US bombing forces. US authorities were concerned with the possibility of interference with the maximum effectiveness of the deterrent. If SAC were forced to withdraw from some of the existing bases closer to the USSR, the US authorities would want it known publicly that compensating arrangements were being made to maintain the effectiveness of the deterrent ... There would be serious consequences if Canada contributed to a lessening of the free world's strength." The credibility of the deterrent was a common feature of departmental reports. Several studies noted that the strengthening of the nuclear deterrent was a *Canadian* interest, not one forced on this country by its more powerful neighbour. In this regard, establishing tanker bases would enhance the deterrent, and therefore the committee recommended that Canada approve the request. While concern was voiced over the prospect of additional American forces on Canadian soil, this issue was of secondary importance. Ultimately, the committee decided that "Canada would be prepared to investigate, in cooperation with the appropriate USAF officers, what existing airfields might be made suitable for this purpose." Within a year, a final agreement with the United States had been negotiated on the establishment of tanker aircraft bases in northern Canada.[41]

The Curious Relationship between Strategic Thought and Defence Policy

The intent of this discussion has been to demonstrate that it is possible to draw a connection between the departmental studies and reports that were examined in earlier chapters and Canadian defence policy decisions that were made in 1950-63. The importance of this observation is clear: it reveals that Canadian strategic thought was not simply an intellectual exercise conducted by members of an isolated defence community, but that such thinking had implications for policy decisions as stated in annual departmental statements, speeches, and cabinet deliberations.

The overall importance of Canadian strategic thinking, however, is not determined by the degree of association that can be drawn with decisions of defence policy. In this regard, it should be noted that there are questions in many countries regarding the significance of strategic thinking vis-à-vis the formulation of defence policy. The most obvious example is the United States, where most of the critical advances in postwar strategic thought were conceived. While there is no denying the importance of the work of strate-gists such as Brodie, Wohlstetter, and Schelling, there certainly are doubts regarding the influence that their work had on American defence policy.[42] This is not to suggest that these observers had no influence in Washington, but such influence was frequently muted, and was often overlooked until the supporting evidence was irrefutable (or, in Schelling's case, until he was recruited to work in the US Department of Defense).[43] It might also be noted that, as discussed earlier, influencing policy was not necessarily a primary objective of all American strategists.[44]

The scholarly literature offers several explanations that can account for the uneasy relationship between strategists and policy makers (written largely in the US context). Strategists are often ignorant of the policy makers' "real world," which includes budget cycles, legislative interests and pressures, and the domestic and foreign political problems of governments. Thus, it is hardly surprising that strategists are not especially sensitive to the nuances of that world. However, policy makers tend to disregard that they normally conceive of policies in ignorance of the strategists' "real world," one that revolves around foreign threats, military deployments, and technological trends. As a result, ignorance runs both ways, which helps explain why the two often approach issues from cross purposes. Properly employed, strate-gists can offer a depth of information and understanding that policy mak-ers cannot provide for themselves.[45] Still, it can be difficult convincing a policy maker of this. As Colin Gray has noted of the relationship between the two, "the 'scholarly fallacy' is the mistaken belief that study is the func-tional equivalent of action."[46]

Gray has further written that "policy advice from civilian strategists is hardly ever accepted as a package." Commenting on the US experience, Gray observes that even in the comparatively rare instances where advice is accepted and implemented, only parts of the strategists' original scheme are officially embraced. Hence, the correlation between policy outcomes and the recommendations of particular strategists is nearly always imper-fect.[47] Further, the intentions of politicians and decision makers are amended in the lengthy course of the policy process, so it is highly unlikely that the vision of a strategist could survive official scrutiny and bureaucratic nego-tiation in unaltered form.[48]

One of the most insightful accounts of the relationship between the scholar and the policy maker was written by James Eayrs. In his 1966 monograph *Right and Wrong in Foreign Policy*,[49] Eayrs noted that "an intellectual, dis-placed from his proper preoccupation to advise governments on foreign policy, tends characteristically to under- or over-react ... The history of re-cent international relations is strewn with the litter of the schemes of intel-lectuals-turned-policy-makers, or of intellectuals-turned-policy-advisors:

schemes contrived in haste, put forward in conceit, and abandoned, as soon as may be decently possible, by the professionals in government who know from hard experience what policy-making is all about."[50] Eayrs concluded that scholars and intellectuals should "stay out" of consulting decision makers. By keeping their distance, Eayrs believed that scholars can keep their principles and their faith.

In a final analysis, then, it would be misleading to seek to identify influence through some form of numerical count of concepts adopted and proposals implemented, an observation that holds as true in Canada as it does for other Western countries. However attractive the work of a defence observer/strategist might be, the practice of policy takes a very different form than that of strategic thought. A more productive approach is to recognize the existence of an ongoing dialogue between observers and policy makers, one that can work to the benefit of both.[51] This chapter demonstrated such a dialogue in the Canadian context.

It should also be noted that Canadian defence officials played a role in both agenda and policy setting – measures in which their influence was notable but perhaps less identifiable. In brief, the former refers to influencing the legitimacy and importance of particular issues, while the latter involves narrowing the parameters of choice and thereby effectively determining acceptable policy options.[52] By identifying and conceptualizing the major strategic issues of the day, defence officials helped define which issues were considered by policy makers, and also helped determine the range of options that were contemplated. While the course of action selected was not always consistent with the recommendation of DND officials, options were largely generated as a result of department analysis.

In sum, the evidence provided shows that Canadian Cold War defence policy evolved in a manner that was broadly consistent with Canadian strategic thought. This chapter thus demonstrates that the work of defence officials who formulated Canadian strategic interests was not a bureaucratic exercise, removed from the demands of policy. However, it bears repeating that the influences on defence policy are wide-ranging, and while this chapter has stressed developments in the domestic environment, other environments played a role in influencing Canadian policy as well. With the major questions of the study now answered, attention turns to some final observations and conclusions.

Conclusion

The history of strategic thought in the postwar period has been widely viewed by scholars as the history of American contributions. Analysts have focused on the writings of Bernard Brodie, William Kaufmann, Herman Kahn, and Albert Wohlstetter not because of their nationality, however, but because of the sophistication and breadth of their observations. In recent years, though, scholars have begun examining the strategic contributions made by observers outside the United States.[1] This study has continued that effort, by focusing on the strategic thinking of the closest ally to the United States at a crucial period of the Cold War. It has revealed that Canadian defence officials did think strategically; that their conclusions frequently challenged those reached in the United States; and that they approached defence and security issues from a distinctly Canadian point of view. These findings represent a challenge to the existing literature in the field, which not only asserts that there was no strategic thought in Canada, but that defence officials were incapable of and/or unwilling to identify national strategic interests. More generally, the study raises questions regarding the dominance of both the external environment thesis and the peripheral dependence perspective in Canadian security, as it has demonstrated that foreign commitments and obligations did not dictate either Canadian thinking or the policy decisions that resulted from them. By challenging long-held assumptions in the field, it is the author's hope that the project has identified avenues for further research that can lead to more definitive answers to several outstanding questions.

One question that this project has not considered is whether Canadian strategic thinking influenced literature in the larger security/strategic studies community. The reason for this omission is that no clear answer is possible, nor is one necessary. Several obstacles account for the difficulty in documenting such influence. First, the classified nature of the Canadian studies precluded them from being cited in the open literature even if they had been used by American observers. Second, major authors in the field did not generally acknowledge which works or strategists were most influential on their own thinking. In this regard, the formation of bitter personal rivalries among strategists encouraged a general reluctance to praise the work of colleagues.[2] Indeed, the latter factor makes it difficult to prove direct influence among American strategists, let alone non-Americans. In an environment where important works were constantly being written, evaluated, and critiqued, strategic thought evolved rapidly as dated concepts were replaced with contemporary ones.

A more useful exercise is to determine whether Canadian defence officials had access to their American colleagues, and vice versa. On this question, Chapter 5 noted some of the discussions between Canadian and American officials on arms control. Documents indicate that Canadian specialists visited the arms control section of the Department of Defense, and upon its formation in 1961, the Arms Control and Disarmament Agency.[3] More broadly, though, there were numerous linkages that ensured Canadian views were transmitted to US specialists, and that Canadian defence officials had avenues to American strategists at both the governmental and civilian levels.

Prior chapters have referred to some of the formal and informal linkages between the two countries' militaries, but a more detailed review can be offered here. Among the formal linkages, the key structures were the Canada-US Permanent Joint Board on Defence, the Canada-US Military Cooperation Committee, the Canadian Joint Planning Committee, the Canadian Joint Staff Mission (Washington), the Canada-US Ministerial Committee on Joint Defence (also known as the Joint Committee on Defence), the Canada-US Inter-Parliamentary Group, the Canada-US Combined Policy Committee, and the Canada-US Regional Planning Group.[4] All of these committees offered vehicles whereby the two countries' militaries could share thinking on defence issues.

Informal linkages, though, may have been even more important in the transcontinental transmission of ideas – especially considering that it was in this community where most of the major advances in the United States originated. Documents declassified for this study contain several references to Canadian specialists and groups who paid visits to defence establishments in the United States, where they participated in various conversations and exchanges.[5] For example, both the Operational Research Group and the Defence Systems Analysis Group of the Defence Research Board visited the RAND Corporation's main office in Santa Monica, California, to discuss an array of strategic issues.[6] The reports that resulted were just two of many that documented Canadians' visits to American think-tanks and the sharing of views. Through such contacts, Canadian concepts and understandings – like those identified by any other strategists – would have been examined and discussed, and ultimately adopted, if enough observers agreed with the basic findings.

That noted, though, it must be emphasized that the literature of the day was so prolific (in both classified and unclassified forms), and most strategists so vigilant in monitoring the works that were published, that it would be meaningless to seek to identify nuggets of thinking as being derived from particular individuals and/or sources.[7] What can be done is to identify the critical contributions in specific sub-fields, and to accept the fact that ideas quickly generated further discussion and debate. Accepting this criterion, this study has demonstrated that Canadians made important and original observations that, like other contributions of the period, helped move the dialogue in new and unexpected directions.

There is a further difficulty of note in trying to draw direct indications of influence in the larger strategic studies community. Simply stated, the absence of direct evidence of influence does *not* indicate that such work was of little importance. As discussed in both Chapters 3 and 6, Bernard Brodie, the most important strategist of the postwar period, was a frequently ignored figure in the American defence community, his observations often drawing criticism and scorn from colleagues and policy makers. However, this isolation should not be interpreted as signifying Brodie's lack of importance or influence – quite the contrary in fact. Summing up Brodie's contributions to postwar strategic thought, Ken Booth has noted, "It is not surprising that Brodie's direct influence on the making of American strategy from the mid-1940s until the late-1970s was limited. But does influence matter? Who now worries whether Clausewitz had any influence on those around him? What counts is the enduring worth of what he wrote ... The influence Brodie wielded was indirect rather than direct and philosophical rather than technical. His writing and teaching helped to shape the sensibilities of numerous individual strategists ... He was not a 'maker' of modern strategy in a direct sense; [rather], he was influential in a more general and indirect sense."[8] Whether or not the observations of Canadian defence officials were as influential as those of Brodie, the conceptual understandings that were reached reveal a sophisticated grasp of the strategic environment, and compare favourably with many of the principal works from the period. Indeed, the true importance of the observations reached in Canada lies not in some numerical count of how many American studies were influenced, but in their enduring legacy. In this regard, the Canadian understanding of deterrence and strategic stability has certainly stood the test of time. Underlining that point, I would argue that R.J. Sutherland deserves to be considered among the most original and thoughtful strategists of the 1950s and 1960s.

The challenge that this study thus presents to the existing literature is considerable. In his critical 1971 study bemoaning the lack of Canadian strategic thought, Colin Gray observed that "Canadians must reject strategic theoretical tutelage by strategic analysts from the United States and elsewhere ... Without the protection of a living and fairly independent strategic debate, Canadian governments have been at the mercy both of foreign governments, strategic theory better versed in the subject, and of individual services pursuing military technological modernization."[9]

In demonstrating that Canadian defence officials did think strategically, this study has countered Gray's thesis – which was also developed in works by Adrian Preston and John Gellner.[10] Canadian conceptual thinking on deterrence, strategic stability, the nuclear balance, and arms control did *not* mimic the appreciations reached elsewhere. Rather, Canadian studies and reports reflected a different set of assumptions, beliefs, and expectations. Further, Canadian thinking on air defence and the domestic nuclear weapons debate was conceived from a Canadian point of view. While officials in National Defence and External Affairs frequently disagreed about the choices and preferences facing the Canadian government, they shared a belief that their recommendations would further Canada's long-term security interest.

Brief final comments can be offered on the findings of each of the archival chapters. Chapter 2, which examined Canada's air defence debate, revealed that defence officials believed enhanced air defence cooperation with the United States would serve Canadian strategic interests, most crucially the strengthening of the nuclear deterrent. This was as much of a Canadian interest as it was an American one, and defence officials were not as concerned about the politics of military cooperation as were officials in the Department of External Affairs. For their part, DEA officials emphasized the political costs of any joint air defence command, and believed that its establishment raised an opportunity for closer bilateral consultation and cooperation. The chapter also indicated that the CF-105 Arrow was cancelled for a variety of reasons, most of which focused on the military roles that Canada could realistically play in the Cold War. Documents reveal that the aircraft was the source of a bitter intraservice debate, and that both the army and navy identified numerous reasons justifying cancellation. Last, additional DND air defence studies were examined that revealed a military establishment grappling with several critical developments, including the changing strategic environment and the consequences of the nuclear buildup.

Chapter 3 revealed that Canadian defence officials, led by R.J. Sutherland and his colleagues in the Joint Ballistic Missile Defence Staff, helped identify and articulate some of the key strategic concepts of the nuclear age, most notably mutual deterrence theory and strategic stability. The chapter demonstrated that Canadians approached nuclear deterrence quite differently from their American colleagues, and began to emphasize its mutual nature around 1950. This approach was not initially accepted in the United States, where observers largely stressed the political/strategic advantages that would result from nuclear superiority and the possible dangers that would come from a balance of power between the superpowers. The discussion also revealed that Canadians identified an array of other key strategic issues – including first- and second-strike weapons and the concept of mutual assured destruction – at roughly the same time or slightly before observers in the United States. Canadians thus contributed to the identification of several strategic concepts of the nuclear age.

Chapter 4 examined the domestic nuclear weapons debate of the 1950s and early 1960s, and found that, contrary to the existing literature, DND officials identified a range of reasons favouring nuclear acquisition. Both political and military reasons were identified – politically, acquisition would move Canada back into the Western camp, an allegiance that many in the department believed the country was moving away from; militarily, acquisition would ensure that Canadian forces would not be at a disadvantage in possible future engagements in Europe and North America. DEA officials, however, came to a completely different conclusion, for External Affairs believed that Canadian nuclear acquisition would damage this country's international reputation and was strategically destabilizing. While the conclusions the two departments reached were fundamentally different, both recommended courses of action that they believed would most effectively contribute to international stability and order, the common goal.

Chapter 5 revealed that defence officials identified conceptual problems with arms control, and that while not entirely opposed to the concept, Canadians were far more cautious in their evaluation of it than their American colleagues. The chapter examined several studies prepared by G.D. Kaye of the DRB that utilized game theory, an emerging tool of quantitative analysis at the time. Essentially, Kaye and other DND officials believed that reduced holdings of nuclear weapons would not necessarily result in greater strategic stability, as large and redundant nuclear forces ensured effective retaliation regardless of which side struck first and the degree of strategic surprise achieved. Defence officials appreciated some of the benefits that arms control could offer, but they tended to emphasize that negotiations needed to be carefully evaluated and agreements closely monitored.

By way of comparison, attention might also be drawn to the overall consistency of Canadian strategic thinking on the two conceptual issues examined – nuclear weapons and arms control. Defence officials believed that nuclear deterrence rested on strategic stability. They further believed that strategic stability could be jeopardized by agreements to limit nuclear arms, as the certainty of effective retaliation is reduced as force levels decline. Thus, arms control threatened the entire edifice upon which deterrence rested. While arms control could, under certain conditions, encourage better political relations, it could also destabilize the larger strategic environment. That is why Canadian defence officials were so cautious in their analysis of it, and revealed their preference for maintaining the strategic environment they knew over one they did not. In essence, Canadian thinking on both issues was designed to avoid a nuclear armageddon, an outcome that defence officials feared was possible, but one that they nonetheless believed was unlikely if the correct interpretations and understandings were reached.

Similarly, it is interesting to note that the concept of strategic "sufficiency" generated little support among defence officials in Canada. The concept emerged gradually in the United States in the late 1950s and 1960s, and reached its conceptual peak under Defense Secretary Robert McNamara.[11] DND officials were reluctant to identify what a "sufficient" force might look like, or how it was to be achieved. This is not to suggest that DND believed in totally unrestrained nuclear expansion – on the contrary, they identified the need for large enough strategic forces so that a retaliatory capability would not be in doubt, but showed no enthusiasm for a completely unbridled arms competition. While the documents reviewed for this study do not contain an explanation for this divergence from the Americans, it is possible that there was concern that a sufficient nuclear force might not be one that US allies necessarily supported. For example, in the early 1960s McNamara repeatedly explained to North Atlantic Treaty Organization countries how the emerging US nuclear force would accomplish Western strategic goals, and yet his plans to "rationalize" the US military frequently generated criticism and uncertainty in Europe. At the same time, it should be recalled that several DND studies had proclaimed that an era of strategic stability had arrived in the early 1960s, and thus it is possible that officials saw little need to define sufficiency at a time when the nuclear balance was effectively stable.

In a more general sense, by identifying a distinctive body of Canadian strategic thought, this study calls for a reconsideration of the utility of peripheral dependence in the field of Canadian defence and security. Indeed, considering that security is one of the areas in which the applicability of peripheral dependence is argued to be strongest, this challenge is fundamental. A nation's defence policy is perhaps the most concrete expression of its sovereignty, the area in which national differences are perhaps easiest to see. By articulating strategic interests that challenged those in the United States, this study asserts that a reconceptualization of Canada's freedom of movement in the Cold War is called for. This conclusion is further underlined upon realization that, with some notable exceptions, peripheral dependence remains the hegemonic paradigm of Canadian security scholars. Works such as Joseph Jockel's 1987 study *No Boundaries Upstairs* have partly chipped away at the framework, but the broad field of Canadian security continues to largely defy conceptual challenge.

Even though it's a useful approach to explaining some aspects of Canada's distorted development, peripheral dependence makes too many assumptions and overlooks some critical considerations. For example, it fails to realize that all countries – even the most powerful – conceive their defence and security policies in the context of an anarchic international system. Canada is therefore hardly the only country that must formulate its policy in a harsh and uncertain environment. In addition, far from being the innocent bystander caught in the game of international politics that peripheral dependence asserts, Canada *chose* to become allied to the West. While there were several countries that had little direct say in their defence policies during the early years of the Cold War, Canada was not one of them. Last, in contrast to what the theory predicts, Canada played an important role in Western defence in the 1950s and 1960s, and the military decisions that this country made were carefully considered and evaluated by other states.

In the postwar period, the main Canadian interest, both political and military, was international stability and order. This goal was articulated in an array of policy papers and speeches. Canada could focus on the international environment because, unlike most states, its security was not directly threatened by hostile neighbours but rather by the prospect of a large-scale conflict involving the superpowers. There was thus no inherent contradiction between Canada's alliance interests and its domestic security concerns. Rather, the two could – and did – advance Canada's principal interest.

In aligning with the United States and in committing itself to two American-dominated military organizations, Canada adopted the military strategy of the West as the basis of its own defence policy.[12] This does not mean that Canada had no voice in the formulation of that policy, or lacked the ability to take independent action. Successive Canadian governments devoted special attention to peacekeeping, for example, and this was one role that Ottawa undertook largely on its own initiative. In addition, disarmament and arms control became an important focus of Canadian security policy in the early 1960s. By identifying distinctive roles and initiatives, Canada asserted its independence and autonomy.

It is also clear, though, that core Canadian security interests did not challenge larger Western goals. The simple fact that successive Canadian governments believed that Canada's main security interests were consistent with those of the West does *not* indicate that Canada was subservient to any other actor. Indeed, a link can be drawn between these arguments and the one that suggests that most decisions the Canadian government makes are attempts at satisfying other countries, so great are the pressures that it must deal with. In this study, we have seen how observers have used this argument to explain the "real" reason behind the cancellation of the Arrow, that is, American pressure and some ill-defined larger conspiracy. The continued popularity of this thesis is testament to its deep-seated appeal, and to the perception that as a small country bordering a superpower, Canada operates under extraordinarily harsh restrictions. This premise is simplistic and self-serving in that Canadian failures can always be explained by larger "global" pressures; its assertion in an array of contexts also conceals the very real ability of this country to make its own decisions.

In a broad sense, this project represents an attempt at presenting Canada as a fully sovereign, independent country, where the external commitments that it made were no more important to its defence and security choices than comparable commitments were for other countries. While that is a seemingly simple statement, the existing literature maintains that Canadian defence choices are more constrained than those of other countries. Such studies constitute a disservice to students and observers, because they portray this country as essentially incapable of articulating national interests.

At the same time, though, it would be misleading to suggest that external developments had little impact on the Canadian defence debate and on the articulation of strategic interests. Thus, attention here focuses on two such concerns – technological developments and the Western alliance – that together helped shape and define the issues that Canadian defence officials considered.

It would be difficult to overstate the dramatic nature of the technological changes that took place between 1950 and 1963. The development and subsequent introduction of nuclear weapons and long-range delivery systems revolutionized military strategy. Power suddenly lost its strict relation to the size of military forces. Strategists who had been concerned with seizing the initiative, carrying the fight to the enemy, and emerging victorious now became more concerned with deterrence and the threat of force. Thus, conventional military assumptions and concepts, first discussed and popularized in the West by Jomini and Clausewitz, were believed to have been nullified, relegated to the dustbin of strategy through a technological revolution that had, literally overnight, required the creation of new concepts of the use of force.

Changes in weapons technology exert a powerful influence on perceptions of stability in the international system, but the most direct impact is on the roles and tasks of the military. In the first quarter-century of the postwar era, Canada's armed forces made both passive and active contributions to the protection of the American nuclear deterrent. Once early warning radars had been installed on Canadian territory, this country helped provide warning time to the Strategic Air Command. And with bombers constituting the main Soviet threat, the Royal Canadian Air Force made an active contribution to the protection of the deterrent by giving high priority to interceptor forces. Advances in technology in the 1960s altered the need for such forces, and Canada began making contributions in air- and spaceborne surveillance and detection.

Throughout this period, though, Canada was hardly a hostage to technology. To keep up with modern weapons developments, a state needs a sophisticated technological infrastructure, an advanced industrial base, and sufficient economic resources. Canada had all three and a proven ability in the high-technology field. Canadian scientists helped develop the atomic bomb and went on to produce an advanced nuclear energy industry; Canadian engineers designed the sophisticated CF-100 and CF-105 aircraft; and Canada had sufficient wealth to afford all but the most expensive weapons systems. However, maintaining a comprehensive Canadian defence research and manufacturing capability was simply not a priority of the government. Thus, Canada rejected atomic weapons in 1945, refused to pay the price of the CF-105 in 1959, and began reducing defence spending in the late 1950s. There were other, non-defence-related domestic priorities, and it was decided that the acquisition of some weapons systems did not provide benefits commensurate with the costs.

The archival chapters revealed that technology was a dominant concern of Canadian defence officials throughout this period. Technological advances not only played an important role in determining which issues were examined, but even affected the formation of defence staff groups designed to review particular innovations – the JBMDS being the best example. And while Canadian officials never lost sight of the fact that strategy in the nuclear age retained a critical political dimension, attention was directed to tracking technical innovations and ensuring that the latest advances in weaponry were well understood. In addition to the examples already discussed, technological advances that received considerable departmental attention included air defence systems, missile defences, and the advent of submarine-launched ballistic missiles in the early 1960s.

An additional influence on Canadian strategic thinking during this period was the Atlantic alliance. NATO was a military organization with responsibility for conducting war; as such, the plans that it made, the military concepts that it followed, and the roles that it advocated all played a powerful part in determining the posture of Canada's armed forces and the broad thinking that underlay Canadian defence policy. Through an exchange of information and opinion between the member states on the political problems facing the alliance, the drawing together of intelligence estimates of Warsaw Pact capabilities, and the direct diplomacy of member states and senior NATO figures, the alliance affected the perceptions of Canadian defence officials and policy makers on a wide array of strategic questions.

During the time frame that this book covers, NATO's influence in Canada was at its peak (and vice versa). From 1949 until 1957, if gross national product is accepted as the principal measure, Canada gave proportionately more money and material to NATO than any other ally.[13] Canada's European divisions were well equipped, the Mutual Aid Programme helped several countries, and the NATO Air Training Program spent hundreds of millions of dollars on the training of European pilots. Corresponding to the era of intense international tension, this was the period in which NATO was the repository of hopes for a new North Atlantic partnership.[14]

The Canadian military enthusiastically supported NATO because, through the integrated alliance force, it was making a real contribution to Western defence. While some national military contingents were uncomfortable at being under a supranational commander and abiding by directives that might not have had unanimous domestic support, this was not the case for Canada, which had a history of sending troops to serve under foreign commands. In addition, the Canadian military and the NATO Strategic Command had a common interest in the maintenance of strong Canadian armed forces. Just as the American military has traditionally had well-placed allies in the US Congress who were willing to put pressure on the executive to maintain strong defences, so the Canadian military had an ally in NATO.[15] In order to perform the missions that Canada had committed itself to, regular purchases of sophisticated military equipment were required, and NATO commanders made sure that successive Canadian governments were aware of these commitments.

Several crucial defence decisions of the period had a NATO connection, including the adoption of the strike/reconnaissance mission and the acquisition of nuclear weapons. Ironically, though, it was DND that consistently stressed the political costs of failing to honour alliance commitments. This task would normally have been performed by External Affairs, but was not during the period 1958-63 because of that department's political orientation and growing anti-American sentiment. Thus, during the years of the nuclear weapons dispute, DEA strongly challenged DND's analysis, indicating the difficulties that many in the department had over the basic direction of Canadian security policy.

One question that remains is how to account for the divergence in strategic thought between Canadian and American defence officials and observers. The literature on learning offers one possibility. This body of scholarship asserts that the articulation of national interests can be transformed as a result of cognitive change. In this sense, to learn is to develop knowledge by study and/or experience.[16] New information alters existing beliefs about the world, but its reception and interpretation are affected by prior beliefs. The extent and accuracy of learning depends upon the strength of the prior beliefs and the quantity and quality of new information.

There are different degrees of learning along a continuum of the ends-means relationship, from very simple to highly complex. Simple learning uses new information merely to adapt the means, without altering any deeper goals. Complex learning, by contrast, involves recognition of conflicts among means and goals in causally complicated situations, and leads to new priorities and trade-offs. Simple learning is relatively easy for an observer to assess, but complex learning is often more elusive, particularly when changes in deeper goals may have occurred.[17]

Given this distinction, one can argue that Canadian defence officials made more effective use of new information and changes to the international strategic environment, which was revealed by their assessment of the nuclear relationship (i.e., complex learning). Information about Soviet technological and scientific advances led to an early realization in Canada that emerging victorious in a nuclear conflict was not a plausible goal, and thus a new approach was required – one that emphasized the mutual risks that nuclear weapons and nuclear conflict posed to both sides. In contrast, early American strategic thinking made greater use of the simple learning model. Thus, for example, the strategy of massive retaliation can be explained as an attempt to utilize American military dominance in reaction to a series of Soviet advances. Unlike the thinking that developed in Canada, then, early American strategic thought confirmed existing goals and objectives in the new security environment – that is, emerging victorious in any future conflict.

The initial American failure to appreciate the reality of the altered strategic environment may be linked to traditional American attitudes toward conflict. In a nation that prided itself on having never "lost" a war, analysts in the United States had a difficult time adapting to an environment in which victory was no longer possible, and in which any attempt to "win" a nuclear conflict would effectively result in mutual suicide. It is therefore possible that American attitudes regarding victory in warfare were so entrenched that they effectively precluded analysts from accurately evaluating the nuclear environment, with the result that whatever learning occurred was distorted and misleading. Thus, the literature on learning offers some possible insight into how Canadians and Americans came to such different findings.

It was not only in the articulation of strategic thought that Canadians and Americans disagreed. This is not the place to examine bilateral political and foreign policy differences in detail, but it should be noted that Canada-US differences over Cuba, Vietnam, China, and the Soviet Union in the years that followed all pointed to an emerging sense of independence, which reached its most noticeable level when Pierre Trudeau was prime minister (1968-79, 1980-4).[18] In a range of foreign policy issues, Canada developed positions that were at odds with the United States and that resulted in the weakening of the bilateral relationship, which had improved considerably under Pearson.

It was during Trudeau's years in office that the combination of policy differences with the Americans and the emerging sense of Canada's growing power led to a series of academic studies that suggested Canada had risen to the first rank of nations, and thus had escaped the "middle power" characterization that had dominated analysis of Canadian foreign policy in the postwar period.[19] While individual arguments varied, the central thesis of this approach was that Canada had joined an elite group of countries, each of which contained the necessary power resources to, in the words of David Dewitt and John Kirton, "act autonomously in pursuit of their own interests."[20] It is therefore possible to see how the discussion of differences in strategic thought can be linked to a much larger body of literature that suggested that the Canadian state has considerable freedom of movement and is certainly capable of acting on its own when its interests diverge from those of its friends and allies.[21]

The existence of Canadian strategic thought was essentially proclaimed in a 1962 article by R.J. Sutherland. This paper, "Canada's Long Term Strategic Situation," largely summarized Sutherland's thinking on many of the issues that he was analyzing at the time for the department in classified studies.[22] Sutherland's main intent was to predict the international security environment through to the end of the twentieth century, and particularly Canada's role within that environment. The central thesis was that even in times of "drastic and revolutionary change," as Canada found itself in during the early 1960s, stable foundations for national security policy could be found in the "invariants" of Canada's strategic situation. Sutherland located these invariants in Canada's geography, economic potential, and broad national interests.[23]

In spite of overwhelming American economic and military power, Sutherland asserted that it was in the best interests of both countries for defence and security arrangements to be established on a cooperative basis, a development that owed as much to similar interests and traditions as it did to the potentially costly perception of the US bullying a much weaker neighbour. With Canada's allegiance to the West already determined, the most important question about future strategic developments was therefore not

the direction that Canada would take in international politics but whether
"we will be a powerful and effective ally or a weak and reluctant one."[24]
Sutherland further examined the "strategic significance of Canadian geography," and considered various scenarios involving the threat and use of
force on or over Canadian territory. Through its examination of both the
political and military dimensions of Canadian security, Sutherland's article
was the most visible example of Canadian strategic thought in the public
domain, which makes its subsequent invisibility in the studies by Preston,
Gellner, and Gray all the more difficult to explain.[25]

In many ways, Sutherland's 1962 article foreshadowed some of the findings of the following years' Report of the Ad Hoc Committee of Defence
Policy (known in DND as the "Sutherland Report," because it was prepared
under Sutherland's leadership).[26] This report examined Canada's political
and military interests in a rapidly changing global environment.[27] The strategic nature of the exercise was highlighted in the report's opening sentence, which noted: "The purpose of this paper is to discuss the major
alternatives available to Canada in the field of defence policy and to analyze
the factors bearing upon the choice between alternatives. The paper is therefore concerned with two problems; the nature of the available alternatives
and the criteria by which these alternatives should be judged." The report
observed that the external environment limited the "freedom of choices"
available to Canada, and that Canada therefore had to respect certain "political realities." As for the roles and missions of the Canadian military, the
report noted the restraining influence of limited resources, but concluded
that "an even more important set of limitations is imposed by Canadian
national policy and by Canadian national interests."[28]

The study found that Canadian defence policy needed to satisfy three
"basic criteria" before being adopted. First, its economic feasibility in terms
of available resources needed to be evaluated. Second, its technical and lo-
gistic feasibility needed to be determined. And third, its strategic relevance
in relation to the policy objectives of the Canadian government needed to
be considered. In the postwar period, Canada had chosen to prioritize alliance diplomacy, and this decision had been a central influence in the subsequent determination of Canadian security policy. As a result, Canada's
alliance commitments needed to be at the forefront of any analysis, because they represented the principal security objective of the Canadian
government.

Setting aside the influence of NATO, however, there were four areas in
which Canada possessed a "certain liberty of choice." These were: (1) questions of national policy; (2) the basis of Canada's participation in NATO; (3)
organization and management of DND; and (4) roles and missions of the
Canadian armed forces. The report discussed each of these in turn, but its

central focus was on Canada's fundamental security interest. Mirroring Sutherland's DND report of the same year (see Chapter 4), the study noted that
"Canada is one of the few nations of any consequence in the world which is
in a position to pursue an isolationist policy."[29] But the price of any such
choice would be high – too high, according to the report. Canada would
lose considerable "stature and influence," most notably in Washington, while
the gains would be negligible. This was an unacceptable price, especially
given Canada's history, interests, and larger political goals. While the study
recognized that Canada was not a central player in Western defence, it had
a role broadly commensurate with its size and abilities. The key consideration in future Canadian security policy was not how Canada's allies would
view the country's choices, "but the effect upon Canada's international
position and upon Canadian national interests."

The 1963 report in many ways accurately describes the contemporary
Canadian security environment. Canada continues to have the luxury of
having no identifiable enemy, and while this permits the country considerable freedom, it also poses challenges. The bilateral relationship with the
United States remains the focus of Canadian external relations, but, as in
the 1950s, continues to be the centre of much anxiety and apprehension.[30]
This is magnified by the unquestioned American political, economic, and
military hegemony – dominance that is actually *increasing* at the beginning
of the new century. While the end of the Cold War has resulted in greater
freedom of choice, this country's security continues to be governed by its
relations with the West and by Canada's desire to remain an international
actor capable of mobilizing resources whenever the nation perceives its larger
security interests to be at risk – as in the 1991 Gulf War and the 1999 NATO
war over Kosovo. Last, Canada still occasionally has difficulty identifying
its "national interests," particularly when they appear to challenge those of
the country's allies.

It bears repeating that this study has not been intended to be of purely
historical interest. A primary goal has been to determine what Cold War
strategic thought can tell us about the contemporary defence and security
debate. Indeed, while many of the early understandings of the nuclear age
may appear to lack relevance, it would be a mistake to assume that the
works of the 1950s and 1960s have little to offer the modern field of strategic studies. This can be seen most clearly with regard to the current debate
over the US national missile defence (NMD) program. As the controversy
over this issue directly relates to strategic concepts developed during the
period of concern for this study, the context of the missile defence program
needs to be established.

Although President Ronald Reagan's Strategic Defense Initiative was effectively dead when Bill Clinton took office in 1993, the notion of theatre

missile defences (the sister program of NMD) generated considerable support during the 1991 Gulf War.[31] After the war, the US Congress passed the National Missile Defense Act, which mandated the development and deployment of an ABM (anti-ballistic missile) Treaty-compliant NMD system as soon as the technology became available.[32] Subsequently, in 1994, the Republican majority in Congress authorized the completion of a national missile defence system by 2003.

Support for NMD grew in 1998, as both Iran and North Korea surprised the US intelligence community with missile tests that showed rapid progress of their respective programs. Iran launched the medium-range Shahab 3, while North Korea fired its multistage Taepo Dong 1 rocket, and immediately began work on a successor that could potentially strike targets in North America. That summer also saw the release of a congressionally mandated commission report by the former US secretary of defence, Donald Rumsfeld (who was reappointed to the post by President George W. Bush in 2001).[33] The report concluded that countries such as Iran, North Korea, and Iraq might soon develop long-range missiles that could threaten American territory.[34]

In January 1999, the Clinton administration formally asked Russia to begin renegotiating the 1972 ABM Treaty, after concluding that the threat of a strike from a "rogue" state justified deploying a limited number of ground-based interceptor missiles capable of destroying incoming missiles (and that such a system would violate the treaty).[35] However, Russia quickly rejected the overture, and emphasized that the terms of the treaty were non-negotiable.[36] Russian officials suggested that the entire US-Soviet (now Russian) arms control regime would be undermined if the Americans unilaterally deployed an NMD system, as they warned they might do in the event of failure to reach a mutually acceptable resolution. For the remainder of the Clinton presidency, US NMD plans were uncertain; the period culminated in a September 2000 announcement – just weeks before the November presidential election – that the United States would not begin deployment of the system, which effectively passed the decision to the next president.[37]

Following the protracted election controversy, President George W. Bush announced in May 2001 that his administration would proceed with an ABM shield, beginning with the placing of 100 missile interceptors in Fort Greely, Alaska.[38] The Russian reaction to the American announcement was predictably hostile: President Vladimir Putin warned the United States not to proceed unilaterally, and noted that the ABM Treaty remained the "cornerstone of the modern architecture of international security."[39] Putin further warned that in response to any US missile shield, Russia would "augment" its nuclear forces without regard to past treaties, and that both the START I and START II treaties would be negated.[40] By the late summer of 2001, the United States was poised to withdraw from the ABM Treaty, as sporadic negotiations with Russia to amend it had failed.⁴¹ Following the failure of a last-ditch meeting between US secretary of state Colin Powell and Russian president Vladimir Putin in early December 2001, the United States gave Russia formal six months' notification that it would withdraw from the treaty.⁴²

In an effort to persuade Russia that the proposed NMD system should not be viewed as a strategic threat, both the Clinton and Bush administrations have used arguments conceptually linked to the notion of mutual assured destruction developed in the early 1960s in the United States, and in the 1950s in Canada. For example, American officials have tried to convince Russian planners that the defence system being contemplated, while adequate to intercept a few missiles from rogue states, could easily be overwhelmed by Russia's strategic missile forces.⁴³ In April 2000, Pentagon officials briefed Russian Foreign Minister Igor Ivanov and explained in detail how Russia's nuclear arsenal could nullify the radar technology at the heart of the proposed system. Officials further suggested that technical limits to the system would not allow the United States to simply add more interceptor missiles, as the Russians feared.⁴⁴ At the June 2000 summit between Clinton and Putin, similar arguments were again raised, and special emphasis was placed on how the "principles of strategic stability" would not be disrupted by the proposed system.⁴⁵ Last, during the summer of 2001, US officials reassured the Russians that the proposed system would be virtually useless against the Russian strategic force for at least twenty-five years, a point that President Putin appeared to accept in June.⁴⁶

The clear intent of these assurances is to persuade Russia that the system of stability based on MAD will remain in effect even *after* the deployment of the proposed NMD system. Thus, despite forty years of advances in weapons technology and changing defence strategies, the twenty-first-century debate over NMD indicates that the understandings reached decades ago continue to have an important effect on the contemporary strategic dialogue.⁴⁷ The model of strategic stability based on mutual vulnerability, born at the height of the Cold War, has proved to be equally important in the post-Cold War environment. It continues to be at the centre of the US-Russian defence relationship, and appears destined to remain so for as long as both sides have nuclear weapons and force is still regarded as a possible instrument in resolving political disagreements.⁴⁸

However, strategic stability based on mutual vulnerability is only one example of the continuing relevance of Cold War strategic thought from the 1950s and early 1960s. Limiting this discussion to Canadian strategic contributions, Chapter 5 noted that the early Canadian critique of arms control remains relevant today, as the notion that neither the United States nor Russia can reduce their strategic forces below the level at which deterrence is called into doubt is a fundamental principle of contemporary arms control (and appears to be a major stumbling block to any proposed START III treaty). Similarly, DND's initial analysis regarding the formation of a bilateral air defence command with the United States also remains relevant, as in June 2000 the North American Aerospace Defence Command (NORAD) was once again renewed for a five-year term, for reasons that were comparable to those offered at NORAD's formation in 1958.[49] While NORAD's mission and functions have changed since its initial signing, it remains a cornerstone of Canada-US defence cooperation.[50] It is also a continuing signal to potential enemies that an attack against North America will trigger a coordinated response. It might also be noted that the current concern over command-and-control issues as a result of the proposed US NMD system are in many ways similar to those raised in the 1950s, and once again raise questions of Canadian involvement in US defence strategies.[51]

Finally, it is interesting to note how DND and DEA – now renamed the Department of Foreign Affairs and International Trade (DFAIT) – approach nuclear weapons today, some four decades after the interdepartmental dispute that essentially split the Canadian government. While Canada has not had nuclear weapons since 1984, the two departments continue to emphasize positions that they developed in the late 1950s (revealing either the wisdom of their initial approaches, or signifying impressive cases of bureaucratic inertia!). DND continues to stress that Western nuclear weapons are necessary, and that they perform a critical deterrent function in an environment where the proliferation of weapons of mass destruction is a major concern; this is clearly seen in the department's continuing refusal to support a "no first use" alliance declaration. For its part, DFAIT still emphasizes the destabilizing effect of nuclear weapons, and continues its effort to persuade NATO to completely renounce them.[52] Thus, the two departments remain as opposed today on the question of nuclear weapons as they were four decades ago.

In a final analysis, then, an observer comparing the contemporary strategic environment with the one of the 1950s would conclude that while many of the specific issues have changed, the threat and use of force remains an intrinsic part of the fabric of international politics. While thinking on deterrence, mutual vulnerability, and nuclear weapons can hardly be expected to have remained static over the past forty years, what is perhaps most surprising is that in spite of immense political and military developments, early concepts and understandings not only remain relevant, but are indeed crucial to the contemporary strategic environment.[53]

Focusing attention back on the present-day Canadian defence debate, some key developments and concerns should be noted. Canada is still closely allied with the United States and NATO, and it continues to derive its security policy through its ties to both. Furthermore, the external environment remains highly uncertain, and while the monolithic power blocs of the Cold War have long since disappeared, states are still faced with difficult security choices. How they make those choices still carries enormous political importance. Thus, better understanding how and why Canada chose the defence options that it did during the Cold War might alert us to similar debates at present, and if possible, help prevent Canada from making similar mistakes. Indeed, at a time when many observers are calling for a total reconsideration of Canada's defence and security policy,[54] and when this country's position on nuclear weapons remains the subject of intense scrutiny (as indicated by the ongoing bureaucratic disagreement), the importance of having an accurate picture of previous defence debates is underlined. In this regard, it might be noted that while the December 1998 parliamentary report on nuclear weapons received widespread public attention in Canada, there was little reference to the history of Canada-US nuclear differences, or for that matter, to the issues, events, and decisions that led to those differences in the first place.[55]

That last point, and particularly what it tells us about the knowledge of Canada's strategic history, deserves highlighting. It is my belief that Canada cannot identify a security policy for the new century unless it fully understands the choices made in the one just ended. Rather than continuing to accept assumptions about Canadian security that have gone untested for decades, the challenge facing students and observers of Canadian defence is to re-examine established dogmas and the "truths" that result from them. By shedding new light on some "old" issues, this study has underlined the importance of questioning the prevailing thinking and the conclusions that flow from it.

In sum, this examination of Canadian strategic thought during the early phase of the Cold War reveals a country that was trying to determine how it could best contribute to Western security and defence. Canadians were capable of identifying independent strategic interests, although they were also conscious of American approaches and understandings. The Canadian experience in dealing with the influence of the United States was doubtlessly repeated elsewhere, as many countries were faced with the hegemonic strategic views of the United States. While those views were not always applicable, they dominated the debate and largely determined the general parameters of the strategic dialogue. If the experience of the 1950s and early 1960s tells Canadians anything, it is that this country has security interests of its own, but that it still faces the challenge of convincing a frequently disinterested populace that issues of security demand continuing attention and occasional action.

Notes

Introduction

1 John Baylis and John Garnett, eds., *Makers of Nuclear Strategy* (London: Pinter Publishers, 1991), 1.

2 Bernard Brodie, ed., *The Absolute Weapon: Atomic Power and World Order* (New York: Harcourt Brace, 1946), 75-6. Emphasis added.

3 One strategist who shared Brodie's conviction was B.H. Liddell Hart. See *The Revolution in Warfare* (London: Faber, 1946). Among those who challenged this conception, see P.M.S. Blackett, *The Military and Political Consequences of Atomic Energy* (London: Turnstile Press, 1948) and Vannevar Bush, *Modern Arms and Free Men* (New York: Simon and Schuster, 1949).

4 The "golden age" thesis asserts that these years saw the initial formulation of several of the key strategic concepts in the nuclear age. Major studies of the period include (in order of publication) Bernard Brodie, "Nuclear Weapons: Strategic or Tactical?" *Foreign Affairs* 32, 2 (1954): 217-19; William Kaufmann, *The Requirements of Deterrence* (Princeton, NJ: Center for International Studies, 1954); Brodie, "Strategy Hits a Dead End," *Harper's* 3, 11 (1955): 33-7; Kaufmann, ed., *Military Policy and National Security* (Princeton, NJ: Princeton University Press, 1956); Robert Osgood, *Limited War: The Challenge to American Strategy* (Chicago: University of Chicago Press, 1957); Henry Kissinger, *Nuclear Weapons and Foreign Policy* (New York: Harper and Row, 1957); Albert Wohlstetter, "The Delicate Balance of Terror," *Foreign Affairs* 37, 2 (1959): 211-34; Brodie, *Strategy in the Missile Age* (Princeton, NJ: Princeton University Press, 1959); Herman Kahn, *On Thermonuclear War* (Princeton, NJ: Princeton University Press, 1960); Thomas C. Schelling, *The Strategy of Conflict* (New York: Oxford University Press, 1960); and Robert Gilpin, *American Scientists and Nuclear Weapons Policy* (Princeton, NJ: Princeton University Press, 1962).

5 Major works in the field include James Eayrs, *In Defence of Canada*, 5 vols. (Toronto: University of Toronto Press, 1964-83); Colin Gray, *Canadian Defence Priorities: A Question of Relevance* (Toronto: Clarke Irwin, 1972); Jon B. McLin, *Canada's Changing Defence Policy, 1957-1963: The Problems of a Middle Power in Alliance* (Baltimore, MD: Johns Hopkins Press, 1967); Joseph Jockel, *No Boundaries Upstairs: Canada, the United States and the Origins of North American Air Defence, 1945-1958* (Vancouver: UBC Press, 1987); and D.W. Middlemiss and J.J. Sokolsky, *Canadian Defence: Decisions and Determinants* (Toronto: Harcourt Brace Jovanovich, 1989). While not focused on Canadian security policy per se, John Holmes's *The Shaping of Peace: Canada and the Search for World Order, 1943-1957*, 2 vols. (Toronto: University of Toronto Press, 1979 and 1982) also deserves mention. Among the best-known "critical" studies (i.e., those that challenge traditional explanations), see James Minifie, *Peacemaker or Powder-Monkey: Canada's Role in a Revolutionary World* (Toronto: McClelland and Stewart, 1960) and John Warnock, *Partner to Behemoth: The Military Policy of a Satellite Canada* (Toronto: New Press, 1970).

6 The phrase "unmilitary people" can be traced to George Stanley. See *Canada's Soldiers: The Military History of an Unmilitary People* (Toronto: Macmillan, 1960).

7 Since 1990, an array of Department of National Defence and External Affairs records have been declassified, both at the National Archives of Canada (NAC) and DND's Directorate of History (DH). Among the individual collections that have been opened, the most significant is the DH Raymont Collection, file 73/1223.

8 This observation was asserted in a range of fields, but the most widely cited (and controversial) works were in the areas of foreign policy/defence and economics. With regard to the former, key studies included Minifie, *Peacemaker or Powder-Monkey*; Stephen Clarkson, ed., *An Independent Foreign Policy for Canada* (Toronto: McClelland and Stewart, 1968); Warnock, *Partner to Behemoth*; and Andrew Brewin, *Stand on Guard: The Search for a Canadian Defence Policy* (Toronto: McClelland and Stewart, 1966).

9 See Adrian Preston, "The Higher Study of Defence in Canada: A Critical Review," *Journal of Canadian Studies* 3, 3 (1968): 17-28; Colin Gray, "The Need for Independent Canadian Strategic Thought," *Canadian Defence Quarterly* 1, 1 (1971): 6-12; and John Gellner, "Strategic Analysis in Canada," *International Journal* 33, 3 (1978): 493-505.

10 Gray noted that "strategic theoretical parasitism is the legacy of Canada's military past; such a posture of dependence for intellectual nourishment upon the debates of others mortgages the future effectiveness of national defence and foreign policies." Gray, "The Need for Independent Canadian Strategic Thought," 7.

11 Ibid., 6.

12 Ibid., 7.

13 Gray did not identify the observers/authors who made up this group. However, in a note at the end of the article he singled out Clarkson's *An Independent Foreign Policy for Canada* as "one of the worst examples of the 'false alternatives' phenomenon."

14 Gray wrote that "lest these comments be thought too strong, let any doubter seek to compile a book list upon the subject of 'The Development of Strategic Thought (or practice) Since 1945' from Canadian sources." Gray, "The Need for Independent Canadian Strategic Thought," 11.

15 Only a handful of scholars have even approached the subject of Canadian strategic thinking since the early 1970s, and not one has directly addressed Gray's thesis. See, for example, Christian Jaekl and David Bellamy, "On 'Home-Grown' Strategic Thought," *Canadian Defence Quarterly* 14, 1 (1985): 33-6; Paul Buteux, "Sutherland Revisited: Canada's Long-Term Strategic Situation," *Canadian Defence Quarterly* 23, 1 (1994): 5-9; and Donald Macnamara, "Canada's Domestic Strategic Interests," *Canadian Defence Quarterly* 23, 4 (1994): 13-16. Two studies on DND's R.J. Sutherland do challenge the conventional wisdom. See James Lee and David Bellamy, "Dr. R.J. Sutherland: A Retrospect," *Canadian Defence Quarterly* 17, 1 (1987): 41-6; and Andrew Richter, "The Sutherland Papers: A Glimpse into the Thinking of Canada's Preeminent Strategist," *Canadian Defence Quarterly* 27, 1 (1997): 28-33.

16 Both Preston and Gellner made many of the same points. Preston argued that Canada's long-standing colonial/deferential relationship with Britain had resulted in a military establishment that was quite willing to forgo an independent identity and copy the strategic analysis developed elsewhere. While Gellner suggested that "Colin Gray's accusation of 'strategic theoretical parasitism' is perhaps too harsh," he agreed that Canada had failed to identify independent strategic interests. He explained this failure, however, as being tied to Canada's larger (and long-standing) inability to assert its political/military independence. It was in this broader context that Gellner believed that this country's strategic failing should be considered.

17 This notion is popular among both "mainstream" and "critical" works in the field. Among the former, Eayrs's *In Defence of Canada* series, McLin's *Canada's Changing Defence Policy*, and Brian Cuthbertson's *Canadian Military Independence in the Age of the Superpowers* (Toronto: Fitzhenry and Whiteside, 1977) all accept the idea of a strategically impotent Canada. Among more recent studies, Howard Langille's *Changing the Guard: The Search for a Canadian Defence Policy* (Toronto: University of Toronto Press, 1990); Douglas Bland's *Chiefs of*

Defence: Government and the Unified Command of the Canadian Armed Forces (Toronto: Brown Book Company and the Canadian Institute of Strategic Studies, 1995); and Ann Denholm Crosby's *Dilemmas in Defence Decision-Making: Constructing Canada's Role in NORAD, 1958-1996* (New York: St. Martin's Press, 1998) continue to accept the argument without significant qualification.

18　There are two main reasons why this study focuses on the records of National Defence: (1) as this study is a challenge to the works by authors Preston, Gray, and Gellner, its emphasis is on the department where the failure to articulate strategic interests was alleged to be most notable; and (2) several secondary studies (as well as personal memoirs) have been published that reveal the thinking of key DEA officials on a variety of strategic issues. See, for example, James Eayrs, *In Defence of Canada: Peacemaking and Deterrence* (Toronto: University of Toronto Press, 1972) and *In Defence of Canada: Growing up Allied* (Toronto: University of Toronto Press, 1980); J.L. Granatstein, *The Ottawa Men: The Civil Service Mandarins, 1935-1957* (Toronto: Oxford University Press, 1985) and *A Man of Influence: Norman A. Robertson and Canadian Statecraft, 1929-1968* (Toronto: Deneau, 1981). Personal memoirs include Lester B. Pearson, *Mike: The Memoirs of the Right Honourable Lester B. Pearson,* 3 vols. (Toronto: University of Toronto Press, 1972-5); Escott Reid, *Radical Mandarin* (Toronto: University of Toronto Press, 1989); Holmes, *The Shaping of Peace*; H. Basil Robinson, *Diefenbaker's World: A Populist in Foreign Affairs* (Toronto: University of Toronto Press, 1989); George Ignatieff, *Memoirs: The Making of a Peacemonger* (Toronto: University of Toronto Press, 1985); Arnold Heeney, *The Things That Are Caesar's: Memoirs of a Canadian Public Servant* (Toronto: University of Toronto Press, 1972); and Dana Wilgress, *Memoirs* (Toronto: Ryerson Press, 1967).

19　The external environment argument maintains that the broad parameters of Canadian defence policy are set outside Canada, the result of this country's fundamental weakness and willingness to accept the defence policies identified for it by others. This argument, or variations of it, can be found in most of the major works in Canadian security. See, in particular, Eayrs's *In Defence of Canada* series; Gray, *Canadian Defence Priorities;* and McLin, *Canada's Changing Defence Policy.* The argument itself is reviewed in Middlemiss and Sokolsky, *Canadian Defence: Decisions and Determinants.*

20　For an overview, see David Dewitt and John Kirton, *Canada As a Principal Power: A Study in Foreign Policy and International Relations* (Toronto: John Wiley, 1983). Peripheral dependence is directly linked to the theory of dependency, which is itself grounded in classical Marxism. Other observers in the field have used the phrase "Canada as a satellite" to indicate the same behaviour, that is, an inability to act in an autonomous or independent way. See, for example, Kim Richard Nossal, *The Politics of Canadian Foreign Policy* (Scarborough: Prentice Hall Canada, 1989) and Michael Hawes, *Principal Power, Middle Power, or Satellite? Competing Perspectives in the Study of Canadian Foreign Policy* (Toronto: York University Research Program in Strategic Studies, 1984).

21　For a general introduction to the subject of dependency, see F.H. Cardoso and E. Falleto, *Dependency and Development in Latin America* (Berkeley: University of California Press, 1979) and A.G. Frank, *Capitalism and Underdevelopment in Latin America* (New York: Monthly Review Press, 1967). Dependency theory has frequently been utilized in the Canadian context to explain the particular evolution of Canadian economic development. For an introduction to the subject of modern Canadian political economy (from the "critical" perspective), see Leo Panitch, ed., *The Canadian State: Political Economy and Political Power* (Toronto: University of Toronto Press, 1977).

22　Dewitt and Kirton, *Canada As a Principal Power,* 32. The two key works that made this argument were Minifie, *Peacemaker or Powder-Monkey* and Warnock, *Partner to Behemoth.*

23　Dewitt and Kirton, *Canada As a Principal Power,* 199-204.

24　Ibid., 204-7.

25　In January 1951, the government announced a three-year, five-billion-dollar rearmament program. Further, the total active strength of the three services increased by 70 percent between 1949 and 1951.

26　The tension in Canadian foreign policy during this period has been widely examined. See, for example, J.L. Granatstein, *Canada 1957-1968: The Years of Uncertainty and Innovation* (Toronto: McClelland and Stewart, 1986).

27 The best study of these developments is Jockel, *No Boundaries Upstairs.*

28 The study that best examines these decisions remains McLin's *Canada's Changing Defence Policy.*

29 The nuclear weapons controversy has been examined by several Canadian scholars, but has to date avoided systematic investigation. Among major works, see Peyton Lyon, "Defence: To Be or Not to Be Nuclear?" in *Canada in World Affairs, 1961-1963* (Toronto: Oxford University Press, 1968); McLin, *Canada's Changing Defence Policy*; and Howard Lentner, "Foreign Policy Decision Making: The Case of Canada and Nuclear Weapons," *World Politics* 29, 1 (1976): 29-66. Two recent studies by John Clearwater examine the weapons themselves, but avoid the larger debate that they sparked. See *Canadian Nuclear Weapons: The Untold Story of Canada's Cold War Arsenal* (Toronto: Dundurn Press, 1998) and *U.S. Nuclear Weapons in Canada* (Toronto: The Dundurn Group, 1999).

30 For a thorough account of the Canadian role in the crisis, see Peter T. Haydon, *The 1962 Cuban Missile Crisis: Canadian Involvement Reconsidered* (Toronto: Canadian Institute of Strategic Studies, 1995). During the last week of January 1963, the Tory government came close to collapse over the nuclear weapons issue, with several cabinet ministers threatening to resign. The best account of the crisis is by Granatstein, *Canada 1957-1967.* Unfortunately, Diefenbaker's memoirs add little to our understanding of these events. See *One Canada,* vol. 3, *The Tumultuous Years, 1962-1967* (Toronto: Macmillan, 1977).

31 In January 1963, the US State Department issued a press release that was sharply critical of Canada. Its most explosive accusation was that the "Canadian government has not as yet proposed any arrangement sufficiently practical to contribute effectively to North American defense." The release is reprinted in Arthur E. Blanchette, ed., *Canadian Foreign Policy 1955-1965: Selected Speeches and Documents* (Toronto: McClelland and Stewart, 1977), 177-9. For a review of the episode, see Jocelyn Maynard Ghent, "Did He Fall or Was He Pushed? The Kennedy Administration and the Collapse of the Diefenbaker Government," *International History Review* 1, 2 (1979): 246-70.

32 R.J. Sutherland, "The Strategic Significance of the Canadian Arctic," in *The Arctic Frontier,* ed. R.St.J. Macdonald (Toronto: University of Toronto Press, 1966), 272.

33 Between 1950 and 1963, the US nuclear stockpile grew some fortyfold, from 450 weapons to 18,000, while Soviet nuclear forces grew, on a percentage basis, even more rapidly, increasing from about 25 weapons to 2,000. Figures from Marek Thee, *Military Technology, Military Strategy, and the Arms Race* (London: Croom Helm, 1986), 5.

34 The impact of weapons technology on military strategy and defence decision making has been well explored in the literature. See, for example, Colin Gray, "Does Theory Lead Technology?" *International Journal* 33, 3 (1975): 506-23; John Garnett, "Technology and Strategy," in *Contemporary Strategy: Theories and Concepts,* 2nd ed. (New York: Holmes and Meier, 1987); Bernard Brodie and Fawn Brodie, *From Crossbow to H-Bomb* (Bloomington: Indiana University Press, 1973); and Martin van Creveld, *Technology and War: From 2000 BC to the Present* (New York: Free Press, 1989).

35 This in no way implies that the strategic contributions and writings of non-Americans were unimportant. It is simply a recognition of the crucial role that US analysts played in the evolution of postwar strategic thought. Indeed, there is widespread agreement on the centrality of the United States in this field. For example, both Lawrence Freedman's *The Evolution of Nuclear Strategy* (London: Macmillan, 1981) and Fred Kaplan's *The Wizards of Armageddon* (New York: Simon and Schuster, 1983) largely concentrate on American strategists. There are two primary explanations for this dominance: (1) the growth of a large civilian defence community in the United States; and (2) the size and scale of the US defence establishment, which required the development of an analytic community that could offer advice on a wide range of strategic issues. For a discussion on these points, see Colin Gray, *Strategic Studies and Public Policy: The American Experience* (Lexington: University of Kentucky Press, 1982). It is widely accepted in the literature that most major advances in American strategic thought were first articulated by civilian strategists (as opposed to officials in the Department of Defense), a group that included Bernard Brodie, William Kaufmann, and Thomas Schelling. See, for example, Kaplan, *The Wizards of Armageddon,* and Gregg Herken, *Counsels of War* (New York: Alfred A. Knopf, 1985). While American

strategic analysis was frequently altered (and/or disregarded) by the policy makers and various officials in DoD (see Chapter 6), a comparison between Canadian DND officials and US government officials would be of questionable utility, as few original strategic contributions were articulated by the latter group. Similarly, a comparison between civilian strategists in the two countries would also be unproductive, as Canada largely lacked a non-governmental defence community (discussed in Chapter 3).

Chapter 1: The Defence and Security Environment, 1945-9

1 James Eayrs, *In Defence of Canada: Peacemaking and Deterrence* (Toronto: University of Toronto Press, 1972), 86. These figures may be contrasted with those achieved during the war. The army had peaked at just under 500,000 men, the navy at about 100,000, and the air force at 250,000. In total, the three armed services had enlisted more than one million men during the war.

2 Tom Axworthy, "Soldiers without Enemies: A Political Analysis of Canadian Defence Policy, 1945-1975" (PhD diss., Queen's University, 1978), 41.

3 For a discussion, see Eayrs, *In Defence of Canada: Peacemaking and Deterrence*, 91-2.

4 Department of National Defence, *Canada's Defence: Information on Canada's Defence Achievements and Organization* (Ottawa: Queen's Printer, 1947), 7.

5 Ibid., 11-12.

6 Douglas Bland, *The Administration of Defence Policy in Canada, 1947-1985* (Kingston, ON: Ronald P. Frye, 1987), 15. In James Eayrs's opinion, the speech was "the first rationale of military expenditure to come from the Government since the end of the Second World War." Eayrs, *In Defence of Canada: Peacemaking and Deterrence*, 95.

7 Axworthy, "Soldiers without Enemies," 919.

8 Eayrs, *In Defence of Canada: Peacemaking and Deterrence*, 101.

9 Joseph Jockel, *No Boundaries Upstairs: Canada, the United States, and the Origins of North American Air Defence, 1945-1957* (Vancouver: UBC Press, 1987), 38.

10 David Bercuson, *True Patriot: The Life of Brooke Claxton, 1898-1960* (Toronto: University of Toronto Press, 1993), 177. For a review of naval policy during this period, see James Boutilier, ed., *The RCN in Retrospect, 1910-1968* (Vancouver: University of British Columbia Press, 1982). The sense of naval despair reached its climax in 1949, when minor mutinies erupted on HMCS *Magnificent* (a carrier acquired from Britain shortly after the war) and two destroyers. An investigation revealed a service prone to imitating British practices, as well as problems of pay and morale.

11 Axworthy, "Soldiers without Enemies," 108.

12 Ron Purver, "The Arctic in Canadian Security Policy, 1945 to the Present," in *Canada's International Security Policy,* ed. David Dewitt and David Leyton-Brown (Scarborough: Prentice Hall Canada, 1995), 85.

13 The North Atlantic Treaty was signed 4 April 1949. Perhaps the most critical provision was Article 5, which stipulated that an armed attack against one of the members would be regarded as an armed attack against all. Canada's principal contribution was Article 2 (known as the "Canadian article"), which stressed non-military cooperation. The article, championed by External Affairs officials Escott Reid and Lester Pearson, was effectively forced into the treaty over the opposition of the United States. For a discussion, see Escott Reid, "The Birth of the North Atlantic Alliance," *International Journal,* 22, 3 (1967): 426-40; and Lester B. Pearson, *Mike: The Memoirs of the Right Honourable Lester B. Pearson,* vol. 2 (Toronto: University of Toronto Press, 1973).

14 Department of National Defence, *Canada's Defence Programme, 1949-1950* (Ottawa: DND, 1949). The first and third objectives – defending Canada and working with other countries – remained essentially unchanged from 1947, but the second was quite different. The 1947 second purpose, to assist the civil power in maintaining law and order, was now dropped in favour of a recognition that Canada's existing forces were intended to be the base from which a much larger force would be constructed should the need arise.

15 Department of National Defence, *Canada's Defence Programme, 1949-1950,* 15.

16 The study that best examines Canada's early nuclear history is Robert Bothwell, *Nucleus: The History of Atomic Energy of Canada Limited* (Toronto: University of Toronto Press, 1988).

See also D.G. Hurst, "The Canadian Nuclear Project," in *No Day Long Enough: Canadian Science in World War II*, ed. George R. Lindsey (Toronto: Canadian Institute of Strategic Studies, 1997).

17 This point is made by Ian Clark and Nicholas Wheeler, *The British Origins of Nuclear Strategy, 1945-1955* (Oxford: Clarendon Press, 1989). While the formal British decision to produce nuclear weapons was not taken until 1947, Clark and Wheeler note that the key decisions were actually made in 1945-6. For more on the early British debate on nuclear weapons, see Andrew J. Pierre, *Nuclear Politics: The British Experience with an Independent Strategic Force, 1939-1970* (London: Oxford University Press, 1972).

18 The memo is the subject of an article by J.A. Munro and A.I. Inglis. See "The Atomic Conference 1945 and the Pearson Memoirs," *International Journal* 29, 1 (1973-4): 90-109. All subsequent quotations in the text are attributable to this article. Pearson briefly discusses the memo in the first volume of his memoirs, although his comments do not shed much insight. See *Mike: The Memoirs of the Right Honourable Lester B. Pearson*, vol. 1 (Toronto: University of Toronto Press, 1972), 259-63.

19 Eayrs has described the memo as deserving "a place among the great diplomatic state papers." *In Defence of Canada: Peacemaking and Deterrence*, 279.

20 John Holmes has written that "there has rarely been such evidence of the docility of the Canadian public as during the period on atomic questions ... This was a subject on which the public seemed to accept government leadership with little questioning." See *The Shaping of Peace: Canada and the Search for World Order, 1943-1957*, vol. 1 (Toronto: University of Toronto Press, 1979), 224.

21 Jon B. McLin, *Canada's Changing Defence Policy, 1957-1963: The Problems of a Middle Power in Alliance* (Baltimore, MD: Johns Hopkins Press, 1967), 125. It might be noted that Pierre's *Nuclear Politics* reached much the same conclusion as McLin. Pierre wrote that "Britain and Canada, with roughly equal atomic facilities and capabilities, and at approximately the same time, made opposite decisions on manufacturing nuclear weapons. The differential factor which appears to have led them to their respective responses was their comparative sense of security. For the Canadians, security was guaranteed by their geographical location next to the United States. An attack on Canada, it was felt, would assuredly activate American retaliation, as all of North America was within the sphere of the vital interests of the US" (77).

22 Brian Buckley, *Canada's Early Nuclear Policy: Fate, Chance, and Character* (Montreal: McGill-Queen's University Press, 2000).

23 Baruch's plan proposed the creation of an International Atomic Development Authority to control the manufacture and use of atomic energy. This authority would either manage or own all atomic energy activities. Only after the means to control atomic energy had been agreed upon would the manufacture of nuclear weapons cease and existing bombs be destroyed. The plan is discussed in Melvyn Leffler, *A Preponderance of Power: National Security, the Truman Administration, and the Cold War* (Stanford: Stanford University Press, 1992).

24 Albert Legault and Michel Fortmann, *A Diplomacy of Hope: Canada and Disarmament, 1945-1988* (Montreal: McGill-Queen's University Press, 1992), 80.

25 See Eayrs, *In Defence of Canada: Peacemaking and Deterrence*, 302-7.

26 See Bothwell, *Nucleus*.

27 Legault and Fortmann, *A Diplomacy of Hope*, 82. King's use of the term "custodian" was linked to a controversial 1949 proposal that would have seen British nuclear weapons stored in Canada. For a review, see Eayrs, *In Defence of Canada: Growing Up Allied* (Toronto: University of Toronto Press, 1980), 240-1.

28 The principal US air bases in Canada were Goose Bay in Labrador, and Harmon Field and Fort Pepperell, NF; the main naval base was Argentia, NF. Each of these bases was US-owned and -operated, and personnel stationed at them were protected by American extra-territorial rights and laws. This point is discussed in Lawrence Aronsen, "American National Security and the Defence of the Northern Frontier, 1945-1951," *Canadian Review of American Studies* 14, 3 (1983): 259-77. As for Canada's plutonium sales, in 1959 Canadian uranium production peaked with more than 12,000 tons exported, with a value of $300 million. See Gordon Edwards, "Canada's Nuclear Industry and the Myth of the Peaceful Atom," in

Canada and the Nuclear Arms Race, ed. Ernie Regehr and Simon Rosenblum (Toronto: James Lorimer, 1983), 126.

29 Much of this concern can be linked to US behaviour on the three major wartime continental projects: the Alaska Highway, the North-West Staging Route, and the Canol pipeline project. In total, the projects employed 30,000 Americans, mostly in remote areas where there was little direct Canadian observation. Books that examine continental wartime projects and general American attitudes toward Canada include K.S. Coates and W.R. Morrison, *The Alaska Highway in World War II: The US Army of Occupation in Canada's Northwest* (Toronto: University of Toronto Press, 1992) and Shelagh D. Grant, *Sovereignty or Security? Government Policy in the Canadian North, 1936-1950* (Vancouver: UBC Press, 1988).

30 The PJBD, established by the Ogdensburg Declaration of August 1940, consisted of Canadian and American sections each headed by a civilian, representatives of the services, and a secretary. The board's primary responsibility was the drafting of plans for the joint defence of North America. For a review, see Christopher Conliffe, "The Permanent Joint Board on Defence, 1940-1988," in *The US-Canada Security Relationship: The Politics, Strategy, and Technology of Defense,* ed. David Haglund and Joel Sokolsky (Boulder, CO: Westview Press, 1989). The MCC comprised the diplomatic and military personnel of the PJBD and members of the planning staffs of the services. The Canadian members of the committee were senior staff officers from each of the three branches of the armed forces and a foreign service officer from External Affairs. The American members were senior officers, but they had, at best, only indirect ties with the American Joint Chiefs of Staff. The MCC's air defence plan called for the construction of numerous air bases, a large increase in air forces, and a variety of both active and passive air defences.

31 Prime Minister Mackenzie King's reaction to the MCC's proposals was particularly harsh. He noted in his diary that "it became perfectly apparent, I think, to all as we listened, that Canada simply could not do what was necessary to protect itself. Our country would be a mere pawn in the world conflict." As cited in Joseph Jockel, "The United States and Canadian Efforts at Continental Air Defence, 1945-1957" (PhD diss., Johns Hopkins University, 1978), 76.

32 Purver, "The Arctic in Canadian Security Policy," 83.

33 William Willoughby, *The Joint Organizations of Canada and the United States* (Toronto: University of Toronto Press, 1979), 130.

34 In June 1946, the *Financial Post* printed a story that suggested the US government had presented Canada with an ultimatum to build a string of northern air bases. The story quickly led to fears that the United States was on the verge of taking unilateral action.

35 Holmes, *The Shaping of Peace,* 87.

36 Axworthy, "Soldiers without Enemies," 69.

37 Eayrs, *In Defence of Canada: Peacemaking and Deterrence,* 352.

38 Willoughby, *The Joint Organizations of Canada and the United States,* 129.

39 As cited in Eayrs, *In Defence of Canada: Peacemaking and Deterrence,* 355. For more on the Goose Bay negotiations, see Aronsen, "American National Security and the Defence of the Northern Frontier, 1945-1951" and David Bercuson, "SAC vs. Sovereignty: The Origins of the Goose Bay Lease, 1946-1952," *Canadian Historical Review* 70, 2 (June 1989): 206-22.

40 Eayrs, *In Defence of Canada: Peacemaking and Deterrence,* 355.

41 This is not to suggest that Canadian officials always agreed with their US counterparts on the nature and severity of the Soviet threat. Indeed, as Chapter 2 demonstrates, officials in the Department of External Affairs struggled with this question, and their failure to adequately resolve it probably contributed to bureaucratic confusion/tension regarding the NORAD agreement. In brief, DEA officials feared a US-led anti-communist crusade as much as any aggression by the Soviet Union. See Don Page and Donald Munton, "Canadian Images of the Cold War, 1946-47," *International Journal* 32, 3 (1977): 577-604.

42 Perhaps the classic liberal argument of the Cold War is Arthur Schlesinger Jr., "Origins of the Cold War," *Foreign Affairs* 46, 1 (1967) 22-52.

43 Among revisionist works, see Christopher Lasch, "The Cold War, Revisited and Re-visioned," *New York Times Magazine,* 14 January 1968; and Wilfrid Knapp, "The Cold War Revised," *International Journal* 23, 3 (1968): 344-56.

44 Joseph Levitt, *Pearson and Canada's Role in Nuclear Disarmament and Arms Control Negotiations, 1945-1957* (Montreal: McGill-Queen's University Press, 1993), 12.

45 Ibid., 12.

46 John Lewis Gaddis, *The United States and the Origins of the Cold War, 1941-1947* (New York: Columbia University Press, 1972).

47 Leffler, *A Preponderance of Power,* 103.

48 The article was published under the pseudonym "x." See "The Sources of Soviet Conduct," *Foreign Affairs* 25, 4 (1947): 566-82.

49 Leffler, *A Preponderance of Power,* 108.

50 Gaddis, *Strategies of Containment: A Critical Appraisal of Postwar American National Security Policy* (New York: Oxford University Press, 1982), 19.

51 Ibid., 21.

52 According to Janice Gross Stein, Richard Ned Lebow, and Robert Jervis, challenges to deterrence often occur under such circumstances – that is, when the political dangers of inaction are believed to outweigh the possible consequences of any use of military force. See *Psychology and Deterrence* (Baltimore, MD: The Johns Hopkins University Press, 1985).

53 As cited in Leffler, *A Preponderance of Power,* 264.

54 Ibid., 264.

55 As cited in Samuel R. Williamson Jr. and Steven L. Rearden, *The Origins of US Nuclear Strategy, 1945-1953* (New York: St. Martin's Press, 1993), 135.

56 NSC-68, "United States Objectives and Programs for National Security," in *Foreign Relations of the United States (FRUS), 1950: National Security Affairs, Foreign Economic Policy,* vol. 1 (Washington, DC: US Government Printing Office, 1977), 237-8.

57 Leffler, *A Preponderance of Power,* 357. For interpretations of NSC-68, see Ernest R. May, ed., *American Cold War Strategy: Interpreting NSC 68* (New York: St. Martin's Press, 1993).

58 Holmes, *The Shaping of Peace,* 14.

59 Ibid., 14.

60 Ibid., 29.

61 One of the first studies to benefit from the release of previously classified documents on various aspects of US nuclear strategy was by David Alan Rosenberg. See "The Origins of Overkill: Nuclear Weapons and American Strategy, 1945-1960," *International Security* 7, 4 (1983): 3-71. The article was reprinted in *Strategy and Nuclear Deterrence,* ed. Steven E. Miller (Princeton, NJ: Princeton University Press, 1984). Also see Marc Trachtenberg, *History and Strategy,* particularly Chapter 3, "A 'Wasting Asset': American Strategy and the Shifting Nuclear Balance, 1949-1954" (Princeton, NJ: Princeton University Press, 1991).

62 Rosenberg in *Strategy and Nuclear Deterrence,* 124.

63 The term is used in ibid., 129.

64 Ibid., 124.

65 Rosenberg, "US Nuclear Stockpile, 1945 to 1950," *Bulletin of the Atomic Scientists* 38, 5 (1982), 26.

66 Williamson and Rearden, *The Origins of US Nuclear Strategy,* 170.

67 See Simon Duke, *US Defence Bases in the United Kingdom: A Matter for Joint Decision?* (New York: St. Martin's Press, 1987). For an overview of US strategy and interests in overseas bases, see James R. Blaker, *United States Overseas Basing: An Anatomy of the Dilemma* (New York: Praeger Publishers, 1990).

68 For a review of American strategic bombers, see Michael Brown, *Flying Blind: The Politics of the US Strategic Bomber Program* (Ithaca, NY: Cornell University Press, 1992).

69 Williamson and Rearden, *The Origins of US Nuclear Strategy,* 102. As these authors note, prior to the changes SAC was an "ill-equipped, ill-trained, and ill-organized operation, barely able to pose a credible threat to any would-be aggressor."

70 Lawrence Freedman, *The Evolution of Nuclear Strategy* (New York: Macmillan, 1981), 63.

71 As late as the summer of 1949 – just weeks before evidence of the Soviet nuclear test was uncovered – US intelligence was reporting that a Soviet bomb was still up to five years away. Indeed, President Truman's senior military advisor (and former director of the Manhattan Project), General Leslie Groves, believed that a Soviet bomb was at least ten years away, if one was even possible. For a discussion of the Soviet bomb project, see

David Holloway, *The Soviet Union and the Arms Race* (New Haven: Yale University Press, 1983).

72 Colin Gray, *Strategic Studies and Public Policy: The American Experience* (Lexington: University of Kentucky Press, 1983), 37.

73 Freedman, *The Evolution of Nuclear Strategy,* 63.

74 Among the advisors in favour of the "super," the most prominent were scientist Edward Teller; Lewis Strauss, the commissioner of the Atomic Energy Commission; and Dean Acheson, the Secretary of State. Among the group opposed were George Kennan, senior policy analyst at the State Department; Robert Oppenheimer, the scientific head of the Manhattan Project and the leader of the General Advisory Committee to the AEC; and David Lilienthal, former chairman of the AEC.

75 Freedman, *The Evolution of Nuclear Strategy,* 67. The issues that the hydrogen bomb raised have been reviewed in Herbert York, *Race to Oblivion: A Participant's View of the Arms Race* (New York: Simon and Schuster, 1970).

76 Levitt, *Pearson and Canada's Role in Nuclear Disarmament,* 27.

77 In December 1954, MC 48 was passed at a North Atlantic Treaty Organization ministerial meeting. The directive specifically recognized that tactical nuclear weapons would be required in Europe in the event of a Soviet ground attack. The directive (along with others of the period) is discussed in Chapter 5.

78 Levitt, *Pearson and Canada's Role in Nuclear Disarmament,* 30.

79 A few months after the end of the war three men were commissioned to examine the implications of the bomb for the future of the US Air Force: General Carl Spaatz, the Air Force Chief of Staff; Senator Hoyt Vandenberg; and Lauris Norstad, the Air Force Vice-Chief of Staff. For a discussion of their report, see Freedman, *The Evolution of Nuclear Strategy.*

80 This discussion is largely from Freedman, *The Evolution of Nuclear Strategy,* 50-1.

81 For example, the 1948 Air Force HARROW war plan contemplated dropping 50 bombs on 20 Soviet cities. By late 1949, Joint Emergency War Plan OFFTACKLE called for attacks on 104 urban targets with 220 atomic bombs, plus a force reserve of a further 72 weapons, an increase of more than 400 percent in just one year. By the following year, SAC's war plan called for the delivery of almost 300 nuclear weapons. See both Rosenberg in *Strategy and Nuclear Deterrence,* 126, and Williamson and Rearden, *The Origins of US Nuclear Strategy,* 165.

82 Freedman, *The Evolution of Nuclear Strategy,* 54.

83 Levitt, *Pearson and Canada's Role in Nuclear Disarmament,* 31.

84 Williamson and Rearden, *The Origins of US Nuclear Strategy,* 102.

85 See Freedman, *The Evolution of Nuclear Strategy,* 58-62.

86 As cited in Levitt, *Pearson and Canada's Role in Nuclear Disarmament,* 32.

87 Early Soviet thinking on nuclear weapons was discussed in a series of books by Raymond L. Garthoff. See *Soviet Strategy in the Nuclear Age* (New York: Praeger Publishers, 1959); *Soviet Military Doctrine* (New York: Free Press, 1953); and *Soviet Images of Future War* (Washington: Public Affairs Press, 1958).

Chapter 2: Canada's Air Defence Debate

1 "Soviet Intentions and Capabilities," 22 November 1949, National Archives of Canada (NAC), Record Group (RG) 2, vol. 2751, file 8.

2 As stated in "Notes for Chairman, Chiefs of Staff," 22 February 1951, NAC, Manuscript Group (MG) 32, B5, vol. 94 (records of Brooke Claxton).

3 "Anti-Aircraft Defence in Canada," 6 February 1952, NAC, RG 24, vol. 20,751, file 5:11:7, part 1.

4 "General Air Staff Requirement for Surface-to-Air Guided Missiles as Part of Canadian Air Defence System," 26 April 1954, NAC, RG 24, vol. 18,138, file 981-100, vol. 2.

5 At the 584th meeting of the Chiefs of Staff Committee (1 November 1955), Air Marshal C.R. Slemon, chief of the air staff, noted: "It seemed evident that the war-making capacity of this continent could not tolerate more than 50 successfully delivered thermo-nuclear bombs." Department of National Defence (DND), Directorate of History, Raymont Collection (hereinafter DHRC), File 73/1223.

6 "Aide Memoire for Minister of National Defence for Meeting of Cabinet Defence Committee," 14 August 1958, DHRC, file 73/1223, #11.

7 Joseph Jockel, *No Boundaries Upstairs: Canada, the United States, and the Origins of North American Air Defence, 1945-1958* (Vancouver: UBC Press, 1987).

8 "USAF-RCAF Plan for the Extension of the Presently Authorized Air Defence Radar Systems of the Continental United States and Canada," 8 February 1951, NAC, RG 24, vol. 20,790, file 6.5. It might be helpful if the key DND committees of the period were identified. The two most important were the Cabinet Defence Committee and the Chiefs of Staff Committee; the former made recommendations that went to full cabinet, while the latter discussed virtually all major issues of the day. Important secondary committees included the Canada-US Military Cooperation Committee; the Joint Planning Committee, whose members also served as the Canadian section of the MCC; the Joint Intelligence Committee, chaired by a representative of External Affairs; the Canadian Joint Staff; the Joint Ballistic Missile Defence Staff; the Defence Systems Analysis Group, a subcommittee of the Defence Research Board; and the Director of Military Operations and Plans (DMO&P). The defence liaison division of External Affairs also provided detailed analysis of many of the major issues facing DND. The division comprised one section that examined defence issues, and another that focused on matters of security and intelligence. The best departmental review of the committee structure appears in a 1979 DND report. See Colonel R.L. Raymont, "The Evolution of the Structure of the Department of National Defence, 1945-1968" (Report to the task force on Review of Unification of the Canadian Armed Forces), DH. Among published works, see Douglas Bland, *The Administration of Defence Policy in Canada, 1947 to 1985* (Kingston, ON: Ronald P. Frye, 1987).

9 Jockel's *No Boundaries Upstairs* reviews the array of air defence directives and procedures that took effect between 1950 and 1955. The two main ones were: (1) PJBD Recommendation 51/6, which stated that in an emergency both US Air Force and Royal Canadian Air Force air defence commanders had authority to order air re-enforcements to cross the border; and (2) Recommendation 53/1, which provided that either country's fighters could intercept a hostile aircraft over the other's territory when the latter was unable to do so.

10 See "Canada-US Air Defence Mutual Re-enforcement," 5 November 1951, NAC, RG 2, vol. 2751, vol. 10.

11 "The Summer Study on Air Defence at Project Lincoln," September 1952 (Operational Research Group Internal Memorandum No. 12), DHRC, file 73/1223, #101.

12 The idea of a DEW line was first proposed in the 1952 report of the Lincoln Summer Study Group, a US effort that called for two separate radar lines to be located in the Far North, at the seventieth and seventy-fifth parallels. The group included two Canadians, John Foster of McGill University and George Lindsey of the DRB.

13 "Defence in depth" involves constructing several different zones of conflict, each independent of the other and supplied with different weapons systems. Against a mass raid, each zone would attain some measure of attrition, the result being greater attrition than if there had been only one defence area.

14 "Command of Continental Defence Forces," 14 July 1954, DHRC, file 73/1223, #89.

15 The four proposals were: (1) the appointment of a supreme allied commander, Canada-US region; (2) the appointment of a commander-in-chief, Canada-US; (3) the appointment of a commander-in-chief, air defence, Canada-US, responsible to Canada-US Regional Planning Group; and (4) the appointment of a commander-in-chief, air defence, Canada-US, responsible to Canadian and US Chief of Staff Committees.

16 "Integration of Operational Control of the Continental Air Defences of Canada and the US in Peacetime," 22 October 1956, DH, file 79/24. This document was jointly prepared by a group of RCAF and USAF officers, and its findings were reported to the Canada-US Military Study Group.

17 "Integration of Operational Control of Canadian and Continental US Air Defence Operations in Peacetime," 23 July 1957, DHRC, file 73/1223, #84.

18 "Continental Radar Defence," 5 October 1953, DHRC, file 73/1223, #89.

19 This description is from John Hilliker and Donald Barry, *Canada's Department of External Affairs: Coming of Age, 1946-1968* (Montreal: McGill-Queen's University Press, 1995), 109.

20 In 1956, the Canadian-US Military Study Group created a binational ad hoc committee of air force officers to devise a joint command. The committee produced its report that December, and the document received MSG approval before year's end. See "The Eighth Report of the Canadian-US Military Study Group, 19 December 1956," DHRC, file 73/1223, #84.

21 Minutes of the 605th Chiefs of Staff Committee meeting, 15 February 1957, DHRC, file 73/1223.

22 NAC, MG 31, E83, vol. 9, file 8.6 (records of Basil Robinson).

23 Letter from Jules Léger to General Charles Foulkes, 10 September 1957, DHRC, file 73/1223, #85.

24 This was undoubtedly linked to the manner in which the original agreement was reached. The normal channel for getting such a proposal approved would have been through the Cabinet Defence Committee. That committee, however, had not been formed and the prime minister was not yet willing to establish it. Rather, acting as his own minister of External Affairs, John Diefenbaker decided, in consultation with Defence Minister George Pearkes and General Charles Foulkes, to approve the arrangement. For more, see Jockel, *No Boundaries Upstairs*, Chapter 5.

25 This letter was a response to one that Foulkes had written to acting undersecretary John Holmes earlier to defend DND's actions during the negotiations and particularly to dispute the assertion that DND had not adequately informed DEA of the status of the air defence negotiations. See "Integration of Operational Control of Canadian and United States Air Defence Forces," 7 August 1957, DHRC, file 73/1223, #85.

26 "NORAD – Political Control," DHRC, file 73/1223, #86.

27 It is difficult to determine what role this report played in the subsequent formation of the Canada-US Ministerial Committee on Joint Defence, the purpose of which was to ensure that there was an effective means of quick consultation between the two countries on defence problems of high political significance.

28 As detailed by Jockel, Prime Minister Diefenbaker decided in October 1957 that a more formal agreement was necessary. Over the next six months, discussions with the United States took place to turn the original agreement into an official diplomatic one. The new agreement was completed on 12 May 1958. For more, see Jockel, *No Boundaries Upstairs*, 106-17.

29 "Continental Air Defence – Foreign Policy Implications," DHRC, file 73/1223, #10.

30 Tom Keating and Larry Pratt, *Canada, NATO, and the Bomb: The Western Alliance in Crisis* (Edmonton: Hurtig Publishers, 1988), 63.

31 A 1952 memo from the defence liaison section to the undersecretary underlined this point. "On our part, I think we should recognize that certain other departments, notably National Defence and Finance, are not very concerned with protecting Canadian sovereignty or autonomy," the memo noted. "Some Observations on Our Defence Policy," 9 July 1952, NAC, RG 25, vol. 4542, file 50030-AG-1-40, part 5.

32 A.V. Roe Canada was formed in 1945, having purchased the Victory Aircraft company that produced Lancaster bombers during the war. The following year, the company acquired Turbo-Research Limited, which was conducting research on jet engines. In 1954, the company was split into separate airframe and engine companies, renamed Avro Aircraft and Orenda Engines. The company continued expanding, and by 1956 it had also acquired Canadian Steel Improvements and the Canadian Car and Foundry to ensure a sufficient supply of advanced composite materials required for aircraft production.

33 According to the original submission to the Cabinet Defence Committee on the CF-105, the required performance characteristics of the new plane were stated as: a radius of action of 300 nautical miles (including a supersonic combat radius of 200 nautical miles); a combat ceiling of 18,000 metres; a maximum speed of Mach 2; a rate of climb of six minutes to 15,000 metres; a manoeuvrability of two G at Mach 1.5 at 15,000 metres without loss of speed or altitude; twin-engined; and designed for a crew of two. These specifications were considerably more demanding than comparable American aircraft of the time (i.e., the "century" series: the F-101, F-102, and F-106). See "Supersonic All-Weather Interceptor

Aircraft – CF 105 for the RCAF," 30 November 1953, NAC, Cabinet Defence Committee Document No. 49-53, RG 24, vol. 20,711, file 2:3:7, part 5. These requirements would later become RCAF specification Air 7-4.

34 With regard to the engines, Orenda had begun design work on an advanced turbine in 1954, and within a year the test results convinced DND that it would be both more powerful and economical than comparable American engines. Concerning the fire-control and weapons systems, the RCAF's very demanding requirements as well as difficulties with American manufacturers resulted in the decisions to pursue both of these projects in Canada.

35 "Reappraisal of the CF-105 Development Programme" (Appendix A – Plans and Analysis and Requirements Group), 4 November 1955, DH, File 112.3M2.009 (D180).

36 A 1953 External Affairs study had noted that "it may be very difficult indeed for the Canadian government to reject any major defence proposals which the United States Government presents with conviction as essential for the security of North America." Cited in D.W. Middlemiss and J.J. Sokolsky, *Canadian Defence: Decisions and Determinants* (Toronto: Harcourt Brace Jovanovich, 1989), 21.

37 "Report on the Development of the CF-105 Aircraft and Associated Weapon System, 1952-1958," 19 August 1958, DHRC, file 73/1223, #632.

38 American ground-to-air missiles including the Hawk and Bomarc, while not yet operational, were already attracting attention for their performance potential. The Bomarc in particular was being touted, as early as 1955, as the air defence weapon of the future, a system that could purportedly do much the same task as an aircraft but at a cheaper cost and with less risk.

39 Minutes of the 574th Chiefs of Staff Committee meeting, 11 February 1955, DHRC, file 73/1223.

40 Minutes of the 584th Chiefs of Staff Committee meeting, 1 November 1955, DHRC, file 73/1223.

41 "Review of Air Defence," 14 October 1958, prepared by D. Arty in conjunction with DMO&P and the Canadian Army Operational Research Establishment, DH, file 121.1.003 (D14).

42 At the 623rd meeting of the Chiefs of Staff Committee on 10 June 1958, O.M. Solandt, chairman of the DRB, proposed a northward extension of the Canadian air defence system. The plan involved moving certain radars farther north and repositioning air bases and proposed locations of Bomarc missiles sites. According to a DRB memo prepared on 3 July 1958, it was the board's opinion that the current concept of air defence would result in much of the air battle occurring above or near major Canadian population centres. The RCAF responded that not only was the proposal impractical and expensive, but if carried out it would result in a "disconnected" air defence system. See "Review of the DRB Proposal for Northern Extension of the Air Defence Combat Zone," 3 July 1958, DHRC, file 73/1223, #10; and "DRB Proposals for Northward Extension of the Air Defence System" (prepared by Air Marshal Hugh Campbell), DH, file 73/1223, #10.

43 This charge would attract widespread attention in the early to mid-1960s, but the first allegations were made at this time. See, for example, Logan Maclean, "RCAF Takes Orders from a US General to Defend Continent," *Saturday Night,* 14 September 1957. The book that popularized this charge was James Minifie's *Peacemaker or Powder-Monkey? Canada's Role in a Revolutionary World* (Toronto: McClelland and Stewart, 1960).

44 "Future Canadian Air Defence Policy," DH, file 112.1.003 (D14).

45 "Memorandum," 21 August 1958, DHRC, file 73/1223, #11.

46 "Advantages and Disadvantages of Continuing Production of the CF105," 22 August 1958, DHRC, file 73/1223, #11.

47 See "Soviet capabilities and probable courses of action against North America in a major war commencing during the period 1 July 1958 to 30 June 1959," (ACAI [Agreed Canadian-American Intelligence] 46, dated 22 January 1958), National Archives and Records Administration (US), RG 218, Joint Chiefs of Staff files, 1958, box 37, file 334, JIC part 4.

48 DHRC, file 73/1223, #632.

49 The variance between US and Canadian intelligence was reviewed and questioned in "Intelligence Schism," *Aviation Week,* 2 March 1959. The article suggested that the Canadian

conclusion was puzzling, as much of the information on Soviet bomber deployments had originally been supplied by Washington.

50 Minutes of the 120th Cabinet Defence Committee meeting, 14 August 1958, DHRC, file 73/1223.

51 "Record of Cabinet Defence Committee Decision," 21 August 1958, DHRC, file 73/1223.

52 At the time of the cancellation, virtually the whole of Avro's workforce was engaged in the Arrow program. There were, in fact, only two other contracts that the company had in place in February 1959 – the maintenance of the CF-100 and a second contract from the USAF for design work on a circular wing air-cushion vehicle. This "flying saucer" (as it was dubbed) was essentially a test bed for the demonstration of vertical takeoff principles. The project, like the Arrow, was extraordinarily ambitious, and was ultimately cancelled in 1961 out of concern that the design was not technically sound. For a recent look at the project, which was dubbed the Avrocar, see Bill Zuk, *Avrocar: Canada's Flying Saucer: The Story of Avro Canada's Secret Projects* (Erin, ON: The Boston Mills Press, 2001).

53 By the time of cancellation, the Arrow flight test program was well under way. Powered with the American J-75 engines (which produced one-third less thrust than the Canadian-made Iroquois), the Arrow had reached a speed of Mach 1.98 and an altitude of 17,000 metres – it thus had largely met the original RCAF specifications. However, these results had been achieved with the Mark I design, and it was anticipated that Arrow 206 (the first to be powered by the Iroquois) would reach a top speed of Mach 2.5 and a maximum altitude of 22,500 metres. Both would have been records for aircraft of the day.

54 In this regard, Canadian defence officials undoubtedly followed the testing and development of the American B-70 bomber with considerable interest. The B-70 incorporated the high-speed and high-altitude performance of an interceptor with the long-range capabilities of intercontinental bombers. While ultimately cancelled by US Secretary of Defense Robert McNamara in 1961, the aircraft promised a revolutionary increase in performance and capability. See Michael E. Brown, *Flying Blind: The Politics of the U.S. Strategic Bomber Program* (Ithaca, NY: Cornell University Press, 1992).

55 This is one of the themes in the Arrow literature. Essentially, the problem manifested itself in the aircraft's component projects. Avro designed and developed both the airframe and the engine, but was planning to purchase the armament suite from an American manufacturer. In contrast, the RCAF, desiring that Canada develop expertise in electronic and guidance capabilities, insisted that the fire-control system and weapons package also be developed in Canada. Further, the two argued over the plane's range and performance requirements, and the bickering led to a strained relationship. See Peter Zuuring, *The Arrow Scrapbook* (Toronto: Avro Alliance Press, 1999).

56 The published accounts of the Arrow contain so much misinformation and half-truths that this point is not well known. American support took two primary forms: (1) the Arrow was dependent on a large number of parts manufactured in the United States; and (2) the United States loaned the RCAF a B-47 bomber to conduct engine testing, as Canada did not have proper ground-based facilities to conduct such experiments. While the United States certainly doubted (with good reason) Canada's ability to finance the Arrow, and had indicated on several occasions that it was not interested in purchasing the aircraft for American use, the United States did not necessarily oppose the program. Indeed, it might also be noted that in late 1958 and early 1959, the United States considered purchasing completed Arrows as aid for Canada.

57 This argument has been made most prominently by E.K. Shaw, *There Never Was an Arrow* (Ottawa: Steel Rail Educational Publishing, 1981); J. Dow, *The Arrow* (Toronto: James Lorimer, 1979); and Palmiro Campagna, *Storms of Controversy: The Secret Avro Arrow Files Revealed* (Toronto: Stoddart, 1992). Even contemporary historical works continue to make this argument. In *Rogue Tory: The Life and Legend of John G. Diefenbaker* (Toronto: Macfarlane, Walter and Ross, 1995), author Denis Smith concludes that the Arrow decision was "encouraged, welcomed, and effectively dictated by the Pentagon." Despite such assertions, no observer has yet produced credible documentation that supports this contention.

58 "Future Canadian Air Defence Policy," 27 October 1958, DH, file 112.1.003 (D14).

59 While US strategic superiority was clear, decision makers never believed that such superiority gave the United States any demonstrable military advantage. Several congressional committees, including Project East River and the Lincoln Summer Study Group, had recognized the enormous power of the Soviet nuclear force, and the message had apparently been received. See Andreas Wenger, *Living with Peril: Eisenhower, Kennedy, and Nuclear Weapons* (New York: Rowman and Littlefield, 1997); and Peter Roman, *Eisenhower and the Missile Gap* (Ithaca, NY: Cornell University Press, 1995).

60 See "A Balanced Air Defence Policy for Canada," 29 October 1958, NAC, RG 24, Access 1983-84/167, vol. 7586, DRBS 9720-43, part 1.

61 DHRC, file 73/1223, #14.

62 In 1958, the United States proposed a ballistic missile early warning system (BMEWS), which was intended to detect and track an intercontinental ballistic missile (ICBM) attack. Three BMEWS stations were ultimately built in the early 1960s – in Alaska, Greenland, and Northern England. Canada's participation in the program was limited to the provision of communications support.

63 It should be noted that despite the creation of a continental air defence command, the United States never believed that the system would prove very effective in the event of a Soviet attack. As a result, and to minimize the damage that the US strategic force would suffer in a Soviet first strike, the US Strategic Air Command: (1) implemented a system whereby it maintained bombers in the air round the clock; and (2) developed a war plan based on "launch-on-warning," whereby confirmation of a Soviet strike was *not* required in order to launch a retaliatory blow. For a discussion of these (and related) issues, see Lawrence Freedman, *The Evolution of Nuclear Strategy* (London: Macmillan, 1981); Gregg Herken, *Counsels of War* (New York: Alfred A. Knopf, 1985); and Wenger, *Living with Peril*.

Chapter 3: Canadian Views on Nuclear Weapons and Related Issues of Strategy

1 An earlier version of this chapter was published in the Summer 2000 issue of *International Journal* 55, 3. See "'Strategic Theoretical Parasitism' Reconsidered: Canadian Thinking on Nuclear Weapons and Strategy, 1950-1963," 401-26. For a review of the "golden age" of nuclear strategy, see Colin Gray, *Strategic Studies and Public Policy: The American Experience* (Lexington: University of Kentucky Press, 1982) and Ken Booth, "The Evolution of Strategic Thinking," in John Baylis, Ken Booth, John Garnett, and Phil Williams, *Contemporary Strategy: Theories and Policies* (New York: Holmes and Meier, 1975).

2 This is not to suggest that Canada had no civilian defence community in the 1950s, but rather that "membership" in it was quite limited. Members included scholars James Eayrs, Peyton Lyon, Robert Reford, and Richard Preston; journalists Blair Fraser, James Minifie, and Peter C. Newman; and former Department of National Defence officials John Gellner, W.H.S. Macklin, and Guy Simonds. Not only was this community small, but it also appeared largely content to offer general comments on contemporary policy issues, and did not drive the theoretical/conceptual debate of the day.

3 The influx of American civilian strategists into a domain that had previously been the preserve of the military might have been the biggest single change in postwar strategic thought. An array of defence "think-tanks" quickly sprouted, led by the RAND Corporation, an independent research institution that began operations in 1949. The study that best examines this development is Fred Kaplan, *The Wizards of Armageddon* (New York: Simon and Schuster, 1983).

4 The primary objective of the Defence Research Board, formed in 1947, was to advance Canadian scientific knowledge and analytical capability for defence. The board was dissolved in 1974. The best review remains D.J. Goodspeed, *A History of the Defence Research Board of Canada* (Ottawa: Queen's Printer, 1958).

5 The report was prepared by the scientific intelligence division of the DRB, and was dated September 1951. National Archives of Canada (NAC), Record Group (RG) 24, vol. 4221, file 69-301, part 2.

6 NAC, RG 25, vol. 4758, file 50069-C-40, part 1. The telegram was addressed to the secretary of state for external affairs, and was dated 4 December 1950.

7   In a 30 November news conference, President Truman warned that the United States "will take whatever steps are necessary to meet the military situation." When pressed by reporters on whether that could include nuclear weapons, Truman responded that "there has always been active consideration of [their] use ... It is one of our weapons." As cited in Richard Betts, *Nuclear Blackmail and Nuclear Balance* (Washington: Brookings Institution, 1987), 33.

8   Tom Keating and Larry Pratt, *Canada, NATO, and the Bomb: The Western Alliance in Crisis* (Edmonton: Hurtig Publishers, 1988), 92.

9   "Science and Future Warfare," DND, Directorate of History (DH), file 81/674, vol. 1.

10 "The Strategic Concept of the Nuclear Deterrent," 26 March 1955, RG 25, vol. 4541, file 50030-1-40, part 2.

11 "Future Canadian Defence Policy," 14 July 1955, DH, file 112.3M2.009 (D 147).

12 In a memo dated October 1953, Foulkes noted that "if the Soviet Union was successful in carrying out a surprise raid on all SAC bases and catching the aircraft on the ground, the retaliatory power of the US might be seriously reduced." See "Reassessment of the Risk," DH, Raymont Collection (hereinafter DHRC), file 73/1223, #89.

13 The plan envisaged flying SAC units with their equipment from their bases in the United States to those overseas, and then conducting repeated strike missions from those bases. It was estimated that SAC would need approximately seven to ten days to get the bases operational and perform the mission. For more on the "mobility plan," see Samuel R. Williamson Jr. and Steven L. Rearden, *The Origins of US Nuclear Strategy, 1945-1953* (New York: St. Martin's Press, 1993).

14 In 1962, Sutherland published an article that established his reputation in the field. See "Canada's Long Term Strategic Situation," *International Journal* 17, 3 (1962): 199-223. For reviews of Sutherland's work, see James Lee and David Bellamy, "Dr. R.J. Sutherland: A Retrospect," *Canadian Defence Quarterly* 17, 1 (1987): 41-6; and Andrew Richter, "The Sutherland Papers: A Glimpse into the Thinking of Canada's Preeminent Strategist," *Canadian Defence Quarterly* 27, 1 (1997): 28-33.

15 Among the responsibilities of the JBMDS, its original 1959 terms of reference emphasized both the offensive and defensive potential of ballistic missiles. By 1960, changes in technology necessitated changes to the JBMDS, and the group became responsible to the Chiefs of Staff to examine the defence and security implications of both space developments and satellite systems. In 1962, further changes in the defence environment resulted in the need for an entirely new agency, one not limited in outlook to aspects of military technology. This new agency was termed the Directorate of Strategic Studies, which adopted the JBMDS staff. During the course of the JBMDS's existence, the staff published more than sixty reports, studies, and briefs. See "Papers Prepared by the JBMDS," 31 March 1961, DHRC, file 73/1223, #431.

16 "The Effect of the Ballistic Missile upon the Prevention of Surprise Attack," 23 February 1960, prepared by the JBMDS, NAC, General Burns Papers, Manuscript Group (MG) 31, G6, vol. 14; "A Military View of Nuclear Weapons," 28 February 1961, NAC, RG 24, Access 1983-84/167, box 7373, DRBS 170-80/J56, vol. 3; "Strategic Considerations Affecting Ballistic Missile Defence" [probably written in 1962], DH, Sutherland Papers (hereinafter DHSP), file 87/253; "Trends in Strategic Weapons and Concepts" 11 March 1963, DHSP, file 87/253.

17 Countercity targeting refers to a strategy in which the opponent's cities are the principal targets of a nuclear attack, while counterforce emphasizes specific political and military targets, such as missile silos and government buildings. The strategist who first coined the terms was Bernard Brodie.

18 For an overview of Larnder's career, see Ronald G. Stansfield, "Harold Larnder: Founder of Operational Research," *Journal of the Operational Research Society* 34, 1 (1983).

19 "Active Defence for North America," 16 October 1959, NAC, RG 24, vol. 21,754, file 2184.4.D, part 1.

20 Colin Gray and David Alan Rosenberg have examined this question in detail. See Gray, *Strategic Studies and Public Policy*; Rosenberg, "The Origins of Overkill: Nuclear Weapons and American Strategy, 1945-1960," *International Security* 7, 4 (1983): 3-71; and Rosenberg,

"Reality and Responsibility: Power and Process in the Making of United States Nuclear Strategy, 1945-1968," *Journal of Strategic Studies* 9, 1 (1986): 35-52. In the former article, Rosenberg concluded that US nuclear policy of the 1950s and 1960s, in contrast to the coolly rational thinking of the strategists, tended to be "bureaucratic, pragmatic, and often inarticulate." While acknowledging that the conceptual work of the civilian strategists "was important in shaping public perceptions," and that strategists "occasionally influenced the thinking of high policymakers," they generally "had little relevance" among operational planners. The gap between the civilian strategists and policy makers is a focus of Rosenberg's work, but the major studies by Kaplan (*The Wizards of Armageddon*) and Gregg Herken (*Counsels of War* [New York: Alfred A. Knopf, 1985]) paid little attention to this question, and stressed the works of the former group over the latter.

21 Kaplan, *The Wizards of Armageddon*; Herken, *Counsels of War*; and Lawrence Freedman, *The Evolution of Nuclear Strategy* (London: Macmillan, 1981).

22 The origins of the directive have been examined by Ernest R. May, ed., *American Cold War Strategy: Interpreting NSC 68* (Boston: St. Martin's Press, 1993).

23 This document is cited in Marc Trachtenberg, *History and Strategy* (Princeton, NJ: Princeton University Press, 1991), 108.

24 Gray, *Strategic Studies and Public Policy*, 38.

25 Early 1950s American war plans were largely based on a Second World War "city busting" model, but with nuclear weapons doing the damage. In effect, the wartime success of the American air power strategy was simply reformulated to be used against the Soviet Union. Plans specified that up to 1,000 nuclear weapons would be dropped over the Soviet Union *on the first day of fighting*. For a review of US war plans from the period, see Rosenberg, "The Origins of Overkill."

26 National Archives and Records Administration (NARA), US, RG 218, Records of the Joint Chiefs of Staff, Admiral Radford's files, 1953-1957, box 36, file 381 (continental defence).

27 As cited in Freedman, *The Evolution of Nuclear Strategy*, 85.

28 Ibid., 86.

29 As cited in Scott D. Sagan, *Moving Targets: Nuclear Strategy and National Security* (Princeton, NJ: Princeton University Press, 1989), 23.

30 For a recent review of massive retaliation, see Saki Dockrill, *Eisenhower's New-Look National Security Policy, 1953-1961* (London: Macmillan, 1996). Readers should note that criticism of Dulles's original speech led the secretary to issue a "clarifying" article in April 1954. See "Policy for Security and Peace," *Foreign Affairs* 32, 3 (1954): 353-64. In the article, Dulles acknowledged that "massive atomic and thermonuclear [retaliation] is not the kind of power which could most usefully be evoked under all circumstances." Dulles wrote that while the nuclear option would always be available to the United States, it was just one of many that could be used in response to aggression.

31 Bernard Brodie, ed., *The Absolute Weapon: Atomic Power and World Order* (New York: Harcourt Brace, 1946).

32 Bernard Brodie, "Unlimited Weapons and Limited War," *Reporter* 11, 9 (1954): 16-21.

33 See Barry Steiner, *Bernard Brodie and the Foundations of American Nuclear Strategy* (Lawrence: University of Kansas Press, 1991), 118. Brodie further wrote, "I can think of no greater service the Congress could do than to provoke through the right kinds of questions basic thinking about two-way rather than merely one-way nuclear capabilities."

34 Bernard Brodie, "Strategy Hits a Dead End," *Harper's* 211 (October 1955): 33-7.

35 Brodie's isolation is illustrated by the fact that when several RAND analysts were hired to work in Washington as part of Robert McNamara's team of "whiz kids," Brodie was left behind. As Fred Kaplan has noted, "in 1961, Brodie, unlike his friends and colleagues who had soared off to Washington, was offered no official position, nor even asked for his advice. He felt shunned, humiliated." Kaplan, *The Wizards of Armageddon*, 339.

36 Kaplan has noted with respect to Brodie's thinking on nuclear weapons that "in most quarters, Brodie and his reports were scorned," and that Brodie was widely considered a "pariah" by his colleagues. See ibid., 48. It might be noted that while massive retaliation was extensively criticized by American civilian strategists, few of the critiques focused on the idea of mutual vulnerability. There were also charges that massive retaliation was out

of character for the United States, that it would promote the erosion of the Western alliance, and that it falsely offered a technological solution to complex political, economic, and strategic problems. For a discussion, see Gray, *Strategic Studies and Public Policy*, 49-58.

37 Following the departure of several of his RAND colleagues to Washington, Brodie became a fierce critic of the "scientific" approach and systems analysis in general. He claimed that those who used it had "no basis in their training for claiming special political insight of any kind," and that such observers seemed to have a "trained incapacity for giving due weight to social and political imponderables." Quotation from Michael Howard, "Brodie, Wohlstetter and American Nuclear Strategy," *Survival* 34, 2 (1992), 109. Brodie's disapproval of his former colleagues was most apparent in his final book, *War and Politics* (New York: Macmillan, 1973), by which time he had become a vociferous critic of the very profession he had founded.

38 Trachtenberg, *History and Strategy*, 18.

39 SAC Commander General Curtis LeMay was both highly critical and suspicious of studies that examined SAC vulnerability. As Kaplan has noted, LeMay made no secret of the fact that in a serious crisis, he intended to give the attack order to the forces under his command *with or without* formal political approval from Washington. Indeed, LeMay is quoted as saying in 1957: "if I see that the Russians are amassing their planes for an attack, I'm going to knock the shit out of them before they take off the ground." Kaplan, *The Wizards of Armageddon*, 134. The larger question of whether the United States would use its nuclear forces in a preemptive strike against the Soviets reveals a fault line in American strategic thought. While military planners recognized the importance of striking first (hence LeMay's statement), they were also obviously aware of the American pledge not to be first to use military force vis-à-vis the Soviet Union. Thus, over time a compromise position evolved whereby the United States would attack first, but only if it had become convinced that the Soviet Union was preparing to strike. This strategy was effectively confirmed in the 1959 Joint Strategic Objectives Plan, which noted that "US national policy precludes the concept of preventive war or acts intended to provoke war. However, in recognition of the clear differentiation between preventive war and the exercise of the initiative, US forces may be required to take the initiative if so directed by the President in response to knowledge that a Soviet attack against the United States is imminent." Report cited in Scott D. Sagan, "SIOP-62: The Nuclear War Plan Briefing to President Kennedy," *International Security* 12, 1 (1987): 30. Emphasizing the importance of seizing the initiative, President Eisenhower told SAC in 1957 that "we must not allow the enemy to strike the first blow." Quotation from Sagan, *Moving Targets*, 22. For a discussion of the American debate on preventative war, see Trachtenberg, *History and Strategy* and Rosenberg, "The Origins of Overkill."

40 In the early 1950s, the most critical foreign bases were in Canada, Japan, and Britain. By the middle of the decade, SAC bases in the Middle East, North Africa, and Asia had been added. See James R. Blaker, *United States Overseas Basing: An Anatomy of the Dilemma* (New York: Praeger, 1990).

41 Albert Wohlstetter, Fred Hoffman, Robert Lutz, and Henry Rowan, *Selection and Use of Strategic Air Bases* (Santa Monica: RAND Corporation, R-266, 1954).

42 "NSC Briefing on the Vulnerability of SAC," NARA, RG 218, Admiral Radford Papers, 1953-1957, Box 37, file 381.

43 See "NSC Briefing on the Vulnerability of SAC," NARA, RG 218, Radford Papers, 1953-1957, Box 36, file 381.

44 Kaplan, *The Wizards of Armageddon*, 109.

45 Kaplan's assessment of the Brodie-Wohlstetter feud is revealing. As he wrote, "Brodie saw the Wohlstetter style of strategic thought gradually displacing his own preeminent position in the field. The Brodie-Wohlstetter falling-out symbolized the clash between the old and the new – Wohlstetter the mathematical logician versus Brodie the scholar of philosophy and international relations, rigor versus soft-headedness in Wohlstetter's eyes, apolitical scholasticism versus a keen historical sense in Brodie's. As Wohlstetter's star began to shine ... the general image of nuclear strategy changed, and Brodie's own light dimmed." See *The Wizards of Armageddon*, 338-9.

46 Wohlstetter, "The Delicate Balance of Terror," *Foreign Affairs* 37, 2 (1959): 211-34.
47 A Cabinet Defence Committee meeting on 3 November 1953 (one month after Foulkes's memo) formally recognized the possibility of SAC vulnerability. At the meeting, Foulkes discussed how recent Soviet military advances meant that "North America, and particularly the Strategic Air Command bases and atomic energy facilities, [had become] increasingly attractive targets." DHRC, file 73/1223.
48 James Eayrs, *In Defence of Canada: Peacemaking and Deterrence* (Toronto: University of Toronto Press 1972), 74.
49 "Initial Survey of the Ballistic Missile Defence Problem," NAC, RG 24, vol. 21,752, file 2180.2, part 1.
50 Lawrence Freedman, "The First Two Generations of Nuclear Strategists," in *Makers of Modern Strategy: From Machiavelli to the Nuclear Age,* ed. Peter Paret (Princeton, NJ: Princeton University Press 1986), 754.
51 Ibid., 757.
52 In fact, it was not McNamara but strategist Donald Brennan who first coined the acronym "MAD." A staunch critic of McNamara and American defence policy under President Johnson, Brennan argued that the government "evidently preferred dead Russians to live Americans." See Donald Brennan, "Symposium on the SALT Agreements," *Survival* (September/October 1972). For more, see Herken, *Counsels of War,* 248.
53 Freedman, "The First Two Generations of Nuclear Strategists," 758. This point has been developed at length by Robert Jervis. See *The Meaning of the Nuclear Revolution: Statecraft and the Prospect of Armageddon* (Ithaca, NY: Cornell University Press, 1989), Chapter 3.
54 Richard Betts's assessment of this change is worth noting. He has written that "American leaders came to endorse nuclear parity, but with an embrace that for most was initially grudging ... They let go of superiority less because it appeared to lack value, than because there seemed no way to hold on to it." See *Nuclear Blackmail and Nuclear Balance,* 182-3.
55 As cited in Sagan, *Moving Targets,* 32. McNamara spent much of his remaining term as defense secretary (a position he held until 1968) ensuring that US strategic forces steadily increased, but that this expansion was constrained by both strategic and financial considerations. Thus, costly air force programs such as the B-58 and B-70 bombers were curtailed and/or cancelled, as were a variety of missile projects (including the Skybolt, Jupiter, and Hound Dog), while the navy's Polaris submarine program was accelerated. For a discussion, see Kaplan, *The Wizards of Armageddon.*
56 Brodie noted that deterrence "must involve a power which guarantees not only vast losses but also utter defeat." Brodie, *Strategy in the Missile Age* (Princeton, NJ: Princeton University Press, 1959), 276.
57 Trachtenberg, *History and Strategy,* 25. A book by Glenn Snyder examined strategic stability in detail. See *Deterrence and Defense: Toward a Theory of National Security* (Princeton, NJ: Princeton University Press, 1961). Snyder wrote that "stability ... is a function of two factors: the extent to which either side's strike-back capability exceeds the necessary minimum, and the attacker-to-target ratio" (98).
58 Thomas C. Schelling, *The Strategy of Conflict* (New York: Oxford University Press, 1960), Chapter 6.
59 Speech as cited in Freedman, *The Evolution of Nuclear Strategy,* 235.
60 Ibid., 235.
61 Sagan, *Moving Targets,* 30.
62 Critics noted that a strategy focusing on military targets would be effective only if such targets were attacked first; that is, a counterforce strategy was, by definition, a first-strike strategy. In addition, to be effective the strategy was dependent on mutual agreement with the Soviets that certain "ground rules" would be respected in a nuclear exchange, a possibility that Soviet strategists quickly dismissed. For a review of McNamara's speech and the reaction it generated, see Andreas Wenger, *Living with Peril: Eisenhower, Kennedy, and Nuclear Weapons* (New York: Rowman and Littlefield, 1997).
63 See, for example, "Future Canadian Air Defence Policy," 27 October 27, 1958, DH, file 112.1.003 (D14); and "Some Considerations Affecting Air Defence Policy," February 1959, DHRC, file 73/1223, #14.

64 In *The Strategy of Conflict,* Schelling starts with the assumption of rationality, but recognizes that departures from rationality can sometimes be more of a help than a hindrance in a bargaining relationship. It is important to note, however, that Schelling's discussion is limited to various abstract and theoretical scenarios of rationality (several of which involve the "emotionally unbalanced"), and does *not* make the leap into the US-Soviet nuclear relationship. Thus, Sutherland's writings attempted to utilize Schelling's conceptual premise to more specifically explain the superpower deterrent relationship. See *The Strategy of Conflict,* 16-18.

65 The notion of limited war entered mainstream strategic thought in the mid-1950s following academic dissatisfaction with the American strategy of massive retaliation. Essentially, limited war strategies would take advantage of US strategic superiority by carefully controlling the Soviet targets to be attacked in the event of war. The intent was to ensure that if hostilities began, all-out devastation could be avoided. One of the first major studies was by Robert Osgood, *Limited War: The Challenge to American Strategy* (Chicago: University of Chicago Press, 1957).

66 Brodie was listed as one of nine "makers" of nuclear strategy in a 1991 book. See John Baylis and John Garnett, eds., *Makers of Nuclear Strategy* (London: Pinter Publishers, 1991). Brodie himself examined the influence that civilian strategists had had on US defence policy in Chapter 10 of *War and Politics.*

Chapter 4: The Canadian Debate on the Acquisition of Nuclear Weapons

1 None of the major works in Canadian security has focused on how the Department of National Defence approached the acquisition of nuclear weapons, although some general comments have been offered. See, in particular, Jon B. McLin, *Canada's Changing Defence Policy, 1957-1963: The Problems of a Middle Power in Alliance* (Baltimore, MD: Johns Hopkins Press, 1967) and Peyton Lyon, "Defence: To Be or Not to Be Nuclear?" in *Canada in World Affairs, 1961-1963* (Toronto: Oxford University Press, 1968). In contrast, there are several accounts of how the Department of External Affairs approached the issue, including J.L. Granatstein, *A Man of Influence: Norman A. Robertson and Canadian Statecraft, 1929-1968* (Toronto: Deneau, 1981); Granatstein, *Canada 1957-1967: The Years of Uncertainty and Innovation* (Toronto: McClelland and Stewart, 1986); and Albert Legault and Michel Fortmann, *A Diplomacy of Hope: Canada and Disarmament, 1945-1988* (Montreal: McGill-Queen's University Press, 1992). Also see Donald Munton, "Going Fission: Tales and Truths about Canada's Nuclear Weapons," *International Journal* 51, 3 (1996): 506-28; and Howard Lentner, "Foreign Policy Decision Making: The Case of Canada and Nuclear Weapons," *World Politics* 29, 1 (1976): 29-66. Two recent books by John Clearwater, *Canadian Nuclear Weapons: The Untold Story of Canada's Cold War Arsenal* (Toronto: Dundurn Press, 1998) and *U.S. Nuclear Weapons in Canada* (Toronto: The Dundurn Group, 1999), while welcome additions to the literature, largely review the technical characteristics associated with nuclear weapons storage and placement in Canada.

2 These directives have been examined in Ian Clark and Nicholas Wheeler, *The British Origins of Nuclear Strategy, 1945-1955* (Oxford: Clarendon Press, 1989).

3 See David J. Bercuson, "SAC vs. Sovereignty: The Origins of the Goose Bay Lease, 1946-1952," *Canadian Historical Review* 72, 2 (June 1989): 206-22. Among departmental documentation, see "A Brief on the RCAF's Position and Responsibilities at Goose Bay," DND, Directorate of History (DH), September 1960, file 88/46.

4 The Cabinet Defence Committee considered defence questions and reported to the full cabinet on major matters of policy relating to the maintenance and employment of the armed services. The Chiefs of Staff Committee advised the minister of national defence and the CDC on matters of defence policy and prepared strategic appreciations and military plans as required. For a discussion on both committees and the evolution of their roles, see Douglas Bland, *The Administration of Defence Policy in Canada, 1947 to 1985* (Kingston, ON: Ronald P. Frye, 1987). It should be noted that, while a few departmental reports from this period are reviewed in this chapter, the general failure of both DND and DEA to examine nuclear weapons acquisition makes such a review difficult.

5 National Archives of Canada (NAC), "Implications of MC 48," 15 July 1955, Record Group (RG) 25, vol. 4541, file 50030-AG-1-40, part 2.

6 The Lisbon meeting of the North Atlantic Council in February 1952 resulted in the establishment of new force-level goals for NATO. The program aimed at increasing NATO's strength from the then-current level of 34 divisions and 2,900 aircraft to 96 divisions and almost 10,000 aircraft within two years. For a discussion, see Samuel R. Williamson Jr. and Steven L. Rearden, *The Origins of US Nuclear Strategy, 1945-1953* (New York: St. Martin's Press, 1993), 174-7.

7 DH, Raymont Collection (hereinafter DHRC), file 73/1223.

8 Ibid.

9 Under the 1946 Atomic Energy Act (the McMahon Act), the United States was prohibited from sharing nuclear-related information with other countries. The act was revised in 1954, and the limited sharing of information on weight, size, yield, and effects of nuclear weapons was permitted.

10 The first request to store American nuclear weapons at Goose Bay was received in 1950, when the US Air Force sought permission to move one bomber group there. By the following year, the USAF had embarked on ordnance-storage, warehousing, and troop-housing construction at the base. However, for half a century it remained unclear whether the United States actually stored nuclear weapons in the absence of formal Canadian approval. Given that the base was US-operated and -run, it had long been considered possible (perhaps even probable) that American weapons had been stored without the Canadian government being so informed. However, a recent article in the *Bulletin of the Atomic Scientists* has ended the uncertainty. The story reveals that nuclear weapons were stored at Goose Bay in the summer of 1950, although "very few members of the Canadian government" were aware of the "arrangement." See Robert S. Norris, William M. Arkin, and William Burr, "Where They Were," *Bulletin of the Atomic Scientists* 55, 6 (1999): 26-35. Clearwater has reached much the same conclusion in *U.S. Nuclear Weapons in Canada*.

11 DHRC, file 73/1223.

12 Ibid.

13 Canada's European Air Division consisted of twelve squadrons of F-86s and CF-100s. The air defence role that the division performed was important, but territorial issues (mainly connected with French opposition to NATO military integration) made the role increasingly difficult. See Mclin, *Canada's Changing Defence Policy*, 114-16; and Marilyn Eustace, *Canada's European Force, 1964-1971: Canada's Commitment to Europe* (Kingston, ON: Centre for International Relations, Queen's University, 1982).

14 In testimony before the House of Commons Special Committee on Defence in 1963, General Foulkes indicated that NATO had first recommended that Canada accept the strike role in 1956. He stated that the St. Laurent government received the proposal "unenthusiastically" and postponed any decision on the matter until after the federal election, which the Liberals subsequently lost. Thus, Air Marshal Slemon's comments were probably triggered by uncertainty within DND over the request and its precise status in the wake of the Tory election victory. See *Minutes of Proceedings and Evidence*, 22 October 1963, 499.

15 In the aftermath of Sputnik, NATO representatives met in Paris in December 1957 to determine the alliance reaction. At the meeting, the United States offered to enter into bilateral negotiations with each member of the alliance for the purpose of stationing medium-range missiles on their territory. For a review, see Philip Nash, *The Other Missiles of October: Eisenhower, Kennedy, and the Jupiters, 1957-1963* (Chapel Hill: University of North Carolina Press, 1997).

16 "Brief for the Canadian Delegation to the NATO Meetings, December 1957 – Stockpiling of Nuclear Weapons in NATO Countries," NAC, Basil Robinson Papers, Manuscript Group (MG) 31, E 83, vol. 9, file 8.4.

17 DHRC, file 73/1223.

18 "Minutes of a Special Meeting of the Chiefs of Staff Committee," 20 December 1957, DHRC, file 73/1223.

19   In January 1958, the United States and Britain reached agreement over arrangements for the storage of American nuclear weapons. The agreement contained a binational command structure and described a system of reciprocal physical controls based on the dual-key principle, the first such agreement reached with any American ally. See Ian Clark, *Nuclear Diplomacy and the Special Relationship: Britain's Deterrent and America, 1957-1962* (Oxford: Clarendon Press, 1994); and John Baylis, *Ambiguity and Deterrence: British Nuclear Strategy, 1945-1964* (New York: Clarendon, 1995).

20   H. Basil Robinson, *Diefenbaker's World: A Populist in Foreign Affairs* (Toronto: University of Toronto Press, 1989), 86.

21   "Acquisition and Control of Defensive Nuclear Weapons," 6 December 1958, NAC, RG 24, vol. 21,418, file 1855.1, part 4.

22   DHRC, file 73/1223.

23   As cited in Lyon, *Canada in World Affairs, 1961-1963*, 81.

24   See Chiefs of Staff Committee meeting, 30 June 1959, DHRC, file 73/1223. The selection of the Starfighter was controversial, as the aircraft had been designed as an air-superiority day fighter and was not well suited to perform the strike role.

25   In his address to the House of Commons announcing the role, Defence Minister George Pearkes did not state that, by definition, the strike mission involved nuclear weapons. See Tom Axworthy, "Soldiers without Enemies: A Political Analysis of Canadian Defence Policy, 1945-1975" (PhD diss., Queen's University, 1978), 293.

26   The four weapons systems have often been described as constituting proof of the government's commitment to acquire nuclear weapons, as two of them – the Bomarcs and Honest John rockets – were not designed for use with conventional ammunition, while the two aircraft were purchased with the clear understanding that they would be armed with nuclear weapons. The book that first made this argument was McLin's *Canada's Changing Defence Policy*, although it has recently been challenged by Munton's "Going Fission" article.

27   "Record of Cabinet Decision," 15 October 1958, DHRC, file 73/1223.

28   At a cabinet meeting on 9 December 1958, ministers essentially agreed on the command and control arrangements for the weapons. A variant of the "two-key" proposal was adopted, under which the authority of both the Canadian and US governments would be required before the weapons could be fired. See Knowlton Nash, *Kennedy and Diefenbaker: The Feud That Helped Topple a Government* (Toronto: McClelland and Stewart, 1990), 76.

29   C.D. Howe's description of Howard Green might be noted: "A perambulating prognosticator of gloom who stalked the halls of Parliament with Bible in one hand and stiletto in the other." As quoted in the *Victoria Daily Colonist*, 5 June 1959. Quotation from Michael Tucker, "Canada and Arms Control: Perspectives and Trends," *International Journal* 36, 3 (1981): 640.

30   In spite of the largely critical mail that Diefenbaker received on the issue, opinion polls conducted throughout the period revealed that Canadians *favoured* nuclear acquisition by a roughly two-to-one margin. Poll results can be found in Jerome Laulicht and John Paul, *In Your Opinion: Leaders' and Voters' Attitudes on Defence and Disarmament* (Clarkson, ON: Canadian Peace Research Institute, 1963).

31   As cited in Granatstein, *Canada 1957-1967*, 119.

32   "US Requirements for Storage Facilities in Canada for Nuclear Weapons," 16 April 1959, DHRC, file 73/1223, #995.

33   "Memo for Cabinet Defence Committee: Nuclear Weapons for NATO and NORAD Forces," 5 December 1960, NAC, RG 2, vol. 2752, file D-1-6-D.

34   A broad-based public campaign opposed to nuclear acquisition arose in the early 1960s. The major actors included the Canadian Committee for Nuclear Disarmament, the Combined Universities Campaign for Nuclear Disarmament, and the Voice of Women.

35   "Canadian Defence Policy and the Problems of Nuclear Weapons," March 1961, NAC, RG 24, vol. 21,756, file 2195. General Foulkes was replaced as chairman of the Chiefs of Staff Committee by Air Marshal F.R. Miller in May 1960.

36   See, for example, James Minifie, *Peacemaker or Powder-Monkey: Canada's Role in a Revolutionary World* (Toronto: McClelland and Stewart, 1960).

37   "Nuclear Weapons for Canadian Forces," 11 October 1961, DHRC, file 73/1223, #303.

38 An example was the prime minister's remarks to the House of Commons on 26 February 1962. He stated: "we take the stand that in the interests of disarmament, everything must be done to assure success if it can be attained, and that the nuclear family should not be increased so long as there is any possibility of disarmament among the nations of the world ... Our view is that at this moment this [question of Canadian nuclear acquisition] is hypothetical and will continue to be as long as disarmament is to the fore." Quotation from Lyon, *Canada in World Affairs,* 106.

39 For a review of the "stand-by" proposal and the debate that it generated, see McLin, *Canada's Changing Defence Policy;* and Nash, *Kennedy and Diefenbaker.*

40 "Nuclear Weapons for Defence," 6 September 1962, DHRC, file 73/1223, #303.

41 "Acquisition of Nuclear Weapons – Bomarc," DHRC, file 73/1223, #303. The letter was undated, but documents in the file indicate that the probable date was early October 1962.

42 For a thorough account, see Peter T. Haydon, *The 1962 Cuban Missile Crisis: Canadian Involvement Reconsidered* (Toronto: Canadian Institute of Strategic Studies, 1993).

43 McLin, *Canada's Changing Defence Policy,* 158-9.

44 Under this proposal, most parts of each nuclear warhead would be stored in Canada, except for some unspecified part that would be held at a nearby US base.

45 See Nash, *Kennedy and Diefenbaker,* 210-13. Clearwater has suggested that the "stand-by" proposal was indeed implemented by the USAF at Goose Bay, with warheads stored at a base in Massachusetts to be airlifted in the event of hostilities. However, Clearwater notes that the USAF squadron scheduled to transport the warheads did not, in fact, have any warheads in its storage facility. See *U.S. Nuclear Weapons in Canada,* 143. In spite of this suggestion, I am sceptical that the United States responded favourably to either Canadian proposal, as my research did not uncover any evidence that would suggest such a reaction.

46 For a transcript of the news conference, see Lyon, *Canada in World Affairs,* 131-5.

47 Part of Pearson's speech has been reprinted in Arthur E. Blanchette, ed., *Canadian Foreign Policy 1955-1965: Selected Speeches and Documents* (Toronto: McClelland and Stewart, 1977).

48 The news release is reprinted in ibid.

49 "Some Problems of Canadian Defence Policy," 9 January 1963, DH, Sutherland Papers, file 87/253.

50 If the term was defined to include all those countries with joint control agreements with the United States, no fewer than fifteen countries would have been considered nuclear weapons states by 1961. In general, the manner in which the expression was used in Canada greatly exaggerated the importance of the decision facing the government.

51 DEA documents on issues related to command and control and on the expansion of the "nuclear club" are not examined in this account. The available literature has addressed these issues in detail, and thus the department's position on both is already well known. See, in particular, Robinson, *Diefenbaker's World,* and Granatstein, *Canada 1957-1967.* Rather, this discussion will examine some of the other issues that DEA officials raised against acquisition.

52 The determination of the Canadian arms control position was the joint responsibility of National Defence and External Affairs. Despite the official division of responsibility, once Howard Green was appointed to cabinet in 1959, Canadian arms control policy was largely overtaken by External. This practice grew even stronger after the formation of a disarmament division within the department in 1961, and the appointment of General E.L.M. Burns as Canada's first disarmament advisor. For more on the division of responsibility and the bureaucratic conflict that resulted, see Legault and Fortmann, *A Diplomacy of Hope.*

53 This discussion is from Robinson, *Diefenbaker's World,* 108-9.

54 "Storage of Nuclear Weapons in Canada," 29 October 1959, Department of External Affairs, DHRC, File 73/1223, #996.

55 Granatstein, *A Man of Influence,* 341.

56 Granatstein, *Canada 1957-1967,* 111.

57 Readers should note that the chain of events that led to Diefenbaker's signing of the initial air defence accord remains controversial and disputed. When he testified before the House of Commons Special Committee on Defence in 1963, General Charles Foulkes, retired

former chairman of the Chiefs of Staff Committee, acknowledged that DND had "stampeded" Diefenbaker into agreeing to the command, a view shared by Defence Minister George Pearkes. See Granatstein, *Canada 1957-1967,* 104. For his part, Diefenbaker steadfastly maintained that he had dealt with the matter in an appropriate and timely fashion.

58 The official reason given for the Canadian change of heart was the expected disruption to civil air traffic, and the possibility that the exercise would be seen as threatening by Soviet premier Nikita Khrushchev, who was planning to visit the United States in September. See Granatstein, *Canada 1957-1967,* 110.

59 DEA memo, 29 October 1959, NAC, RG 24, vol. 21,418, file 1855.1, part 5.

60 Granatstein, *A Man of Influence,* 342.

61 "Memorandum for the Minister," 5 December 1960, NAC, Basil Robinson papers, MG 31, E 83, vol. 9, file 9.3.

62 In fact, the memo was overly optimistic on this matter. In the fall of 1960, Canadian negotiators at the Ten-Nation Disarmament Committee devised a draft disarmament resolution that was intended to be put before a vote in early 1961. The draft called for the establishment of an advisory committee that would study the "principles of disarmament" and make recommendations to the superpowers. However, the Canadian resolution was never voted on. Commenting on the proposal, Legault and Fortmann note that it was "hardly realistic" to have expected any of the major powers to accept principles developed by other states. See *A Diplomacy of Hope,* 192.

63 According to a memo prepared by General Burns, the division would prepare instructions for the government, correlate questions on disarmament with other departmental divisions, and be a central agency for disarmament information. See "Organization of a Disarmament Division in Department of External Affairs," 23 January 1961, NAC, General Burns Papers, MG 31, G6, vol. 13.

64 Memo addressed to Air Marshal Miller, 18 October 1960, NAC, RG 24, vol. 21,756, file 2195.

65 "Argument against the Spreading of Nuclear Weapons," 8 November 1960, NAC, General Burns Papers, MG 31, G6, vol. 13.

66 Some of these ideas ultimately found their way into the "Burns plan," a largely unwritten set of ideas and proposals that Burns conceived during 1960-1. For a discussion, see Legault and Fortmann, *A Diplomacy of Hope,* 161-9. Burns examined some of his experiences as a disarmament negotiator in his book *Megamurder* (Toronto: Clarke, Irwin, 1966).

67 Legault and Fortmann, *A Diplomacy of Hope,* 187.

68 Norman Robertson prepared several memos on the issue. See "Irish Proposal on the Prevention of the Dissemination of Nuclear Warheads," 28 August 1959, NAC, RG 25, vol. 6006, file 50271-5-40, pt. 1. Also see "Irish Proposal," same file.

69 Robinson, *Diefenbaker's World,* 159-60.

70 This discussion is from ibid., 238.

71 While Robinson does not identify which systems DND examined (outside of saying they included "one British and three American"), the paper almost certainly would have discussed the American F-108 interceptor and B-70 strategic bomber, two programs that had recently been cancelled due to a combination of changing military conditions and enormous cost overruns.

72 This is a reference to a still-classified DEA paper. It is cited in Robinson, *Diefenbaker's World,* 238.

73 For an account of the meeting, see Nash, *Kennedy and Diefenbaker,* 213-17. The Nassau meeting between Kennedy and Macmillan was intended to clarify Britain's strategic nuclear role in the aftermath of the cancellation of the Skybolt missile system in November of that year. As a result of the discussions, the United States agreed to offer Britain the Polaris submarine-launched ballistic missile (SLBM). While the United States maintained that Polaris would be part of a larger Multilateral Nuclear Force, the British position was that Polaris constituted an independent nuclear deterrent.

74 Robinson, *Diefenbaker's World,* 301.

75 Ibid., 305.

76 In the speech, the prime minister finally admitted that Canada had made nuclear commitments, but he claimed that the Nassau communiqué had called them into doubt and thus

more time was needed before NATO's revised military strategy would be fully understood. Indeed, reflecting the genuine uncertainty that the speech created, Defence Minister Harkness and Foreign Affairs Minister Green separately congratulated Diefenbaker after the speech, each believing that the prime minister had finally sided with his department in the dispute.

77 Clearwater's *Canadian Nuclear Weapons* provides fairly precise information regarding when Canada's nuclear weapons systems became operational, and when the weapons were ultimately removed. In brief, DND's first operational nuclear weapons system was the Bomarc surface-to-air missile, followed closely by CF-104 squadrons in Europe, Honest John rockets in Europe, and CF-101s armed with Genie (also known as MB-1) air-to-air missiles in Canada (in 1965). Bomarc missiles were phased out of service between 1971 and 1972, the CF-104 strike role was ended in 1971, Honest John nuclear rockets were withdrawn in 1970, while Genie warheads for the CF-101s remained in active inventory until June 1984. It remains unclear why Genie warheads remained in service so long after the other three nuclear roles had been terminated.

78 Robinson, *Diefenbaker's World*, 229.

79 Ann Denholm Crosby's recent study *Dilemmas in Defence Decision-Making* argued that Canada had little choice but to accept nuclear weapons on the basis of decisions reached elsewhere (primarily in NORAD). See *Dilemmas in Defence Decision-Making: Constructing Canada's Role in NORAD, 1958-1996* (New York: St. Martin's Press, 1998).

Chapter 5: Canadian Conceptual Understanding of Arms Control

1 Despite the important role played by External Affairs in the formulation of Canada's arms control policy, the department's attention was focused on the specific initiatives of the day, and not on examining the conceptual basis of the theory. The two major studies on Canada's arms control history support this contention, as both focus on the determination of Canada's arms control policies. See Albert Legault and Michel Fortmann, *A Diplomacy of Hope: Canada and Disarmament, 1945-1988* (Montreal: McGill-Queen's University Press, 1992) and Joseph Levitt, *Pearson and Canada's Role in Nuclear Disarmament, 1945-1957* (Montreal: McGill-Queen's University Press, 1993). In contrast, the position and orientation of DND toward arms control has not attracted any scholarly attention, outside of a few (largely negative) references in the former work.

2 Colin Gray, *Strategic Studies and Public Policy: The American Experience* (Lexington: University Press of Kentucky, 1982), 73.

3 Disarmament theory takes a direct approach to the problem of war. In its simplest form, it aims to abolish war by stripping states of the weapons with which they fight. One of the first works to examine the concept in detail was Philip Noel-Baker, *The Arms Race: A Programme for World Disarmament* (London: Atlantic Books, 1958).

4 Lawrence Freedman, *The Evolution of Nuclear Strategy* (London: Macmillan, 1981), 196.

5 While it was not widely explained at the time, arms control came to include two quite different activities – operational arms control and structural arms control. Operational arms control seeks to place constraints on the behaviour of armed forces and embraces such possibilities as regulations on weapons deployment. Its general goal is the inhibition of military actions that can increase the risks of war. In contrast, structural arms control (otherwise known simply as arms limitation) addresses the quantity and quality of arms rather than the behaviour regarding their use per se.

6 As cited in Levitt, *Pearson and Canada's Role in Nuclear Disarmament*, 268.

7 See *Daedalus* 89, 4 (1960). Included among the authors were Herman Kahn, Henry Kissinger, Morton Halperin, and Thomas Schelling, each of whom was already an important figure in nuclear strategy.

8 See Donald Brennan, ed., *Arms Control, Disarmament, and National Security* (New York: George Braziller, 1961).

9 Emanuel Adler, "The Emergence of Cooperation: National Epistemic Communities and the International Evolution of the Idea of Nuclear Arms Control," *International Organization* 46, 1 (1992), 114.

10 Colin Gray, "What RAND Hath Wrought," *Foreign Policy* 4 (Fall 1971): 116.

11 Hedley Bull, *The Control of the Arms Race: Disarmament and Arms Control in the Missile Age* (New York: Praeger Publishers, 1961).

12 Two other major works on the subject were also published in 1961. These were Thomas Schelling and Morton Halperin, *Strategy and Arms Control* (New York: Twentieth Century Fund); and David Frisch, ed., *Arms Reduction: Programs and Issues* (New York: Twentieth Century Fund).

13 As listed by Colin Gray, *House of Cards: Why Arms Control Must Fail* (Ithaca, NY: Cornell University Press, 1992), 6-7.

14 Schelling and Halperin, *Strategy and Arms Control,* 2.

15 Readers should note that, as discussed in the text, at the time concern with arms control initially arose, the relevant terminology was still evolving and thus many observers used the terms "arms control" and "disarmament" interchangeably. In point of fact, arms control did not acquire its contemporary meaning until the late 1950s.

16 Legault and Fortmann, *A Diplomacy of Hope,* 69.

17 "United Nations Disarmament Commission: Reduction of Armed Forces," National Archives of Canada (NAC), Record Group (RG) 24, vol. 20,711, file 2:3:2, part 4.

18 "Disarmament Proposals – Canadian Views," NAC, RG 24, vol. 21,263, file 1644.1, part 4.

19 For a review of Canada's position in these talks, see Michael Tucker, "Canada and the Test-Ban Negotiations, 1955-1971," in *An Acceptance of Paradox / Essays on Canadian Diplomacy in Honour of John W. Holmes,* ed. Kim Richard Nossal (Toronto: Canadian Institute of International Affairs, 1982).

20 In March 1954, an American test code-named "Bravo" was conducted on Bikini island in the South Pacific. Bravo was actually a series of tests of newly miniaturized devices (i.e., tactical nuclear weapons) as well as multimegaton behemoths. The tests attracted worldwide attention when it was revealed that a group of Japanese fishermen had been contaminated by the explosions. One year later, in February 1955, the Atomic Energy Commission released a report on the dangers of nuclear fallout that strengthened the public's fear of nuclear tests. As for the Soviets, in 1955 they began testing hydrogen weapons in the upper atmosphere (including the first such weapon that was deliverable by air), and later in the year much of Europe and Japan reported a sharp increase in radioactive rain. For a review of both the tests of the period and the larger debate that they sparked, see Robert A. Divine, *Blowing on the Wind: The Nuclear Test Ban Debate, 1954-1960* (New York: Oxford University Press, 1978).

21 "Memo for the Minister," 18 July 1956, NAC, RG 25, file 50271-A-40, file 4.

22 As cited in Levitt, *Pearson and Canada's Role in Nuclear Disarmament,* 233.

23 "Tests of Nuclear Weapons," 4 April 1956, NAC, RG 24, vol. 4158, file 170-80-J/4.

24 "Disarmament: Limitations on Atomic Tests," 27 September 1956, NAC, RG 24, vol. 4158, file 170-80-J/4.

25 US opposition to the Canadian proposal had been assumed from the start, but the realization that the British were also opposed came as something of a shock to Pearson and the department. For a discussion, see Levitt, *Pearson and Canada's Role in Nuclear Disarmament,* 240. In general, the episode reveals a striking lack of realistic political analysis in DEA, as British and American opposition should have been expected.

26 The registration initiative was jointly undertaken with Norway and Japan. The purpose was to keep actual and expected radiation released under observation. To the surprise of many observers, the United States ultimately agreed to register the dates of nuclear tests and the amount of total energy to be released, and to limit the amount of radioactive material released by each test.

27 General and complete disarmament (GCD) involves the reduction and gradual elimination of both conventional and nuclear forces. The matter first attracted notice in 1957 at a meeting of the UN Disarmament Subcommittee, and GCD quickly became the declared goal of both the United States and Soviet Union.

28 "Disarmament and the Deterrent," 9 May 1960, DND, Directorate of History, Sutherland Papers (hereinafter DHSP), file 87/253. An appendix to this document was titled "Strategic Nuclear Disarmament." Quotations in the text are attributable to both the main document and the appendix.

29 While the Strategic Arms Limitation Treaty (SALT) I largely froze the number of permitted intercontinental ballistic missile (ICBM) and submarine-launched ballistic missile (SLBM) launchers – to a maximum of 2,568 for the Soviet Union, and 1,764 for the United States – it did not prevent further qualitative improvements in forces, nor did it cover strategic bombers. In fact, the number of multiple independently targetable warheads (MIRVs) deployed on missiles by the superpowers in 1977 was four times greater than when the SALT talks began.

30 G.D. Kaye, "A Model for the Study of Stability, Arms Control, and Disarmament," November 1960, Defence Systems Analysis Group, Report 60/6. This paper was acquired from George Lindsey's personal collection. See also "Arms Balance Model," RG 24, Access 83-84/167, DRBS 9700-82-1, part 1, which was written at the same time.

31 While not expressly identified, it seems that Kaye was basing this on the Soviet Union's enormous casualties suffered during the Second World War.

32 The instability measure identifies the degree to which an actor is willing to accept strategic inequality, which raises the possibility of a devastating nuclear strike.

33 G.D. Kaye, "A Guide to Deterrence and Arms Control," *RCAF Staff College Journal* (1961), 86. This article was the journal's 1961 "Prize Essay."

34 Ibid., 87.

35 Joint staff, "Canadian Policy on Disarmament – 1961," January 1961, NAC, RG 24, vol. 21,265, file 1644-1, #15.

36 G.D. Kaye, "Subjective Aspects of the Strategic Nuclear Balance," February 1962, Defence Research Board Systems Analysis Group (SAG Memorandum no. 62), NAC, RG 24, vol. 21,805, file 2406.1, part 2.

37 "Disarmament and Arms Control," [undated paper – probably 1963-4], DHSP, file 87/253.

38 Other important studies from the period include Arthur Lawson, *A Warless World* (New York: McGraw-Hill, 1962); J.W. Spanier and J.L. Nogee, *The Politics of Disarmament: A Study in Soviet-American Gamesmanship* (New York: Praeger, 1962); R.J. Barnet, *Who Wants Disarmament?* (Boston: Beacon Press, 1960); and J. David Singer, *Deterrence, Arms Control, and Disarmament* (Columbus: Ohio State University Press, 1962).

39 Gray, *Strategic Studies and Public Policy*, 76.

40 Bernard Brodie, *Strategy in the Missile Age* (Princeton, NJ: Princeton University Press, 1959).

41 Ibid., 300.

42 Ibid., 300.

43 Ibid., 302.

44 Ibid., 304.

45 Bull, *The Control of the Arms Race*, 39.

46 Ibid., 60.

47 Malcolm Hoag, "On Stability and Deterrent Races," *World Politics* 13, 4 (1961): 505-27.

48 Ibid., 513.

49 Schelling and Halperin, *Strategy and Arms Control*, 4.

50 Phil Williams, "Thomas Schelling," in *Makers of Nuclear Strategy*, ed. John Baylis and John Garnett (London: Pinter Publishers, 1991), 128.

51 Schelling and Halperin, *Strategy and Arms Control*, 6.

52 Ibid., 57.

53 In brief, the talks over a nuclear test ban – which took place between 1958 and 1963, although discussions dated back to 1950 – ended with the signing of the Partial Test Ban (PTB) Treaty, although the success was tempered by the continued allowance of underground testing. The 1958 Surprise Attack Conference ended in disarray, with the two sides unable to even agree on appropriate issues to discuss. The negotiations on general and complete disarmament (1959-62) similarly ended in failure, with both sides tabling very different proposals and seemingly more interested in scoring political points than in resolving their differences. These negotiations are discussed in Albert Carnesale and Richard Haass, eds., *Superpower Arms Control: Setting the Record Straight* (Cambridge: Ballinger Publishing, 1987); and Walter C. Clemens, *The Superpowers and Arms Control: From Cold War to Interdependence* (Lexington: D.C. Heath, 1973).

54   Robin Ranger, *Arms and Politics, 1958-1978: Arms Control in a Changing Political Context* (Toronto: Macmillan, 1979), 11.

55   Originally dubbed the "Peace agency," the Arms Control and Disarmament Agency (ACDA) grew out of the 1960 US presidential election, and the desire of President-elect John Kennedy to have an independent agency that could provide the administration with unbiased analysis on arms control issues. For the next thirty-eight years, the director of ACDA served as the principal advisor to the US president, the National Security Council, and the secretary of state on arms control issues. ACDA became part of the State Department in April 1999. On the agency's creation, see Arthur Herzog, *The War Peace Establishment* (New York: Harper and Row, 1965).

56   Ranger, *Arms and Politics,* 205. For more on the links between the civilian community and ACDA, see Harland B. Moulton, *From Superiority to Parity: The United States and the Strategic Arms Race, 1961-1971* (Westport: Greenwood Press, 1973).

57   This point is the basic thesis of Ranger's *Arms and Politics.*

58   Of course, as with the 1946 Baruch plan discussed in Chapter 1, it has been suggested that official US interest in arms control during the 1950s and early 1960s was largely an exercise in public relations, in that there was little "real" interest in reaching agreements at a time when the United States was still in the midst of building its strategic triad of nuclear forces. Although this argument is a reasonable one, the same charge can be directed toward Soviet proposals of the era; that is, that the Soviets were also trying to score political points – indeed, their efforts in this regard were arguably even more transparent than those of the United States – and that they were no more interested in limiting their strategic forces (which lagged behind those of the West) than was the United States. It is therefore hardly surprising that arms control progress proved difficult, and it was not until the Cuban Missile Crisis of 1962 that this dynamic changed, although it took an additional ten years before the first agreement that actually limited deployments of weapons systems was signed.

59   John von Neumann's most critical book was co-authored with Oskar Morgenstern. See *Theory of Games and Economic Behaviour* (Princeton, NJ: Princeton University Press, 1947). Fred Kaplan has called von Neumann "possibly the most brilliant man – certainly among the broader intellects – of the twentieth century." Quotation from *The Wizards of Armageddon* (New York: Simon and Schuster, 1983), 63.

60   Freedman, *The Evolution of Nuclear Strategy,* 182. Game theory also had its share of critics, the best-known of whom were Anatol Rapoport and Philip Green.

61   Williams, "Thomas Schelling," 121.

62   George W. Downs and David M. Rocke, *Tacit Bargaining, Arms Races, and Arms Control* (Ann Arbor: University of Michigan Press, 1990), 19-26.

63   Thomas C. Schelling, *The Strategy of Conflict* (New York: Oxford University Press, 1960). See Chapter 9.

64   Kaplan, *The Wizards of Armageddon,* 331.

65   Williams, "Thomas Schelling," 122.

66   Schelling, *The Strategy of Conflict,* Chapter 8.

67   Freedman, *The Evolution of Nuclear Strategy,* 188.

68   The basic premises of game theory were challenged in a computer simulation contest in the early 1980s. The results were reviewed in Robert Axelrod's *The Evolution of Cooperation* (New York: Basic Books, 1984). The test revealed that the simplest strategy submitted, "Tit-for-Tat," proved the most effective in encouraging cooperation over the long term. The strategy was submitted by Anatol Rapoport. For more on the use of game theory, see Duncan Snidal, "The Game Theory of International Politics," in *Cooperation under Anarchy,* ed. Kenneth A. Oye (Princeton, NJ: Princeton University Press, 1986) and R. Harrison Wagner, "Theory of Games and International Cooperation," *American Political Science Review* 77, 2 (June 1983): 330-46. For a general introduction to the subject, see Martin Shubik, *Game Theory in the Social Sciences: Concepts and Solutions* (Cambridge: MIT Press, 1983).

69   Seymour Melman, ed., *Disarmament: Its Politics and Economics* (Boston: American Academy of Arts and Sciences, 1962).

70   "Arms Control – Strategic Deterrent Model" (letter from R.S. Eaton), 12 December 1960, NAC, RG 24, Access 1983-84/167, DRBS 9700-82-1, part 1.

71 Two memos clearly reveal this. See "DSAG Visit Report, 60/2," 20 September 1960, NAC, RG 24, vol. 21,754, file 2184.4.D, part 1; and "Discussions on Arms Control" (letter prepared by J. Koop of the DRB for the chairman, O.M. Solandt, 21 June 1960), NAC, RG 24, Access 1983-84/167, DRBS 9700-82-1, part 1. The latter document noted that American analysts were interested in maintaining "regular contact" with Canadian arms control specialists.

72 Gray, *Strategic Studies and Public Policy*, 160.

73 Major Cold War arms control agreements included the 1963 PTB Treaty, the 1968 Nuclear Non-Proliferation Treaty, the 1972 SALT I Treaty, the 1974 Vladivostok Accord, the 1979 SALT II Treaty, the 1987 Intermediate-Range Nuclear Forces Treaty, and the 1991 Strategic Arms Reduction Treaty (START I).

74 Gray, *Strategic Studies and Public Policy*, 163.

75 Other major critics of arms control include Jennifer Sims, Bruce Berkowitz, and Kenneth Adelman. See their respective works: *Icarus Restrained: An Intellectual History of Nuclear Arms Control, 1945-1960* (Boulder, CO: Westview Press, 1990); *A Century of Arms Control: Why It Has Failed and How It Can Be Made to Work* (New York: Simon and Schuster, 1987); and *The Great Universal Embrace: Arms Summitry – A Sceptic's Account* (New York: Simon and Schuster, 1989).

76 Gray, *House of Cards*, 11.

77 Thomas Schelling, "What Went Wrong with Arms Control?" in *Studies of War and Peace*, ed. O. Osterud (Oslo: Norwegian University Press, 1986). More recently, Henry Kissinger has similarly reconsidered his earlier support for arms control. In a 1999 newspaper editorial, Kissinger questioned whether arms control in an age of nuclear proliferation makes strategic sense. As he noted, "traditional arms control agreements ... may have come to the end of the road." See "Arms Control to Suit a New World," *Los Angeles Times*, 21 November 1999.

78 Gray, *House of Cards*, 28-9.

79 Gray subsequently expanded this argument and made it the focus of a book. See *Weapons Don't Make War: Policy, Strategy, and Military Technology* (Lawrence: University Press of Kansas, 1993).

80 This assertion became the basis of a 1982 report titled *Soviet Compliance with Arms Control Agreements*, which became an annual publication during the Reagan presidency. In combination with a further annual report produced by the Department of Defense, *Soviet Military Power* (which was sharply critical of the ongoing Soviet defence buildup), a community of arms control critics took centre stage in Washington.

Chapter 6: Links between Canadian Strategic Thinking and Defence Policy, 1950-63

1 Department of National Defence, *Canada's Defence Programme, 1951-1952* (Ottawa: Queen's Printer, 1951).

2 Peter T. Haydon, *The 1962 Cuban Missile Crisis: Canadian Involvement Reconsidered* (Toronto: Canadian Institute of Strategic Studies, 1993), 49.

3 In 1959, Canada and the United States signed the Defence Production Sharing Agreement. The arrangement involved a limited free-trade regime in defence products, thereby giving Canadian industry access to the American defence market and the armed forces the benefit of lower prices on the larger items produced in the United States. For a review, see Michael Slack and John Skynner, "Defence Production and the Defence Industrial Base," in *Canada's International Security Policy*, ed. David Dewitt and David Leyton-Brown (Scarborough: Prentice Hall Canada, 1995).

4 D.W. Middlemiss and J.J. Sokolsky, *Canadian Defence: Decisions and Determinants* (Toronto: Harcourt Brace Jovanovich, 1989), 24.

5 William Arkin and Richard W. Fieldhouse, *Nuclear Battlefields: Global Links in the Arms Race* (Cambridge: Ballinger, 1985), 78.

6 The importance of this objective is made clear by documents prepared both before and after Pearson's initial meeting with President John F. Kennedy in May 1963. See "Aide Memoire: Prime Minister's Discussions with President Kennedy, May 1963," 7 May 1963, DND, Directorate of History, Raymont Collection (hereinafter DHRC), file 73/1223, #15; "Summary Report," 15 May 1963, DH, file 73/1223, #827; and "Canada-US Relations,"

report prepared by Harry Scott, Consul General, New York, 14 June 1963, DH, file 73/1223, #821.

7 Middlemiss and Sokolsky, *Canadian Defence,* 27.

8 The Canadian public policy literature is extensive, although it largely falls outside the immediate concern of this study. See, for example, Ronald Manzer, "Social Policy and Political Paradigms," *Canadian Public Administration* 24, 4 (1981): 641-8; Ronald Manzer, *Public Policies and Political Development in Canada* (Toronto: University of Toronto Press, 1985); Bruce Doern and Peter Aucoin, eds., *Public Policy in Canada: Organization and Process* (Toronto: Macmillan, 1978); Bruce Doern and Richard Phidd, *Canadian Public Policy: Ideas, Structures, Processes* (Toronto: Nelson Canada, 1992); Bruce Doern and Bryne Purchase, eds., *Canada at Risk? Canadian Public Policy in the 1990s* (Toronto: C.D. Howe Institute, 1990); and Leslie Pal, *Public Policy Analysis: An Introduction* (Scarborough: Nelson, 1992).

9 Department of National Defence, *Canada's Defence Programme, 1955-1956* (Ottawa: Queen's Printer, 1955).

10 Ibid., 4

11 Ibid., 4.

12 For example, *Canada's Defence Programme, 1952-1953* noted that "we are convinced that the best way to avoid a war of annihilation is to make plain to a potential aggressor that collectively we have the strength to defend ourselves and that we value our freedoms sufficiently to fight for them."

13 Department of National Defence, *Report on National Defence* (Ottawa: Queen's Printer, 1957), 6.

14 Department of National Defence, *Canadian Defence Policy* (Ottawa: DND, 1960), 5.

15 Joseph T. Jockel and Joel J. Sokolsky, "Canada's Cold War Nuclear Experience," in *Pondering NATO's Nuclear Options: Gambits for a Post-Westphalian World,* ed. David G. Haglund (Kingston, ON: Queen's Quarterly and the Centre for International Relations, Queen's University, 1999).

16 For a review of McNamara's thinking on nuclear strategy, see Andreas Wenger, *Living with Peril: Eisenhower, Kennedy, and Nuclear Weapons* (New York: Rowman and Littlefield, 1997) and Lawrence Freedman, *The Evolution of Nuclear Strategy* (London: Macmillan, 1981). For an examination of the US SIOP of the early 1960s, see Peter Pringle and William Arkin, *SIOP: The Secret U.S. Plan for Nuclear War* (New York: W.W. Norton, 1983).

17 Presidential Directive 59 attracted particular attention because of its stated intent in locating and attacking Soviet leaders in their bunkers. This came after US intelligence estimated that more than 100,000 key Soviet government officials would be moved to hardened shelters in the early stages of a conflict, and thus had a good chance of surviving a nuclear exchange. For more on the directive, see Fred Kaplan, *The Wizards of Armageddon* (New York: Simon and Schuster, 1983) and Scott D. Sagan, *Moving Targets: Nuclear Strategy and National Security* (Princeton, NJ: Princeton University Press, 1989). Kahn's ideas on escalation were outlined in *On Escalation: Metaphors and Scenarios* (New York: Praeger Publishers, 1965).

18 In a widely cited 1983 article, Albert Wohlstetter argued that MAD "has never [influenced] operational policy." See "Bishops, Statesmen, and Other Strategists on the Bombing of Innocents," *Commentary* 75, 6 (1983): 15-35. Similarly, both David Alan Rosenberg and Robert Jervis have concluded that US war planning never actually reflected the MAD model. See their respective works, "The Origins of Overkill: Nuclear Weapons and American Strategy, 1945-1960," *International Security* 7, 4 (1983): 3-71; and *The Meaning of the Nuclear Revolution: Statecraft and the Prospect of Armageddon* (Ithaca, NY: Cornell University Press, 1989).

19 Gregg Herken, *Counsels of War* (New York: Alfred A. Knopf, 1985), 259. It should be noted that several years earlier Laird had written a book that advocated an American first-strike capability against the Soviet Union. See *A House Divided: America's Security Gap* (New York: Henry Regnery, 1962).

20 Pringle and Arkin have noted that "the gap between the rhetoric and the actual war plans has been an enduring characteristic of the [Single Integrated Operational Plan]." See *SIOP,* 175.

21 This point was extensively examined in Chapter 3, n. 39.

22 This argument is strengthened if one examines the intended targets of Canadian nuclear weapons. For the air force, the strike/reconnaissance role was primarily aimed at military bases, airfields, and radar facilities in central and Eastern Europe; the Honest Johns were battlefield tactical weapons to be used against Soviet land forces; and the nuclear weapons based in Canada, the Bomarcs and the Genie warheads for the CF-101s, were to be used in an air defence role. Clearly, none of the Canadian weapons were directed at Soviet strategic forces, targets that could have called into question the ability of the Soviets to conduct a retaliatory strike. For a review, see John Clearwater, *Canadian Nuclear Weapons: The Untold Story of Canada's Cold War Arsenal* (Toronto: Dundurn Press, 1998).

23 Department of National Defence, *White Paper on Defence* (Ottawa: Queen's Printer, 1964), 10.

24 The white paper noted that "the question of nuclear weapons for the Canadian armed forces is subordinate to that of Canada's political responsibility as a member of a nuclear-armed alliance. NATO is a nuclear-armed defensive alliance, which dare not be otherwise as long as it is confronted by a nuclear-armed potential opponent ... A share in the responsibility for [nuclear-based] policies is a necessary concomitant of Canada's membership in NATO. One cannot be a member of a military alliance and at the same time avoid some share of responsibility for its strategic policies" (13). The Sutherland reference in the text is to "Some Problems of Canadian Defence Policy," 9 January 1963, DH, Sutherland Papers, file 87/253.

25 See "Address by the Honourable Ralph Campney, Minister of National Defence, before the United Services Institute," 27 February 1956, DH, file 72/918.

26 "Nuclear War and the Deterrent," 20 June 1956, DH, file 72/918.

27 See "Address by the Honourable Douglas S. Harkness, Minister of National Defence," 17 February 1961, delivered to the Royal Canadian Military Institute, DH, file 81/674, vol. 4.

28 This belief was linked to the emerging body of literature in arms control and especially disarmament, much of which asserted that force was an outmoded aspect of global politics. For a review, see Chapter 5.

29 "Remarks by Air Marshal C.R. Dunlap," 19 July 1963, delivered to the National Defence College, DH, file 74/425.

30 R.J. Sutherland, "The CF-104 Follow-On Order," 5 July 1963, DHRC, file 73/1223, #130.

31 In the early 1960s, France reached an impasse with the United States on nuclear policy (and on the specific issue of the stationing of American nuclear weapons in France), and the Canadian European Air Division was essentially caught in the crossfire. While France was willing to allow Canada to station quick-reaction aircraft, it was not willing to allow them to store "Special Ammunition," that is, nuclear weapons (unless the weapons were wholly under French control). In combination with an array of other concerns – including American dominance in NATO, doubts regarding extended nuclear deterrence, and a desire to play a more independent role in the superpower conflict – French President Charles de Gaulle began considering alternative security measures. In 1966, the French government announced that it would formally withdraw from NATO's military command, and that all allied staffs should be removed by 1 April 1967. For a review of the France-NATO dispute, see Helga Haffendorn, *NATO and the Nuclear Revolution: A Crisis of Credibility, 1966-1967* (Oxford: Clarendon Press, 1996). France's difficulties with NATO were examined in Appendix C of Sutherland's CF-104 report. See "Possible Solution to the Problem Created by Refusal of France to Accept Nuclear Weapons on French Bases."

32 Sutherland, "The CF-104 Follow-On Order," 5.

33 "The Vulnerability of ACE Air Strike Forces to Ballistic Missile Attack," 7 March 1960, National Archives of Canada (NAC), Record Group (RG), 24, vol. 21,805, file 2406.1, part 2.

34 An additional report prepared by the Defence Systems Analysis Group concluded that all of the aircraft deployed on European air bases would probably be destroyed by missiles and aircraft in a surprise Soviet attack. See G.D. Kaye, G.R. Lindsey, and S.B. Brown, DSAG Report 60/3, "The Vulnerability of the NATO Strike Force to Ballistic Missile Attack," NAC, RG 24, vol. 21,754, file 2184.4.D, part 1.

35 The secondary literature suggests that it was Canadian political officials who first raised concerns about the nuclear role. Indeed, many scholars assert that Canadian acceptance of

the strike mission is a further indication of the uncritical manner in which Canada accepted the strategic analysis of other countries during the Cold War. See, for example, John Gellner, "Strategic Analysis in Canada," *International Journal* 33, 3 (1978): 493-505.

36 Cabinet Defence Committee minutes, 96th meeting, 3 November 1953, DHRC, file 73/1223.

37 See "Reassessment of the Risk," DHRC, file 73/1223, #89.

38 Cabinet Defence Committee minutes, 103rd meeting, 24 January 1955, DHRC, file 73/1223.

39 Cabinet Defence Committee minutes, 110th meeting, 13 June 1956, DHRC, file 73/1223.

40 This request dated back to 1954, when the US Air Force first informed Canadian defence officials that it was vital there be forward bases in northern Canada where tanker aircraft could be stationed. In April 1956, the Royal Canadian Air Force identified three considerations that would need to be satisfied before approval could be granted: (1) each base should be under the command and control of a Canadian officer; (2) each base should be some distance away from centres of population and industrial complexes; and (3) the US government had to bear the full cost of the project, including annual recurring costs, with Canada retaining title to all immoveables. See "Aide Memoire – USAF Operating Requirement in Canada-SAC Tanker Bases," 9 April 1956, DHRC, file 73/1223, #1085.

41 In February 1957, cabinet granted final authorization for the establishment of four tanker bases: Frobisher, Churchill, Cold Lake, and Nameo. Authorization was also granted for joint engineering studies aimed at identifying five additional bases. See Cabinet Defence Committee minutes, 113th meeting, 6 and 7 February 1957, DHRC, file 73/1223. In January 1958, cabinet agreed to expand the program, and the United States was granted permission to enlarge the bases. However, the changing technological environment of the period (and the introduction of long-range B-52 bombers) resulted in the rapid de-emphasis of tanker aircraft, and the program was abandoned in the early 1960s.

42 On this point, it is widely accepted in the strategic studies literature that the writings of Bernard Brodie, the dean of postwar American strategists, had little policy relevance. Barry Steiner's *Bernard Brodie and the Foundations of American Nuclear Strategy* (Lawrence: University Press of Kansas, 1991) examines this question in detail, and concludes that Brodie's status as the proverbial "outsider," his tendency to question accepted practices and decisions, and his penchant for altering his positions on key issues as strategic conditions changed led policy makers to challenge his work. While strategists such as Wohlstetter and Schelling were certainly not ignored to the extent that Brodie was, they frequently expressed frustration that their work was not accorded the policy relevance they felt it deserved. Rosenberg has also examined this question. See "The Origins of Overkill" and "Reality and Responsibility: Power and Process in the Making of United States Nuclear Strategy, 1945-1968," *Journal of Strategic Studies* 9, 1 (1986): 35-52.

43 Perhaps the most obvious example was Wohlstetter's basing study, which was not accepted by the Washington defence establishment for more than two years after its completion, in spite of overwhelming evidence that its basic finding was true. Similarly, it took years for the criticisms of the policy of massive retaliation to be formally accepted. The inertia of the US Department of Defense on both these issues clearly reveals the limited authority and influence that civilian observers had. See Kaplan, *The Wizards of Armageddon,* and Herken, *Counsels of War.*

44 Colin Gray has identified ten distinct roles that civilian strategists played in the US defence policy community, including policy innovator, problem-solving expert, friendly critic, and scholar. While each was at least partly connected to the broad defence policy environment, direct influence was, at best, an indirect goal of many of them. See *Strategic Studies and Public Policy: The American Experience* (Lexington: University Press of Kentucky, 1982), Chapter 11.

45 Ibid., 178.

46 Ibid., 176.

47 Ibid., 178.

48 Ibid.

49 James Eayrs, *Right and Wrong in Foreign Policy* (Toronto: University of Toronto Press, 1966).

50 Ibid., 54.

51 Gray, *Strategic Studies and Public Policy,* 184.
52 See Denis Stairs, "Public Opinion and External Affairs: Reflections on the Domestication of Canadian Foreign Policy," *International Journal* 33, 1 (1977-8): 128-49.

Conclusion

1 See, for example, Ian Clark, *Nuclear Diplomacy and the Special Relationship: Britain's Deterrent and America, 1957-1962* (Oxford: Clarendon Press, 1994); Martin S. Navias, *Nuclear Weapons and British Strategic Planning, 1955-1958* (Oxford: Clarendon Press, 1991); Stephen Twigge and Alan Macmillan, "Britain, the United States, and the Development of NATO Strategy, 1950-1964," *Journal of Strategic Studies* 19, 2 (1996): 260-81; Beatrice Heuser, "The Development of NATO Nuclear Strategy," *Contemporary European History* 4, 1 (1995): 37-66; John Baylis, *Ambiguity and Deterrence: The United Kingdom and Nuclear Weapons, 1945-1964* (Oxford: Clarendon Press, 1995); and Jan Melissen, "Nuclearising NATO, 1957-1959: The 'Anglo-Saxons,' Nuclear Sharing, and the Fourth Country Problem," *Review of International Studies* 20, 3 (1994): 253-76.
2 The most bitter such rivalry was between Bernard Brodie and Albert Wohlstetter. For a discussion, see Fred Kaplan, *The Wizards of Armageddon* (New York: Simon and Schuster, 1983).
3 See, for example, "DSAG Visit Report, 60/2," National Archives of Canada (NAC), Record Group (RG) 24, vol. 21,754, file 2184.4.D, part 1; and letter from J. Koop, Defence Research Board (DRB), to Chairman, DRB, "Discussion on Arms Control," 21 June 1960, NAC, RG 24, Acc. 83-84/167, DRBS-9700-82-1, part 1.
4 For a departmental review of these linkages, see "Committees and Agencies Concerned with Canada-United States Defence Collaboration," 5 August 1954, NAC, Manuscript Group (MG) 32, B5, vol. 126.
5 George Lindsey, a former head of Operational Research and Analysis and member of the Operational Research Group of the DRB, told me that meetings between Canadian defence officials and members of the American civilian defence community in the late 1950s and early 1960s were "common," and that the Americans paid close attention to what Canadians had to say. Lindsey also noted that because of the array of institutional linkages between the two countries' militaries, Americans paid closer attention to the views and interpretations of Canadians than to those of any other group of foreigners, including the British. Telephone interview, 7 December 1997.
6 See both the Report of the Defence Systems Analysis Group, Visit to the Rand Corporation, 13-14 November 1961, "Central and Limited War," SAG Visit report 62/VI, January 1962, NAC, RG 24, vol. 21,754, file 2184.4.D, part 2; and Letter from B.A. Walker, DRB, to Chairman, DRB, "Visit to the Rand Corporation," 10 June 1959, NAC, RG 24, Acc. 83-84/167, vol. 7586, DRBS-9720-43, part 1.
7 Colin Gray, *Strategic Studies and Public Policy: The American Experience* (Lexington: University Press of Kentucky, 1982), 178-9.
8 Ken Booth, "Bernard Brodie," in *Makers of Nuclear Strategy,* ed. John Baylis and John Garnett (London: Pinter Publishers, 1991), 51.
9 Colin Gray, "The Need for Independent Canadian Strategic Thought," *Canadian Defence Quarterly* 1, 1 (1971), 12.
10 See Adrian Preston, "The Higher Study of Defence in Canada: A Critical Review," *Journal of Canadian Studies* 3, 3 (1968): 17-28; and John Gellner, "Strategic Analysis in Canada," *International Journal* 33, 3 (1978): 493-505.
11 "Sufficiency" was first publicly discussed in the United States by Donald Quarles, Dwight D. Eisenhower's secretary of the air force. According to Quarles, a "sufficiency of force" was that required to perform a retaliatory mission, and the United States was rapidly achieving this capability. During Robert McNamara's tenure, the US government cancelled a series of procurement projects (including the B-70 bomber, the nuclear-powered aircraft, and the Skybolt missile) largely because the defence secretary was not convinced that they would add appreciably to the American nuclear triad. However, under President Richard Nixon, the term began to acquire a more sinister meaning: a 1972 White House memorandum defined strategic sufficiency as the forces necessary "to ensure that the United States would

emerge from a nuclear war in discernibly better shape than the Soviet Union." This conception was consistent with the views of Defense Secretary Melvin Laird, who opposed the concept of stability through mutual vulnerability. Discussion from Robert Jervis, *The Meaning of the Nuclear Revolution: Statecraft and the Prospect of Armageddon* (Ithaca, NY: Cornell University Press, 1989), 17; and Gregg Herken, *Counsels of War* (New York: Alfred A. Knopf, 1985), 112 and 266.

12   D.W. Middlemiss and J.J. Sokolsky, *Canadian Defence: Decisions and Determinants* (Toronto: Harcourt Brace Jovanovich, 1989), 212.

13   John Gellner, *Canada in NATO* (Toronto: Ryerson Press, 1970), 30.

14   Tom Axworthy, "Soldiers without Enemies: A Political Analysis of Canadian Defence Policy, 1945-1975" (PhD diss., Queen's University, 1978), 667.

15   Ibid., 669-70.

16   Joseph S. Nye Jr., "Nuclear Learning and US-Soviet Security Regimes," *International Organization* 4, 3 (1987), 378.

17   Ibid., 380.

18   For reviews of Canadian foreign policy under Trudeau, see J.L. Granatstein and Robert Bothwell, *Pirouette: Pierre Trudeau and Canadian Foreign Policy* (Toronto: University of Toronto Press, 1990) and Ivan Head and Pierre Elliott Trudeau, *The Canadian Way: Shaping Canada's Foreign Policy, 1968-1984* (Toronto: McClelland and Stewart, 1995).

19   Among studies to argue that Canada was a major power, see David Dewitt and John Kirton, *Canada As a Principal Power: A Study in Foreign Policy and International Relations* (Toronto: John Wiley, 1983) and Norman Hillmer and Garth Stevenson, eds., *Foremost Nation: Canadian Foreign Policy and a Changing World* (Toronto: McClelland and Stewart, 1977). The literature on middle powers is considerable, but key studies include Carsten Holbraad, *Middle Powers in International Politics* (London: Macmillan, 1984) and Holbraad, "The Role of Middle Powers," *Co-operation and Conflict* 7, 2 (1971). For works in the Canadian context, see King Gordon, ed., *Canada's Role as a Middle Power* (Toronto: Canadian Institute of International Affairs, 1966); John Holmes, "Most Safely in the Middle," *International Journal* 39, 2 (1984): 366-88; and most recently, Adam Chapnick, "The Canadian Middle Power Myth," *International Journal* 55, 2 (2000): 188-206.

20   Dewitt and Kirton, *Canada As a Principal Power,* 4.

21   A recent study has again suggested that Canada has far greater capabilities than it is commonly given credit for (in this case in the area of financial markets). See John Kirton, "Canada As a Principal Financial Power," *International Journal* 54, 4 (1999).

22   R.J. Sutherland, "Canada's Long Term Strategic Situation," *International Journal* 17, 3 (1962): 199-223.

23   Ibid., 201.

24   Ibid., 223.

25   As Sutherland's article predated the studies by Preston, Gellner, and Gray by several years, it might have been expected to attract some comment. But, puzzlingly, it was not even *cited* in any of the three studies.

26   "Report of the Ad Hoc Committee on Defence Policy," Department of National Defence, Directorate of History, file 72/153. The committee consisted of R.J. Sutherland, A.C. Grant (deputy minister's staff), Captain V.J. Wilgress (Royal Canadian Navy), Brigadier D.A.G. Waldock (army), and Group Captains J.K.F. MacDonald and C.H. Mussells (Royal Canadian Air Force).

27   Chapter headings included "Canada's Foreign Policy, 1945-1963," "Canada's Defence Policy, 1945-1963," "Outstanding Problems of Canadian Defence," and "The World of 1963-1990."

28   "Report of the Ad Hoc Committee on Defence Policy," 162.

29   Ibid., 163.

30   Two separate incidents in 1999 threatened to drive a wedge in the Canada-US defence relationship, which had already been weakened by the consistent reduction in Canadian defence spending under the government of Jean Chrétien. In April, amid widespread concerns about technology "leakage" to third parties, the US Congress passed a series of changes to the International Traffic in Arms Regulations, which effectively ended Canada's favoured status as a defence and aerospace trading partner. While a partial re-instatement

was negotiated in July 2000, the episode revealed a perceptible shift in security dynamics between the two countries. Further, in December, Ahmad Ressam, an Algerian citizen who had been living in Montreal for three years under a suspended deportation order, was arrested at the BC-Washington border carrying sophisticated triggering devices and chemicals used to produce explosives. The incident drew American attention to Canada's relatively lax refugee claimants system and generated considerable fear that Canada was being used as a "staging ground" for terrorism attacks on the United States. See "Official Denies Ottawa Is Snoozing over Terror," *National Post,* 29 January 2000, and "Border with Canada Must Be Tightened, US Expert Says," *National Post,* 24 February 2000. American concerns over Canada's refugee system were heightened following the 11 September 2001 terrorist attacks, although Canadians were quick to note that few of the suspected hijackers had any connection to Canada. For a recent general overview of the Canada-US defence relationship, see Alex Macleod, Stephane Roussel, and Andri van Mens, "Hobson's Choice: Does Canada Have Any Options in Its Defence and Security Relations with the US?" *International Journal* 55, 3 (2000): 341-54.

31 During the war, both the US Department of Defense and the Raytheon Corporation, the manufacturer of the Patriot missile, claimed that Patriot had achieved a near-perfect record of interception over Saudi Arabia and Israel. Subsequent analysis taken from both video recordings and telemetry data suggested that the missile had been far less successful, and that the earlier claims had been based on a misreading of the evidence. The primary critic of the Patriot has been Theodore Postel, a professor at MIT. See "Lessons of the Gulf War Experience with the Patriot," *International Security* 16, 3 (1991-2): 119-71.

32 The 1972 Treaty on the Limitation of Anti-Ballistic Missile Systems – the ABM Treaty – allows each side two ABM systems (at least 1,300 km apart) limited to 100 ABM launchers and 100 ABM missiles, together with their associated radars. However, the treaty is explicit that such defences should also be limited in terms of coverage, and that interceptors are supposed to defend only the nation's capital or an intercontinental ballistic missile field (thus, Russia to this day maintains an outdated ABM defence around Moscow that is permitted under the treaty). No *national* defence of any kind is permitted. Given that the intent of an American national missile defence (NMD) system would presumably be coverage of the continental United States (as well as Hawaii and Alaska), it is widely accepted that this will be impossible without substantial revisions to the treaty. In June 2000, US administration lawyers were reported to be considering various interpretations that would determine at precisely which point the United States would be in technical "violation" of the ABM treaty, should a decision on deployment be given. See "Clinton Lawyers Give a Go-Ahead to Missile Shield," *New York Times,* 15 June 2000. The debate became moot in December 2001, when the United States decided to withdraw from the treaty (see n. 42).

33 Donald Rumsfeld, *Executive Summary of the Report of the Commission to Address the Ballistic Missile Threat to the United States* (Washington: US House of Representatives, July 1998). The report can be viewed at the Federation of Atomic Scientists Web site <www.fas.org/irp/threat/bm-threat.htm>, (18 December 2001).

34 For a review of the report from the perspective of someone who served on the committee, see Richard L. Garwin, "The Rumsfeld Report: What We Did," *Bulletin of the Atomic Scientists* 54, 6 (1998): 40-5. For a critique, see Lisbeth Gronlund and David Wright, "What They Didn't Do," *Bulletin of the Atomic Scientists* 54, 6 (1998): 46-51.

35 "US Asking Russia to Ease the Pact on Missile Defence," *New York Times,* 21 January 1999.

36 For example, in May 2000, General Leonid Ivashov, head of the Russian military's international relations department, stated that American proposals to amend the ABM Treaty "are not constructive and cannot be a subject of further consultations." See "Russian Criticizes US Missile Plans," *New York Times,* 5 May 2000.

37 See "President Decides to Put off Work on Missile Shield," *New York Times,* 2 September 2000.

38 President Bush has several different options for an ABM system, although as of January 2002 a final decision had not been made. Options include a ground- or navy-based system, or an airborne laser program. The cost of the project is unclear, although estimates range as high as $100 billion.

39 See "Putin Urges Bush Not to Act Alone on Missile Shield," *New York Times,* 17 June 2001.
40 The Russian president noted that following the deployment of any US shield, Russia "will reinforce our capability by mounting multiple warheads on our missiles," and the "nuclear arsenal of Russia will be augmented multifold." See "Putin Says Russia Would Counter US Shield," *New York Times,* 19 June 2001.
41 While there appeared to be a change in Russian opposition to amending the ABM treaty at the Bush-Putin meeting in June 2001, any optimism of a breakthrough faded in August when talks between US defense secretary Rumsfeld and Putin failed to reach a compromise. See "Bush and Putin Tie Antimissile Talks to Big Arms Cuts," *New York Times,* 23 July 2001 and "Russians Resolute on ABM Pact," *Washington Post,* 14 August 2001.
42 In a statement, Bush noted that "the ABM Treaty hinders [the United States'] ability to develop ways to protect [American citizens] from future terrorist or rogue-state missile attacks." In an attempt to reassure Russia, the president further noted that "the Cold War is gone. Today we leave behind one of its last vestiges." In response, Russian president Vladimir Putin called the US move "mistaken," but said that it would not threaten Russian national security. Indeed, quickly signalling that the US withdrawal would not lead to an increase in tensions, Putin stated that "the present level of bilateral cooperation between Russia and the United States should not only be preserved but also used for quickly working out new frameworks of strategic cooperation." See "US Sets Missile Treaty Pullout," *Washington Post,* 14 December 2001, and "Putin Calls ABM Move 'Mistaken,'" *Washington Post,* 14 December 2001. Within days of the American move, it was announced that a new round of bilateral arms control talks would begin early in the new year, thereby indicating that the relationship remained cordial. See "Formal Talks on Nuclear Cuts to Begin Next Month," *Washington Post,* 18 December 2001.
43 See "Putin Seeks Allies in Quest to Fight US Missile Plan," *New York Times,* 11 June 2000 and "Russian Foreign Minister Restates Opposition to US Missile Defence System," (CNN interactive Web site, 25 April 2000, cnn.com).
44 "Russians Get Briefing on US Defense Plan," *New York Times,* 29 April 2000.
45 The "principles of strategic stability" was one of the guidelines for future talks that was agreed to at the summit. See "Clinton's Ticking Clock: A Rush for Arms Control," *New York Times,* 5 June 2000.
46 Following the first Bush-Putin meeting, the Russian president said that "I am confident that at least for the coming 25 years" American missile defences "will not cause any substantial damage to the national security of Russia." See "Putin Says Russia Would Counter US Shield."
47 See "ABM Treaty May Be History, but Deterrence Doctrine Lives," *Washington Post,* 16 December 2001. For recent reviews of the NMD system, see George Lewis, Lisbeth Gronlund, and David Wright, "National Missile Defense: An Indefensible System," *Foreign Policy* 117 (Winter 1999-2000), 120-37 and Michael O'Hanlon, "Star Wars Strikes Back," *Foreign Affairs* 78, 6 (1999).
48 It must be noted, though, that Russian opposition to ABM/NMD is largely a result of the fact that it has not been sufficiently convinced of the US assurance(s). Reflecting such concerns, Igor Sergeyev, a security advisor to President Putin and a former defence minister, noted in July 2001 that "to put it simply, the US is seeking to realize unilateral advantages that they have: I can destroy you but you cannot destroy me." See "Russia Says Alaska Test Site Violates ABM Treaty," *New York Times,* 20 July 2001.
49 In a news release announcing the renewal, Canadian Defence Minister Art Eggleton was quoted as saying that "through outstanding cooperation and cohesiveness, NORAD has proven itself effective in watching, warning, and responding ... By adapting to the changing world, NORAD continues to play an important role in the defence of Canada and the United States." See News Release no. 06-00, 21 June 2000, NORAD Web site <www.spacecom.af.mil/norad>, (10 March 2002). A few weeks later, Canadian Lieutenant-General George Macdonald, NORAD deputy commander-in-chief, noted that "the two commands work hand in glove on several key areas." See News Release no. 10-00, 6 July 2000.

50 According to the 1996 renewal (which was extended without change in 2000), NORAD's warning missions include the monitoring of objects in space, and the detection, validation, and warning of attack against North America whether by aircraft, missiles, or space vehicles, while its control missions include the control and surveillance of both Canadian and US airspace.

51 Canada's involvement in the NMD system remains the subject of considerable speculation and uncertainty. While as of January 2002 Canada had still not been formally asked to participate, such an invitation is widely seen as virtually certain (especially given the US decision in December 2001). The government of Jean Chrétien has been very cautious in its comments about NMD, at times emphasizing its disruptive and threatening nature, while at other times suggesting that a re-evaluation of the US-Russian strategic environment is long overdue. In the spring of 2000, the decision facing Canada generated controversy when the US deputy commander of Space Command, Vice-Admiral Herbert Browne, suggested that if Canada declined the (anticipated) American offer, the United States would have no "obligation" to defend Canadian cities from attack. One year later, in May 2001, the *National Post,* citing an unnamed government source, reported that Canada would ultimately cooperate with the US plan. In any event, in fall 2001, Canada's position was still undetermined, with Chrétien saying that it would take "many months and years before we are in a position to make a definite decision." See "Join Missile Defence Plan or We Won't Protect You: US Admiral," *National Post,* 3 May 2000; "Canada to Back Missile Shield," *National Post,* 14 May 2001; "Chrétien Wary of Missile Plan," *National Post,* 14 June 2001; and "Decision on Missile Defence Long Way Off, Official Says," *Globe and Mail,* 19 July 2001.

52 The department's current position was summarized in a recent parliamentary report. See *Canada and the Nuclear Challenge: Reducing the Political Value of Nuclear Weapons for the Twenty-First Century* (Ottawa: Report of the Standing Committee on Foreign Affairs and International Trade, December 1998).

53 It should be noted that this book was completed before the events of 11 September 2001, and thus the "strategic environment" it refers to is the one that existed *prior* to that day. In the aftermath of the terrorist attacks and the subsequent US-led war on Afghanistan and the Taliban regime, it is unclear how that environment will change, but it is apparent that terrorist organizations such as al-Qaeda are increasingly acquiring military equipment that used to be the preserve of states. Indeed, in January 2002 there were several press reports that al-Qaeda was attempting to acquire nuclear weapons, although those efforts to date were believed to have been unsuccessful. In this new environment, strategic thought will have to be altered, but it is premature to predict how it may change. To cite just one example, the concept of deterrence is difficult to apply to a terrorist network, which lacks a clearly defined territory and in any case may include individuals willing, perhaps even eager, to die for their cause. On the other hand, the 1950s DND-DEA debate on air defence appears to be directly relevant, as the current Canadian discussion on border security has largely divided between continentalists who believe that the primary concern is security and nationalists who are equally, if not more, concerned over the sovereignty implications of a common North American perimeter.

54 Two recent studies call for a reconsideration of Canadian security policy in the aftermath of the end of the Cold War. See Joseph Jockel and Joel J. Sokolsky, *The End of the Canada-US Defence Relationship* (Kingston, ON: Centre for International Relations, Queen's University, 1996); and Ann Denholm Crosby, *Dilemmas in Defence Decision-Making: Constructing Canada's Role in NORAD, 1958-1996* (New York: St. Martin's Press, 1998).

55 In December 1998, a parliamentary report was released that called on Canada to redouble its efforts in the promotion of arms control and disarmament, and to use its influence to persuade nuclear weapons states to de-alert their forces. See *Canada and the Nuclear Challenge.*

Selected Bibliography

Newspapers, 1950-63

Hamilton Spectator.
Montreal Gazette.
Montreal Star.
Ottawa Citizen.
Ottawa Journal.
Toronto Telegram.
Globe and Mail (Toronto).
Winnipeg Free Press.
Newspaper Clipping File, "Canadian Defence Policy," Canadian Institute of International Affairs (CIIA), Toronto.

Periodicals, 1950-63

Aircraft Review.
Aviation Week and Space Technology.
Canadian Aviation.
Jet Age Magazine.
Life.
Maclean's.
RCAF Staff College Journal.
Time.

Primary Sources

National Archives of Canada, Ottawa

A.D.P. Heeney Papers.
Defence Production, Record Group 49.
External Affairs, Record Group 25.
Hon. Brooke Claxton Papers.
Hon. C.D. Howe Papers.
Hon. Donald Fleming Papers.
Hon. Douglas Harkness Papers.
Hon. Howard Green Papers.
Hon. Paul Hellyer Papers.
Howard Larnder Papers.
National Defence, Record Group 24.
Norman Robertson Papers.
Privy Council Office, Record Group 2.
R.B. Bryce Papers.
Rt. Hon. J.G. Diefenbaker Papers.

Rt. Hon. L.B. Pearson Papers.
Rt. Hon. Louis St. Laurent Papers.

Department of National Defence, Directorate of History, Ottawa
Air Vice-Marshal Max Hendricks Papers.
Cabinet Defence Committee Records and Files.
Chairman, Chiefs of Staff Committee Records
Col. Raymont Papers.
Gen. Charles Foulkes Papers.
Office of Chief of the Defence Staff Records.
R.J. Sutherland Papers.
Vice Chiefs of Staff Committee Records.

National Archives and Records Administration, Washington, DC
Admiral Radford Papers.
Joint Chiefs of Staff Papers.
National Security Council Papers.
Permanent Joint Board of Defence (PJBD) Papers.
US Air Force Files.

Government Documents, Canada (Department of National Defence)
Canadian Defence Policy. Ottawa: Department of National Defence, 1960.
Canada's Defence Programme, 1951-1952. Ottawa: Queen's Printer, 1951.
Canada's Defence Programme, 1952-1953. Ottawa: Queen's Printer, 1952.
Canada's Defence Programme, 1953-1954. Ottawa: Queen's Printer, 1953.
Canada's Defence Programme, 1954-1955. Ottawa: Queen's Printer, 1954.
Canada's Defence Programme, 1955-1956. Ottawa: Queen's Printer, 1955.
Canada's Defence Programme, 1956-1957. Ottawa: Queen's Printer, 1956.
Defence 1959 (DND white paper). Ottawa: Queen's Printer, 1959.
Minutes of the Chiefs of Staff Committee meetings held between 1950 and 1963. Directorate of History.
Report on National Defence. Ottawa: Queen's Printer, 1957.
White Paper on Defence. Ottawa: Queen's Printer, 1964.

Secondary Sources
Aron, Raymond. *The Great Debate: Theories of Nuclear Strategy.* New York: Doubleday, 1963.
Aronsen, Lawrence. "American National Security and the Defence of the Northern Frontier, 1945-1951." *Canadian Review of American Studies* 14, 3 (1983): 259-77.
Axworthy, Tom. "Soldiers without Enemies: A Political Analysis of Canadian Defence Policy, 1945-1975." PhD diss., Queen's University, 1978.
Ball, Desmond. "The Development of the SIOP, 1960-1983." In *Strategic Nuclear Targeting,* edited by Desmond Ball and Jeffrey Richelson, 57-83. Ithaca, NY: Cornell University Press, 1986.
Baylis, John. *Ambiguity and Deterrence: British Nuclear Strategy, 1945-1964.* New York: Clarendon Press, 1995.
Baylis, John, Ken Booth, John Garnett, and Phil Williams. *Contemporary Strategy: Theories and Policies.* New York: Holmes and Meier, 1975.
Baylis, John, and John Garnett, eds. *Makers of Nuclear Strategy.* London: Pinter Publishers, 1991.
Beaufre, André. *Deterrence and Strategy.* London: Faber and Faber, 1964.
Bercuson, David. "SAC vs. Sovereignty: The Origins of the Goose Bay Lease, 1946-1952." *Canadian Historical Review* 72, 2 (1989): 206-22.
–. *True Patriot: The Life of Brooke Claxton, 1898-1960.* Toronto: University of Toronto Press, 1993.
Blackett, P.M.S. *Atomic Weapons and East-West Relations.* Cambridge: Cambridge University Press, 1956.

–. *Studies of War: Nuclear and Conventional.* London: Oliver and Boyd, 1962.

Blake, Raymond B. "An Old Problem in a New Province: Canadian Sovereignty and the American Bases in Newfoundland, 1948-1952." *American Review of Canadian Studies* 23, 2 (1993): 183-201.

Bland, Douglas. *The Administration of Defence Policy in Canada, 1947 to 1985.* Kingston, ON: Ronald P. Frye, 1987.

–. *Chiefs of Defence: Government and the Unified Command of the Canadian Armed Forces.* Toronto: Brown Book Company and the Canadian Institute of Strategic Studies, 1995.

Booth, Ken. "Bernard Brodie." In *Makers of Nuclear Strategy,* edited by John Baylis and John Garnett, 19-56. London: Pinter Publishers, 1991.

Borden, William. *There Will Be No Time.* New York: Macmillan, 1946.

Bothwell, Robert. *Nucleus: The History of Atomic Energy of Canada Limited.* Toronto: University of Toronto Press, 1988.

Brennan, Donald, ed. *Arms Control, Disarmament, and National Security.* New York: George Braziller, 1961.

Brodie, Bernard. "The Development of Nuclear Strategy." *International Security* 2, 4 (1978): 65-83.

–. *Escalation and the Nuclear Option.* Princeton, NJ: Princeton University Press, 1966.

–. "Implications of Nuclear Weapons in Total War." *RCAF Staff College Journal* (1957): 13-22.

–. "Nuclear Weapons: Strategic or Tactical?" *Foreign Affairs* 32, 2 (1954): 217-29.

–. "On the Objectives of Arms Control." *International Security* 1, 1 (1976): 17-36.

–. "Some Notes on the Evolution of Air Doctrine." *World Politics* 7, 3 (1955): 349-70.

–. "Strategy As a Science." *World Politics* 1, 4 (1949): 467-88.

–. "Strategy Hits a Dead End." *Harper's* 211 (October 1955): 33-7.

–. *Strategy in the Missile Age.* Princeton, NJ: Princeton University Press, 1959.

–. "Unlimited Weapons and Limited War." *Reporter* 11, 9 (1954): 16-21.

–. *War and Politics.* New York: Macmillan, 1973.

–. "Why Were We So (Strategically) Wrong?" *Foreign Policy* 5 (Winter 1971-2): 151-62.

–, ed. *The Absolute Weapon: Atomic Power and World Order.* New York: Harcourt Brace, 1946.

Buckley, Brian. *Canada's Early Nuclear Policy: Fate, Chance, and Character.* Montreal: McGill-Queen's University Press, 2000.

Bull, Hedley. *The Control of the Arms Race: Disarmament and Arms Control in the Missile Age.* New York: Praeger Publishers, 1961.

Buteux, Paul. "NATO and the Evolution of Canadian Defence and Foreign Policy." In *Canada's International Security Policy,* edited by David Dewitt and David Leyton-Brown, 153-70. Scarborough: Prentice Hall Canada, 1995.

–. "Sutherland Revisited: Canada's Long-Term Strategic Situation." *Canadian Defence Quarterly* 23, 1 (1994): 5-9.

Buzzard, Sir Anthony. "Massive Retaliation and Graduated Deterrence." *World Politics* 8, 2 (1956): 228-37.

Campagna, Palmiro. *Storms of Controversy: The Secret Avro Arrow Files Revealed.* Toronto: Stoddart, 1992.

Clark, Ian. *Nuclear Diplomacy and the Special Relationship: Britain's Deterrent and America, 1957-1962.* Oxford: Clarendon Press, 1994.

Clark, Ian, and Nicholas Wheeler. *The British Origins of Nuclear Strategy, 1945-1955.* Oxford: Clarendon Press, 1989.

Clearwater, John. *Canadian Nuclear Weapons: The Untold Story of Canada's Cold War Arsenal.* Toronto: Dundurn Press, 1998.

–. *U.S. Nuclear Weapons in Canada.* Toronto: The Dundurn Group, 1999.

Conant, Melvin. "Canada and Continental Defence: An American View." *International Journal* 15, 3 (1960): 219-28.

–. "Canada and Nuclear Weapons: An American View." *International Journal* 18, 2 (1963): 207-10.

–. *The Long Polar Watch: Canada and the Defence of North America.* New York: Harper, 1962.

Cox, David. *Canada and NORAD 1958-1978: A Cautionary Retrospective.* Ottawa: Canadian Centre for Arms Control and Disarmament, 1985.

Cuthbertson, Brian. *Canadian Military Independence in the Age of the Superpowers.* Toronto: Fitzhenry and Whiteside, 1977.

Dewitt, David, and David Leyton-Brown, eds. *Canada's International Security Policy.* Toronto: Prentice Hall Canada, 1995.

Diefenbaker, John. *One Canada.* Vol. 3, *The Tumultuous Years, 1962-1967.* Toronto: Macmillan, 1977.

Divine, Robert A. *Eisenhower and the Cold War.* New York: Oxford University Press, 1981.

–. *The Sputnik Challenge: Eisenhower's Response to the Soviet Satellite.* New York: Oxford University Press, 1995.

Dockrill, Saki. *Eisenhower's New-Look National Security Policy, 1953-1961.* London: Macmillan, 1996.

Dow, J. *The Arrow.* Toronto: James Lorimer, 1979.

Eayrs, James. "Canada, NATO, and Nuclear Weapons." *RCAF Staff College Journal* (1960): 87-94.

–. *In Defence of Canada: Growing up Allied.* Toronto: University of Toronto Press, 1980.

–. *In Defence of Canada: Peacemaking and Deterrence.* Toronto: University of Toronto Press, 1972.

–. *Northern Approaches: Canada and the Search for Peace.* Toronto: Macmillan, 1961.

Edwards, Gordon. "Canada's Nuclear Industry and the Myth of the Peaceful Atom." In *Canada and the Nuclear Arms Race,* edited by Ernie Regehr and Simon Rosenblum, 122-70. Toronto: James Lorimer, 1983.

Emmott, N.W. "Should We Rely Completely on Guided Missiles?" *RCAF Staff College Journal* (1956): 15-18.

Enthoven, Alain, and Wayne Smith. *How Much Is Enough? Shaping the Defense Program, 1961-1969.* New York: Harper and Row, 1971.

Foulkes, Charles. "Canadian Defence Policy in a Nuclear Age." *Behind the Headlines* 21, 1 (1961).

–. "The Complications of Continental Defence." In L.T. Merchant, *Neighbours Taken for Granted,* 101-33. Toronto: Burns and MacEachern, 1966.

Freedman, Lawrence. *The Evolution of Nuclear Strategy.* London: Macmillan, 1981.

–. "The First Two Generations of Nuclear Strategists." In *Makers of Modern Strategy: From Machiavelli to the Nuclear Age,* edited by Peter Paret, 735-78. Princeton, NJ: Princeton University Press, 1986.

–. "The Strategist's Vocation." *Survival* 25, 4 (1983): 170-4.

Futrell, Robert Frank. *Ideas, Concepts, Doctrine: A History of Basic Thinking in the United States Air Force, 1907-1964.* Maxwell Air Force Base, AL: Air University, 1974.

Gaddis, John Lewis. *Strategies of Containment: A Critical Appraisal of Postwar American National Security Policy.* New York: Oxford University Press, 1982.

–. "The Unexpected John Foster Dulles: Nuclear Weapons, Communism, and the Russians." In *John Foster Dulles and the Diplomacy of the Cold War,* edited by Richard Immerman, 47-77. Princeton, NJ: Princeton University Press, 1990.

Gaddis, John Lewis, and Paul H. Nitze. "NSC-68 and the Soviet Threat Reconsidered." *International Security* 4, 4 (1980): 164-76.

Gallois, Pierre. *The Balance of Terror: Strategy for the Nuclear Age.* Boston: Houghton Mifflin, 1961.

Garthoff, Raymond L. "The Death of Stalin and the Birth of Mutual Deterrence." *Survey* 25, 3 (1980): 10-24.

Gellner, John. "Problems of Canadian Defence." *Behind the Headlines* 18, 5 (1958).

–. "Strategic Analysis in Canada." *International Journal* 33, 3 (1978): 493-505.

Gellner, John, and James Jackson. "Modern Weapons and the Small Power." *International Journal* 13, 2 (1958): 87-99.

Ghent, Jocelyn Maynard. "Canadian-American Relations and the Nuclear Weapons Controversy." PhD diss., University of Illinois at Urbana-Champaign, 1976.

Gilpin, Robert. *American Scientists and Nuclear Weapons Policy.* Princeton, NJ: Princeton University Press, 1962.

Gilpin, Robert, and Christopher Wright, eds. *Scientists and National Policy Making.* New York: Columbia University Press, 1964.

Granatstein, J.L. "The American Influence on the Canadian Military, 1939-1963." *Canadian Military History* 2, 1 (1993): 63-73.

–. *Canada 1957-1967: The Years of Uncertainty and Innovation.* Toronto: McClelland and Stewart, 1986.

–. *A Man of Influence: Norman A. Robertson and Canadian Statecraft, 1929-1968.* Toronto: Deneau, 1981.

Gray, Colin. *Canadian Defence Priorities: A Question of Relevance.* Toronto: Clarke Irwin, 1972.

–. *House of Cards: Why Arms Control Must Fail.* Ithaca, NY: Cornell University Press, 1992.

–. "The Need for Independent Canadian Strategic Thought." *Canadian Defence Quarterly* 1, 1 (1971): 6-12.

–. "Nuclear Strategy: A Case for a Theory of Victory." *International Security* 4, 1 (1979): 54-87.

–. *Nuclear Strategy and National Style.* Lanham, MD: Hamilton Press, 1996.

–. *Strategic Studies and Public Policy: The American Experience.* Lexington: University Press of Kentucky, 1982.

–. "What RAND Hath Wrought." *Foreign Policy* 4 (Fall 1971): 111-29.

Halperin, Morton. *Limited War in the Nuclear Age.* New York: John Wiley, 1963.

Hansen, Chuck. *U.S. Nuclear Weapons: The Secret History.* New York: Orion Press, 1988.

Haydon, Peter T. *The 1962 Cuban Missile Crisis: Canadian Involvement Reconsidered.* Toronto: Canadian Institute of Strategic Studies, 1993.

Heeney, Arnold. *The Things That Are Caesar's: Memoirs of a Canadian Public Servant.* Toronto: University of Toronto Press, 1972.

Herken, Gregg. *Counsels of War.* New York: Alfred A. Knopf, 1985.

–. "The Not-Quite-Absolute-Weapon: Deterrence and the Legacy of Bernard Brodie." *Journal of Strategic Studies* 9, 4 (1986): 15-24.

–. *The Winning Weapon: The Atomic Bomb in the Cold War, 1945-1950.* New York: Alfred A. Knopf, 1980.

Heuser, Beatrice. *NATO, Britain, France, and the FRG: Nuclear Strategies and Forces for Europe, 1949-2000.* New York: St. Martin's Press, 1997.

Hilliker, John, and Donald Barry. *Canada's Department of External Affairs: Coming of Age, 1946-1968.* Montreal: McGill-Queen's University Press, 1995.

Hoag, Malcolm. "On Stability and Deterrent Races." *World Politics* 13, 4 (1961): 505-27.

Holmes, John. *The Shaping of Peace: Canada and the Search for World Order, 1943-1957.* 2 vols. Toronto: University of Toronto Press, 1979 and 1982.

Howard, Michael. "Brodie, Wohlstetter, and American Nuclear Strategy." *Survival* 34, 2 (1992): 107-16.

–. *The Causes of War.* London: Unwin, 1983.

Huntington, Samuel. *The Common Defense: Strategic Problems in National Politics.* New York: Columbia University Press, 1961.

Ignatieff, George. *Memoirs: The Making of a Peacemonger.* Toronto: University of Toronto Press, 1985.

Jackson, J.I. "Air Power and Future Wars." *RCAF Staff College Journal* (1957): 29-35.

Jaekl, Christian, and David Bellamy. "On 'Home-Grown' Strategic Thought." *Canadian Defence Quarterly* 14, 1 (1985): 33-6.

Jervis, Robert. *The Illogic of American Nuclear Strategy.* Ithaca, NY: Cornell University Press, 1984.

–. *The Meaning of the Nuclear Revolution: Statecraft and the Prospect of Armageddon.* Ithaca, NY: Cornell University Press, 1989.

–. "Strategic Theory: What's New and What's True." *Journal of Strategic Studies* 9, 4 (1986): 135-62.

Jockel, Joseph. "The Military Establishments and the Creation of NORAD." *American Review of Canadian Studies* 12, 3 (1982): 1-16.

–. *No Boundaries Upstairs: Canada, the United States, and the Origins of North American Air Defence, 1945-1958.* Vancouver: UBC Press, 1987.

Jockel, Joseph, and Joel J. Sokolsky. "Canada's Cold War Nuclear Experience." In *Pondering NATO's Nuclear Options: Gambits for a Post-Westphalian World,* edited by David G. Haglund, 107-24. Kingston, ON: Queen's Quarterly and the Centre for International Relations, Queen's University, 1999.

Kahn, Herman. *On Thermonuclear War.* Princeton, NJ: Princeton University Press, 1960.

–. *Thinking about the Unthinkable.* New York: Horizon Press, 1962.

Kaplan, Fred. "Strategic Thinkers." *The Bulletin of the Atomic Scientists* 38, 10 (1982): 51-8.

–. *The Wizards of Armageddon.* New York: Simon and Schuster, 1983.

Kaufmann, William. *The McNamara Strategy.* New York: Harper and Row, 1964.

–. *The Requirements of Deterrence.* Princeton, NJ: Center for International Studies, 1954.

–, ed. *Military Policy and National Security.* Princeton, NJ: Princeton University Press, 1956.

Keating, Tom, and Larry Pratt. *Canada, NATO, and the Bomb: The Western Alliance in Crisis.* Edmonton: Hurtig Publishers, 1988.

Keeny, Spurgeon M., and Wolfgang Panofsky. "MAD versus NUTS: Can Doctrine or Weaponry Remedy the Mutual Hostage Relationship of the Superpowers?" *Foreign Affairs* 60, 2 (1981-2): 287-304.

Killian Jr., James R. *Sputnik, Scientists, and Eisenhower: A Memoir of the First Special Assistant to the President for Science and Technology.* Cambridge: MIT Press, 1977.

King, James. "Nuclear Plenty and Limited War." *Foreign Affairs* 35, 2 (1957): 238-56.

Kissinger, Henry. "Force and Diplomacy in the Nuclear Age." *Foreign Affairs* 34, 3 (1956): 349-66.

–. "Missiles and the Western Alliance." *Foreign Affairs* 36, 3 (1958): 383-400.

–. *Nuclear Weapons and Foreign Policy.* New York: Harper and Row, 1957.

Knorr, Klaus. "Canada and Western Defence." *International Journal* 18, 1 (1962-3): 1-16.

–. *On the Uses of Military Power in the Nuclear Age.* Princeton, NJ: Princeton University Press, 1966.

Lee, James, and David Bellamy. "Dr. R.J. Sutherland: A Retrospect." *Canadian Defence Quarterly* 17, 1 (1987): 41-6.

Leffler, Melvyn. *A Preponderance of Power: National Security, the Truman Administration, and the Cold War.* Stanford: Stanford University Press, 1993.

Legault, Albert, and Michel Fortmann. *A Diplomacy of Hope: Canada and Disarmament, 1945-1988.* Montreal: McGill-Queen's University Press, 1992.

Lentner, Howard. "Foreign Policy Decision Making: The Case of Canada and Nuclear Weapons." *World Politics* 29, 1 (1976): 29-66.

Levitt, Joseph. *Pearson and Canada's Role in Nuclear Disarmament and Arms Control Negotiations, 1945-1957.* Montreal: McGill-Queen's University Press, 1993.

Liddell Hart, B.H. *The Defence of the West.* London: Cassell, 1950.

–. *Deterrent or Defence: A Fresh Look at the West's Military Position.* London: Stevens, 1960.

–. *Strategy: The Indirect Approach.* New York: Praeger, 1954.

Lindsey, George. "In Memorium: Omond Solandt." *Canadian Defence Quarterly* 22, 6 (1993): 44.

–. *Research on War and Strategy in the Canadian Department of National Defence.* ORAE Memorandum M113. Ottawa: Department of National Defence, Operational Research and Analysis Establishment, 1983.

–. "When Is Air Defence Worth While?" *RCAF Staff College Journal* (1956): 30-2.

Lyon, Peyton. "Defence: To Be or Not to Be Nuclear?" In *Canada in World Affairs, 1961-1963,* 76-222. Toronto: Oxford University Press, 1968.

–. *The Policy Question: A Critical Appraisal of Canada's Role in World Affairs.* Toronto: McClelland and Stewart, 1963.

McLin, Jon B. *Canada's Changing Defence Policy, 1957-1963: The Problems of a Middle Power in Alliance.* Baltimore, MD: Johns Hopkins Press, 1967.

Maloney, Sean M. "The Canadian Army and Tactical Nuclear Warfare Doctrine." *Canadian Defence Quarterly* 23, 2 (1993): 23-9.

–. "The Mobile Striking Force and Continental Defence, 1948-1955." *Canadian Military History* 2, 2 (1993): 75-88.

Marshall, Andrew, J.J. Martin, and Henry S. Rowen, eds. *On Not Confusing Ourselves: Essays on National Security Strategy in Honour of Alberta and Roberta Wohlstetter.* Boulder, CO: Westview Press, 1991.

Melissen, Jan. "Nuclearising NATO, 1957-1959: The 'Anglo-Saxons,' Nuclear Sharing, and the Fourth Country Problem." *Review of International Studies* 20, 3 (1994): 253-76.

–. *The Struggle for Nuclear Partnership: Britain, the United States, and the Making of an Ambiguous Alliance, 1952-1959.* Groningen, Netherlands: Styx Publications, 1993.

Middlemiss, D.W., and J.J. Sokolsky. *Canadian Defence: Decisions and Determinants.* Toronto: Harcourt Brace Jovanovich, 1989.

Morgan, Patrick. *Deterrence: A Conceptual Analysis.* Beverly Hills: Sage Library of Social Science, 1983.

Munro, J.A., and A.I. Inglis. "The Atomic Conference 1945 and the Pearson Memoirs." *International Journal* 29, 1 (1973-4): 90-109.

Munton, Donald. "Going Fission: Tales and Truths about Canada's Nuclear Weapons." *International Journal* 51, 3 (1996): 506-28.

Nash, Knowlton. *Kennedy and Diefenbaker: The Feud That Helped Topple a Government.* Toronto: McClelland and Stewart, 1990.

Nash, Philip. *The Other Missiles of October: Eisenhower, Kennedy, and the Jupiters, 1957-1963.* Chapel Hill: University of North Carolina Press, 1997.

Navias, Martin S. *Nuclear Weapons and British Strategic Planning, 1955-1958.* Oxford: Clarendon Press, 1991.

Norris, Robert S., William M. Arkin, and William Burr. "Where They Were." *Bulletin of the Atomic Scientists* 55, 6 (1999): 26-35.

Osgood, Robert. *Limited War: The Challenge to American Strategy.* Chicago: University of Chicago Press, 1957.

–. *NATO: The Entangling Alliance.* Chicago: University of Chicago Press, 1962.

Page, Don, and Donald Munton. "Canadian Images of the Cold War, 1946-47." *International Journal* 32, 3 (1977): 577-604.

Paret, Peter, ed. *Makers of Modern Strategy: From Machiavelli to the Nuclear Age.* Princeton, NJ: Princeton University Press, 1987.

Pearson, Lester B. *Mike: The Memoirs of the Right Honourable Lester B. Pearson.* 3 vols. Toronto: University of Toronto Press, 1972-5.

Pennie, A.M. "The Defence Research Board: A Quarter Century of Achievement." *Canadian Defence Quarterly* 1, 4 (1972): 6-15.

Preston, Adrian. "The Higher Study of Defence in Canada: A Critical Review." *Journal of Canadian Studies* 3, 3 (1968): 17-28.

–. "The Profession of Arms in Postwar Canada, 1945-1970: Political Authority as a Military Problem." *World Politics* 23, 2 (1971): 189-214.

Preston, Richard. "The Discussion and Formulation of National Security Policy." *RCAF Staff College Journal,* 1959: 74-83.

Ranger, Robin. *Arms and Politics, 1958-1978: Arms Control in a Changing Political Context.* Toronto: Macmillan, 1979.

Rearden, Steven L. *The Evolution of American Strategic Doctrine: Paul H. Nitze and the Soviet Challenge.* Boulder, CO: Westview Press, 1984.

Reford, Robert. "Making Defence Policy in Canada." *Behind the Headlines* 23, 4 (1963).

Regehr, Ernie. "Canada and the US Nuclear Arsenal." In *Canada and the Nuclear Arms Race,* edited by Ernie Regehr and Simon Rosenblum, 101-21. Toronto: James Lorimer, 1983.

Reid, Escott. *Radical Mandarin.* Toronto: University of Toronto Press, 1989.

Rempel, Roy. "The Canadian Army and the Commitment-Capability Gap: Central Europe, 1956-1961." *Canadian Defence Quarterly* 25, 1 (1995): 22-6.

Richter, Andrew. "'Strategic Theoretical Parasitism' Reconsidered: Canadian Thinking on Nuclear Weapons and Strategy, 1950-63." *International Journal* 55, 3 (2000): 401-26.

–. "The Sutherland Papers: A Glimpse into the Thinking of Canada's Preeminent Strategist." *Canadian Defence Quarterly* 27, 1 (1997): 28-33.

Ritchie, Ronald. "Problems of a Defence Policy for Canada." *International Journal* 14, 3 (1959): 202-12.

Robinson, H. Basil. *Diefenbaker's World: A Populist in Foreign Affairs.* Toronto: University of Toronto Press, 1989.

Roman, Peter. *Eisenhower and the Missile Gap.* Ithaca, NY: Cornell University Press, 1995.

Rosecrance, Richard. "Albert Wohlstetter." In *Makers of Nuclear Strategy,* edited by John Baylis and John Garnett, 57-69. London: Pinter Publishers, 1991.

Rosenberg, David Alan. "The Origins of Overkill: Nuclear Weapons and American Strategy, 1945-1960." *International Security* 7, 4 (1983): 3-71.

–. "Reality and Responsibility: Power and Process in the Making of United States Nuclear Strategy, 1945-1968." *Journal of Strategic Studies* 9, 1 (1986): 35-52.

–. "A Smoking Radiating Ruin at the End of Two Hours: Documents on American War Plans for Nuclear War with the Soviet Union, 1954-1955." *International Security* 6, 3 (1981-2): 3-38.

Ross, Douglas. "American Nuclear Revisionism, Canadian Strategic Interests and the Renewal of NORAD." *Behind the Headlines* 39, 6 (1982).

Rowen, Henry. "The Evolution of Nuclear Strategic Doctrine." In *Strategic Thought in the Nuclear Age,* edited by Lawrence Martin, 131-56. Baltimore, MD: Johns Hopkins University Press, 1979.

Sagan, Scott D. "SIOP-62: The Nuclear War Plan Briefing to President Kennedy." *International Security* 12, 1 (1987): 22-40.

Schelling, Thomas C. *Arms and Influence.* New York: Yale University Press, 1966.

–. *The Strategy of Conflict.* New York: Oxford University Press, 1960.

Schelling, Thomas, and Morton Halperin. *Strategy and Arms Control.* New York: Twentieth Century Fund, 1961.

Schilling, Warner, Paul Hammond, and Glenn Snyder, eds. *Strategy, Politics, and Defense Budgets.* New York: Columbia University Press, 1962.

Sharp, D.E. "North American Defensive Requirements in the Missile Age." *RCAF Staff College Journal* (1958): 49-51.

Shaw, E.K. *There Never Was an Arrow.* Ottawa: Steel Rail Educational Publishing, 1981.

Simon, Paul. "We're Arming against Ourselves If We Take A-Arms for the Bomarc." *Maclean's* 75 (14 July 1962): 20-1.

Slessor, Sir John. *Strategy for the West.* London: Cassell, 1954.

Smith, Bruce. *The RAND Corporation: Case Study of a Non-Profit Advisory Corporation.* Cambridge, MA: Harvard University Press, 1966.

Smith, Denis. *Rogue Tory: The Life and Legend of John G. Diefenbaker.* Toronto: Macfarlane, Walter, and Ross, 1995.

Smith, Sydney. "NATO and the Challenge of the Missile Age." *International Journal* 13, 3 (1958): 165-74.

Snead, David L. *The Gaither Committee, Eisenhower, and the Cold War.* Columbus: Ohio State University Press, 1999.

Snyder, Glenn H. *Deterrence and Defense: Toward a Theory of National Security.* Princeton, NJ: Princeton University Press, 1961.

Solandt, O.M. "The Defence Research Board's Untimely End: What It Means for Military Science." *Science Forum* 8, 5 (1975): 19-25.

Stairs, Denis. "Will and Circumstance and the Postwar Study of Canadian Foreign Policy." *International Journal* 50, 1 (1994-5): 9-39.

Steiner, Barry. *Bernard Brodie and the Foundations of American Nuclear Strategy.* Lawrence: University Press of Kansas, 1991.

Stewart, Greig. *Shutting Down the National Dream: A.V. Roe and the Tragedy of the Avro Arrow.* Toronto: McGraw-Hill Ryerson, 1988.

Sutherland, R.J. "Canada's Long Term Strategic Situation." *International Journal* 17, 3 (1962): 199-223.

–. "The Strategic Significance of the Canadian Arctic." In *The Arctic Frontier,* edited by R.St.J. Macdonald, 256-78. Toronto: University of Toronto Press, 1966.

Trachtenberg, Mark. *History and Strategy.* Princeton, NJ: Princeton University Press, 1991.

–. "Melvyn Leffler and the Origins of the Cold War." *Orbis* 39, 3 (1995): 439-55.

–, ed. *The Development of American Strategic Thought: Writings on Strategy, 1945-1969.* New York: Garland Press, 1988.

Tucker, Michael. "Canada and Arms Control: Perspectives and Trends." *International Journal* 36, 3 (1981): 635-56.

Warner, Geoffrey. "The United States and the Western Alliance, 1958-1963." *International Affairs* 71, 4 (1995): 801-18.

Warnock, John. *Partner to Behemoth: The Military Policy of a Satellite Canada.* Toronto: New Press, 1970.

Watson, Gordon D. "Why the Bureaucrats Secretly Carved up the DRB: It Worked Too Well." *Science Forum* 8, 5 (1975): 22-5.

Wells Jr., Samuel F. "The Origins of Massive Retaliation." *Political Science Quarterly* 96, 1 (1981): 31-52.

–. "Sounding the Tocsin: NSC-68 and the Soviet Threat." *International Security* 4, 2 (1979): 116-58.

Wenger, Andreas. *Living with Peril: Eisenhower, Kennedy, and Nuclear Weapons.* New York: Rowman and Littlefield, 1997.

Whitaker, Reg, and Gary Marcuse. *Cold War Canada: The Making of a National Insecurity State, 1945-1957.* Toronto: University of Toronto Press, 1994.

Whitehouse, Peter. "What Nuclear Bombs Would Do to Canada." *Saturday Night* 74 (29 September 1959): 9-14.

Williams, Phil. "Thomas Schelling." In *Makers of Nuclear Strategy,* edited by John Baylis and John Garnett, 120-35. London: Pinter Publishers, 1991.

Wilgress, Dana. *Memoirs.* Toronto: Ryerson Press, 1967.

Williamson Jr., Samuel R., and Steven L. Rearden. *The Origins of US Nuclear Strategy, 1945-1953.* New York: St. Martin's Press, 1993.

Wohlstetter, Albert, "The Delicate Balance of Terror." *Foreign Affairs* 37, 2 (1959): 211-34.

–. "Nuclear Sharing: NATO and the N+1 Country." *Foreign Affairs* 39, 3 (1961): 355-87.

–. "On the Value of Overseas Bases." *RAND Paper P-1877.* Santa Monica, CA: RAND Corporation, 1960.

Wohlstetter, Albert, and Fred Hoffman. "Protecting US Power to Strike Back in the 1950s and 1960s." *RAND Report R-290.* Santa Monica, CA: RAND Corporation, 1956.

Wohlstetter, Albert, Fred Hoffman, Robert Lutz, and Henry Rowan. "Selection and Use of Strategic Air Bases." *RAND Report R-266.* Santa Monica, CA: RAND Corporation, 1954.

Woodrow, J. "The RCAF Is Unprepared for the Guided Missile Age." *RCAF Staff College Journal* (1958): 45-8.

York, Herbert. *The Advisors: Oppenheimer, Teller, and the Superbomb.* San Francisco: W.M. Freeman, 1976.

Index